The Paradox of American Democracy

ALSO BY JOHN B. JUDIS

Grand Illusion: Critics and Champions of the American Century

William F. Buckley, Jr.: Patron Saint of the Conservatives

★ ★ ★

The Paradox of American Democracy

Elites, Special Interests, and the Betrayal of Public Trust

John B. Judis

Pantheon Books New York

Published in the United States by Pantheon Books,
a division of Random House, Inc., New York, and simultaneously in Canada
by Random House of Canada Limited, Toronto.
Pantheon Books and colophon are registered trademarks of Random House, Inc.

Library of Congress Cataloging-in-Publication Data

Judis, John B.
The paradox of American democracy : elites, special interests, and
the betrayal of public trust / John B. Judis.
p. cm.
Includes bibliographical references and index.
ISBN 0-679-43254-X
1. Political participation—United States—History—20th century. 2. Democracy—United States—History—20th century. 3. United States—Politics and government—20th century. I. Title.
JK1764.J83 2000
320.973'09'045—dc21 99-16821
CIP

Random House Web Address: www.randomhouse.com

Book design by Laura Hammond Hough

Printed in the United States of America
First Edition
2 4 6 8 9 7 5 3 1

For Eleanor and Hilary

Contents

Introduction

America has experienced a steady growth of industry and invention over this century—not interrupted even by the Great Depression. Today, our country is awash in new technology—from the World Wide Web to gene splicing—and abounds in brilliant entrepreneurs, such as Microsoft's Bill Gates, TCI's John Malone, and Federal Express's Frederick W. Smith. Information technology has transformed how Americans work and where they buy and sell their goods and services. Within a decade, innovations in biotechnology may utterly change agriculture and medicine. The burgeoning American trade deficit, once a mark of weakness, now symbolizes the nation's status as the consumer of last resort for other nations mired in recession. In the wake of the Soviet Union's collapse, the United States has also achieved unchallenged military supremacy; it has no credible adversaries. And American culture—from movies to teenage fashion—dominates the world market. In this sense, the American century that Henry Luce predicted in 1941 has truly arrived. But while we have hurtled forward in technology and enjoy global hegemony in cruise missiles and designer jeans, we have not made similar progress in our political institutions. As we look out upon a new century, American politics seems in far worse shape than it did at the last turn of the century.

There are telling signs that something is wrong with America's political system. Voter turnout in the 1996 presidential contest was 48.9 percent, the lowest since 1924, and turnout in the 1998 Congressional races was the lowest since 1942, a wartime election. Perhaps more important, there is a noticeable lack of popular political activity in the country, except, perhaps, for the Christian right in the South and the environmental movement in the West. During the last decade, formidable grassroots organizations have dissolved or been transformed into letterhead groups. The labor movement, once a bulwark of popular power, has continued to lose its hold over America's working class. Political parties have become subordinated to political consultants, media experts, pollsters, and public relations flacks, none of whom are accountable to voters. The political system has become ruled by large contributors, who through loopholes in the porous campaign laws hold the balance of power in elections and popular referenda.

While activity outside Washington has atrophied, activity on or around Washington's K Street has spread and expanded. In 1997, 11,500 lobbyists spent $1.26 billion lobbying Congress—or $2.4 million for each member.[1] There are thousands of lobbying organizations in Washington representing every conceivable interest group, from Alaska crab fishermen and Armenian-Americans (two organizations) to mink exporters and motorcyclists. There are also hundreds of political organizations ranging from the Defenders of Wildlife to Handgun Control to the Conservative Caucus. Very few of these organizations have real members. Instead, they are run by Washington staff and funded by direct mail, and they survive by attempting to capture public attention for single issues. They defy the old-fashioned view that politics rests ultimately on a shared view of the national interest. Far from deepening citizen involvement in politics, the proliferation of these Washington organizations discourages it by making politics the exclusive province of paid hacks and single-issue fanatics.

Congress appears incapable of passing significant reform legislation. In 1993 and 1994, Congress couldn't produce any bill aimed at reducing the growing ranks of Americans who have no health insurance. After the 1996 election, when there was widespread public support for campaign reform, Congress could not even pass the most perfunctory measure. During the 1997–98 session, the only large-scale legislation adopted was a

$218 billion transportation bill that, while needed to modernize crumbling infrastructure, was heavily larded with pork-barrel projects. Even the onset of large budget surpluses, which would allow generous expenditures in education and healthcare, failed to shake Congress's torpor. Much of Congress's time has been consumed by such "hot button" issues as "partial birth" abortion, gay rights in the military, and funding for UN birth control programs and for the National Endowment for the Arts—issues that are of very little concern to most Americans. Serious national issues, such as military intervention in the Balkans, have been debated in a spirit of the most narrow partisanship. Worse still, hearings and investigations into scandals—from the imbroglio over Clarence Thomas's Supreme Court nomination in 1991 to the charges of perjury against President Clinton in 1998—have overshadowed any consideration of the country's future. These scandals have generally not involved the flagrant misuse of government funds or an attempt to subvert the Constitution, but instead petty corruption and inappropriate personal behavior. They have been triggered by partisan struggles for power inside Washington, and arouse only passing or prurient interest outside of Washington. They reached a pinnacle of absurdity in 1999 with the impeachment trial of Clinton—an event driven by partisan fanaticism and opposed by the general public.

The president and the executive branch are equally paralyzed, and not simply by the opposition in Congress. Domestic politics is dominated by public opinion polling. After the defeat of its health care initiative, the Clinton administration limited itself to what campaign consultant Dick Morris called "bite-size programs" that were designed to win popular favor, but even if adopted by Congress had little chance of solving the problems they were intended to address.[2] Foreign policy decisions lacked a widely accepted and understood rationale. Instead, intermittent decisions to use American forces in the Balkans or Middle East appeared to reflect not just interests and ideals, but also transient political pressures and passing diplomatic fancies. And they were conducted in an atmosphere of public uncertainty and partisan bickering.

In the past, the existence of a powerful political establishment could make up for the shortcomings of public institutions and could work to overcome the absence of shared national goals, but there has been a disturbing decline in the quality of the American leadership class—the former public officials, investment bankers, CEOs, and academics who are periodically summoned to lend their wisdom and experience to the government and the country. Former officials who used to provide dispassionate guidance on difficult foreign or domestic policy issues have become lobbyists and consultants for American and foreign businesses. Former Secretaries of State make provocative public statements defending China while not revealing their own financial stake in the current Chinese government. Former senators call for the privatization of Social Security without revealing that they are on the boards of directors of securities firms that would stand to benefit mightily from such a change. Former presidential candidates lobby for businesses that, as politicians, they had denounced only a year before. Bankers, business leaders, and corporate lawyers who, in past generations, might have been driven to devote part of their time to public service and to the greater good confine their public activity to lobbying on behalf of their own firm or industry. And academics and policy intellectuals who brought a spirit of scientific objectivity and disinterest to political deliberations lend their name and expertise to think tanks and policy groups that are dedicated to promoting the narrowest interests of business contributors.

Together, the irresponsibility of the nation's elites, the power and proliferation of special interest groups, and the paralysis of Congress and the executive have contributed to a corrosive public cynicism. Americans, of course, have often been skeptical about government and politicians, but over the last decades, this skepticism has hardened. Political scientist Hugh Heclo writes, "A long-term downward trend in political trust reflects not simply a skepticism toward authority but a much more negative cynicism toward anything that happens in politics. To doubt and question public authority is a time-honored American tradition. Always to expect the worst is not."[3] Put this cynicism together with a certain complacency born of temporarily good times and one has the ingredients for a massive withdrawal from public activity and vital public questions.

These developments suggest that even as the Dow-Jones stock index exceeds a record 10,000, our political system is faltering, and faltering in a way that might eventually undermine our progress as a nation.

Periods of prosperity should provide welcome opportunities to strengthen our institutions to prepare for future adversity, but our political institutions make it impossible to adopt far-reaching policies, particularly if they threaten vested interests. Like holiday travelers, we are prepared for the pleasures of the next stop, but are completely ill-equipped to handle even the smallest crisis, let alone a severe economic downturn or a war. How did this happen, and why, and what can be done about it? These are the questions that this book will attempt to answer.

The Paradox of American Democracy

[1]

The Paradox of Democracy

In the decades after World War II, a great debate took place among political scientists, historians, and philosophers about the nature of American democracy. It was finally abandoned rather than being resolved, as political science was overrun by number crunchers, but it remains critical to understanding what has happened to American politics over this century. There were three competing views—which I will call the electoralist, the pluralist, and the populist/Marxist—of how American politics does work and how it should work.

The first and oldest school of thought, the electoralist, believed that what the government did was primarily determined by which candidates the voters elected and what party prevailed in Washington and in the states. Politicians and parties could defy voters, but voters could then retaliate by throwing them out of office. Labor unions, business groups, environmental organizations, and other kinds of groups had influence on the political process, but were constrained to work through voters, candidates, and their parties. The parties played a critical mediating role among these contentious groups. Clinton Rossiter stated this view succinctly at the beginning of his classic *Parties and Politics in America:* "No America without democracy, no democracy without politics, no politics without parties, no parties without compromise and moderation."[1] This kind of democracy was thought to work best when the two major parties were highly competitive and when a large percentage of Americans participated.

The second, pluralist school of thought evolved out of dissatisfaction with the purely electoral model of democracy. Reflecting real changes in politics during the twentieth century, the pluralists believed that organized groups rather than voters and parties played the dominant role in shaping the actions of government. These groups had enormous influence on the results of elections and on what elected officials did. Borrowing from Newtonian physics, the pluralists imagined government action as the resolution of many different vectors, each representing the force wielded by a large organized group, such as business lobbies or labor unions. As Arthur Bentley, the founder of pluralism, put it in his 1908 work *The Process of Government,* "The balance of the group pressures *is* the existing state of society."[2] The pluralists believed that the ideal society was one of democratic pluralism, where all the major groups within society, including labor as well as business, were adequately represented. They believed that the America of the 1950s approached this ideal.

The third school of thought, composed of populists and Marxists, held that important government decisions were shaped and then made by a small, interlocking group of business, political, and military leaders who prevailed regardless of who won elections. Populists described this group as a "power elite" or "establishment" and Marxists called it a "ruling class." Through the power elite's influence and even control over political parties and media, it was often able to establish a broad consensus through which politicians and interest groups acted; but even when a consensus did not exist, such as during the beginning of the Cold War and the Vietnam War, the elite was still capable of directing government action through its clout within the executive branch. Marxists and populists regarded the electoral view as hopelessly naïve, and saw pluralists as apologists for an undemocratic status quo. Their own alternative was either participatory democracy—a vague term that conjured up direct local control—or some form of democratic socialism. While the electoral view held sway in many high school civics classes and the theory of pluralism in university political science departments, the populist/Marxist theory came into favor among new left activists and intellectuals.

During the time when these three views were hotly debated, they were thought to contradict each other, but in the heat of political conflict, the proponents of these views failed to notice that they were describing complementary, rather than contradictory, aspects of the overall political process. If you start with the electoral view (which makes most sense in the mid-nineteenth century) and then add the dimension of interest groups (which comes into play in the late nineteenth century) and then add to that the role of elites and elite policy groups (which emerge as critical in the early twentieth century), then you have a comprehensive view of how American politics has worked in the twentieth century. You can't understand any era of twentieth-century politics without understanding the distinctive role played by voters and parties, interest groups and elites.

But what of the conflicting view of how American democracy should work? If you look not at an imagined future, but at how American politics has actually worked over this century, American democracy has flourished in those periods when voters actually affected what government did, and when labor and consumers as well as business wielded significant influence. This occurred during the Progressive Era, the New Deal, and the early 1960s. During those periods, elites and elite organizations also played a conspicuous and active role. They did not undermine, but bolstered democratic pluralism. Conversely, during those periods in which democracy flagged, elites and elite organizations have been eclipsed by business lobbies. This integral relationship between elites and democracy is the great paradox of twentieth-century American politics.

Voters and Parties

Political parties and elections first became important during the 1820s. Until then, American politics was dominated by the Virginia dynasty and the Northern Federalists and their descendants. The male vote was still restricted by property qualifications in many states; and to the extent that parties existed, they were predominately legislative caucuses. But over the next decade, a new party system emerged. As the states eliminated property tests for voting, the parties became local and national organizations that chose candidates, erected platforms, raised money for campaigns, and conducted them, often without the participation of the candidate himself. (The election of 1896 was the first in which both major presidential candidates campaigned.) When in power, the parties—which locally aspired to be "machines"—doled out government jobs through patronage and controlled local newspapers, which they funded through publishing legal notices.

Until the late nineteenth century, parties were the only important national political institutions. If a dissenting national movement wanted to contest for power and influence, it had to found its own party. (The exception that proved the rule was the woman-suffrage movement.) Thus, the nineteenth century saw a plethora of third and fourth parties—from the Free-Soil and Know Nothing parties to the National Greenback and Populist parties. The most successful of these was the Republican Party, which displaced the Whigs in 1856 as the principal rival to the Democratic Party. The elections from 1832 to 1860, with their high turnout and mobilization around land, the tariff, immigration, and the expansion of slavery, represented a high-water mark in the importance of parties, politicians, and elections.

After the Civil War, much of what the national government and local and state governments did was dictated by the growing power of wealthy merchants, bankers, and industrialists. The new men of wealth were able to buy off politicians, and sometimes entire state legislatures and the U.S. Congress. Urban politics, and some state politics, were ruled by tightly organized machines that used patronage, the dispensation of social services, and force and bribery to maintain their dominance. In the South, blacks were excluded from the vote. Corruption was rife. Simon Cameron, a Pennsylvania Republican boss and U.S. senator who served briefly as Lincoln's Secretary of War, once quipped, "An honest politician is one who, when bought, stays bought."[3] Electoral turnout was very high after the Civil War, but it didn't necessarily reflect public involvement in government debate. National campaigns were like sporting events, where parties commanded loyalty rather than intellectual conviction. A Chicagoan might be a Democrat rather than a Republican in the same spirit that he later was a Cubs rather than White Sox fan.

Political parties themselves began to decline in importance in the late nineteenth century. In 1883 a coalition of Democrats and dissident Republicans succeeded in getting civil service reform through Congress, which removed many federal jobs from the control of politicians and political parties. Business leaders—partly in response to the growing challenge to their power from the Socialist and Populist parties—got cities to adopt commission and city manager governments that removed administration from politicians and parties.[4] They also championed new electoral rules that made it more difficult for dissident third parties to function. Ironically, populists and progressives also contributed to the decline of the parties. They advocated the initiative and referendum, which allowed voters to bypass the party competition, and the direct election of U.S. senators, which removed an important office from party control. And on the grounds of fighting corruption, they often joined business leaders in trying to strip city councils and state legislators of power. After winning the initiative and referendum and the primary nomination in Oregon, William S. U'Ren, the leader of the People's Power League, fought to make virtually all state offices subject to appointment by an elected governor.[5] (There is a direct line between U'Ren's antipolitical populism and the combination of imperial rule and plebiscitary democracy espoused by Ross Perot in the 1990s.)

The parties also lost control over the press. A new group of newspaper publishers, led by Joseph Pulitzer and William Randolph Hearst, created commercial publications that entertained their readers, while Adolph Ochs's *New York Times* promised to be "nonpartisan."[6] Public officials, beginning with Theodore Roosevelt, established independent relationships with the press and ran their own campaigns. Roosevelt set up a press room in the White House, and Wilson began holding regular press conferences. Politicians also increasingly depended directly upon wealthy individuals rather than upon the party itself to fund their campaigns.

After World War II, the parties were weakened by the onset of television, which changed the nature of campaigning. The party precinct captain was replaced by the adman and pollster, and the political boss by the political consultant.[7] The pollster and the consultant worked for the candidate rather than the party. Even the elected official relied on these experts in public opinion. Jimmy Carter was the first president to appoint both a pollster and an advertising expert as White House advisors. Parties were further weakened by the elimination of the closed-party caucus as a means by which states nominated presidential candidates. The spread of the primary system took the election of presidential and other candidates out of the hands of the party and its convention. It made the party nominating convention—the event that once epitomized the power of party bosses like Chicago's Richard J. Daley—televised spectaculars where the nominee could exhibit his message to a national audience. The final blow, perhaps, was the collapse of the Congressional seniority system and the strict rule of authority that it entailed. Beginning in the 1970s, House and Senate members no longer deferred invariably to their party leaders and committee chairs. A freshman senator like Texas's Phil Gramm could have as much influence as the leader of his party.

The party system did not disappear, but parties no longer played the central role in the political process. In the two most consequential elections of the twentieth century—Franklin Roosevelt's landslide win in 1936 and Ronald Reagan's landslide in 1980—neither candidate campaigned as the leader of his political party. Reagan's avoidance of the Republican label is well known, but according to historian William Leuchtenburg, Roosevelt mentioned that he was a Democrat no more than three times during the entire 1936 campaign.[8] And like Reagan's victory in 1980, Roosevelt's victory strengthened a loose coalition of politicians, intellectuals, political movements, and interest groups that operated through, but often independently of, the party system.

In the 1990s political parties made a minor comeback, thanks to campaign finance loopholes that allowed the parties to spend "soft money" on campaigns without having to adhere to the limits on contributions to candidates. But the party organization itself plays little role in selecting or counseling candidates or in encouraging the support of politics. Candidates operate largely outside any party control. Not only the candidates, but the press itself is much more likely to seek political guidance from pollsters and political consultants than from party officials. Washington pollster Guy Molyneux described the national Democratic Party of the 1990s as a party of political consultants. "Insofar as there is a Democratic Party, it is a network of thirty to forty political consultants. They have the institutional memory and commitment," Molyneux said.[9] In between elections, opinion polls serve as a kind of plebiscitary referendum on policies and politicians. A president will often hesitate to act if opinion polls show a majority of the public is opposed to what he wants to do. House and Senate members will use polling in their districts and states to help them decide how to vote.

But what the public tells pollsters and how it votes is not an independent variable. Interest groups can change public opinion. During the debate over the Clinton health care program in 1993 and 1994, the Health Insurance Association of America spent $15 million on television ads that, though highly misleading, roused considerable opposition to the Clinton plan. Interest groups can even hire pollsters to devise questions that will make it appear the public supports its aims when in fact it does not. The Cato Institute, a Washington think tank funded partly by brokerage firms, financed polls that claimed to show that the public favored the privatization of Social Security, but the questions, which never mentioned the risk incurred by private investment, invited the answers they got.[10] Interest groups can also use campaign contributions to influence politicians. With elections having become increasingly expensive because of the cost of television advertising, candidates have found it increasingly difficult to defy their funders. In considering legislation that fails to receive wide public scrutiny, Congress can be swayed decisively by money. Appropriations bills are filled with provisions that reflect the interest of large donors.[11] In 1995, for instance, the new Republican leadership went out of its way to pay back two major contributors, the Golden Rule Insurance Co. and Amway.[12]

Interest groups can also enter the political arena more directly. They can nominate their representatives for party positions. They can go door-to-door and run phone banks for candidates. They can even run their own "independent" advertising. The modern Christian right began strictly as a policy lobby to change an Internal Revenue Service ruling on church-run segregated schools, but during the 1980s entered the political arena. In the 1990s the Christian Coalition and the AFL-CIO were among the most important forces in electoral politics, even though neither was a political party and both were legally prevented from running their own candidates. This attests to the continuing vitality of the electoral system, but also to the importance within it of interest groups and other nonparty kinds of political organizations.

Interest Groups

The new national interest groups—the American Bankers Association (founded in 1877), the American Federation of Labor (1886), the National Association of Manufacturers (1894), the U.S. Chamber of Commerce (1912), and the American Farm Bureau (1920)—originated at the same time that American industry began to produce for a national market, and when labor unions, following the European example, began to organize across companies and industries and to form national federations. As government itself began to intervene extensively in economic affairs—regulating the currency, curbing monopolies, encouraging conservation, policing food and meat products, and taxing income and profits—businesses and other affected groups organized lobbies to protect their interests. They operated independently of the parties, though they were often aligned more closely with one party than another.

These organizations got a boost during World War I, when government planning boards encouraged private industries to form trade associations to negotiate with the government. By the 1920s such interest groups as the National Coal Association and the Association of American Railroads had become a fixture in American politics. In his pioneering work *Group Representation Before Congress,* political scientist E. Pendelton Herring counted more than a hundred trade organizations in Washington in 1929 and more than 500 groups with representatives. During the New Deal and World War II, still more groups were formed. By 1949 the U.S. Department of Commerce estimated that there were "approximately 4,000 trade, professional, civic and other [national] associations." These in turn included 16,000 local businessmen's organizations, 70,000 labor unions, 100,000 women's organizations, and 15,000 civic and professional groups. All these groups engaged "in lobbying to varying degrees."[13] The next great period of growth occurred during the fierce battles over social, consumer, environmental, labor, trade, and tax legislation that took place during the 1960s and 1970s. Between 1961 and 1982, the number of corporations with Washington offices increased tenfold. The number of attorneys in Washington tripled between 1973 and 1983 alone.[14] During the 1980s, Washingtonians began to refer to the city's array of trade associations, law firms, and public relations firms as "K Street," after the boulevard on or around which many of the firms had their offices.

The development of K Street was by no means inevitable and has not been replicated in Western Europe or Japan. It was spurred initially by the success of progressives, populists, and business leaders in weakening the political parties. Interest groups filled a vacuum left by the declining power of the political parties. In the 1870s, farmers, angered by tight money, formed parties; by the 1920s, farmers, threatened by falling prices, formed national organizations and lobbies. K Street was also made possible by the peculiar way in which the American regulatory state developed. In other countries, state bureaucracies, staffed by civil servants, had authority to make rules and final judgments on complex issues involving business, labor, and consumers. During the 1930s, American public officials in regulatory agencies wielded this kind of power, but after a ten-year battle, businesses, aided by the American Bar Association, persuaded Congress to pass the Administrative Procedure Act in 1946, which made regulatory rulings subject to hearings and then judicial review. The act helped turn the regulatory apparatus into a mini-court and led to the proliferation of lawyers and lobbyists in Washington.[15] From 1960 to 1987, public expenditure on lawyers increased sixfold, and the share of gross national product going to legal services doubled. By 1987 the legal industry had become larger than the auto or steel industries.[16]

The pluralists—Bentley, Herring, and, after World War II, David Truman of Columbia University, Robert Dahl of Yale, and V. O. Key and John Kenneth Galbraith of Harvard—were right to insist that interest groups and lobbies have exerted an enormous influence over American politics. Every piece of tax and regulatory legislation, every government expenditure, and every government initiative in international trade bears their imprint. Indeed, many of the most important bills, such as the 1947 Taft-Hartley Act, were drafted by lobbyists. And the enforcement of every important government rule and regulation is subject to litigation on behalf of competing interest groups. The question is, however, whether all politics can be explained by the competition among interest groups.

Political scientist E. E. Schattschneider made the most telling critique of pluralist theory. He conceded in his classic work *The Semi-Sovereign People* that the pluralists had correctly identified the *origins* of much political conflict—which lay in the conflict between interest groups. But he pointed out that they had moved from this valid observation to the invalid inference that interest groups dominated the *course* of political conflict and its *resolution.* Some conflicts between interest groups—say, over an arcane piece of telecommunications law—might never surface in the public, political arena. They might be fought out in the corridors outside committee hearings. But most conflicts that begin between groups eventually take a political and electoral form. Explained Schattschneider, "Private conflicts are taken into the public arena precisely because someone wants to make certain that the power ratio among the private interests most immediately involved shall not prevail."[17] In 1977 consumer groups led by Ralph Nader stood poised to win Congressional passage of a bill creating a new consumer protection agency. The bill had passed the House three times already, and in November 1977, Democrats had control of the presidency and Congress. Business groups, sensing their initial disadvantage, tried to portray the new agency publicly not as a boon to consumers, but as a new "super-agency" that would cost taxpayers money and would not do anything. As public perceptions changed, politicians who were unsure how to vote sided with the business groups, and the agency lost.[18] Or take what happened in 1996 with the minimum wage. Early that year, the AFL-CIO, facing united business opposition in Washington, decided to conduct a public campaign on behalf of legislation raising the minimum wage. It ran television ads in districts of Republican House members who faced difficult races the next year. When opinion polls revealed that the public, including voters in those districts, strongly favored an increase, Congress finally acceded.

Interest groups themselves have recognized that they cannot usually confine their efforts merely to influencing legislators directly. Since the 1920s, they have hired public relations specialists and employed what was called "grassroots lobbying" to make their case. Wrote Herring in 1929, "The men who seek special favors of Congress rely almost exclusively upon the manipulation of public sentiment. . . . they attempt to make the legislators think that the thing they want is the thing the public wants."[19] Today, what is called K Street is not simply composed of lobbyists and lawyers, but of pollsters and public relations specialists who make their living turning interest group battles into public campaigns. Pluralists could still argue that most conflicts *begin* between interest groups. They could also point out that interest groups attempt to shape and manipulate the electoral arena through public relations and campaign finance, but as Schattschneider demonstrated, they have to concede that the electoral arena is a distinct realm of politics that is also important in determining what government will do.

The pluralists also set out a model for how politics and democracy should work. The liberal pluralists argued that the government should use its power to enable labor unions to organize against the superior power of business—in effect, to create the conditions of a more democratic pluralism. John Kenneth Galbraith argued that political equality would be made possible by the "countervailing power" of business and labor organizations.[20] If combined with the electoral ideal of public participation and accountable parties, this model of democratic pluralism comes very close to defining what we mean by democracy in the twentieth century.

The pluralists also used this model ideologically to defend the American political system against its critics. In the 1920s and 1950s, they responded to critics on the left who charged the government was controlled by business and critics on the right who contended that it was in the hands of labor unions or even Communists. Herring celebrated the "balance of interests" in American society.[21] Dahl wrote in 1956 that the United States had evolved a "political system in which all the active and legitimate groups in the population can make themselves heard at some crucial stage in the process of decision."[22]

These celebrations of American pluralism—as Dahl later acknowledged—were products of the self-congratulatory mood of the 1920s and the 1950s, which blinded political scientists to the inequities in the society and the political system. The balance between business and financial interests on the one hand, and labor and consumer interests on the other, has shifted dramatically with each new political epoch. Labor was its peak of strength during World War I and from 1936 to 1946. Business was clearly stronger than its critics in the 1950s. In the 1920s and 1980s, business lobbies would virtually reign supreme, undermining the promise of democratic pluralism. Which groups or lobbies were in the ascendancy made all the difference in what kind of things government did during a particular period.

During the fifties, the pluralist model also failed to take account of a different kind of policy group and political institution. The Council on Foreign Relations, the Brookings Institution, and the Ford Foundation exercised considerable influence over policy. These groups, organizations, or institutions were run primarily, but not exclusively, by Americans drawn from the upper rungs of business, finance, the academy, and labor. But they were not dedicated to defending the particular interests of their members. Rather, they stood for what their members believed to be the national interest. They didn't fit easily within either the electoral or the pluralist model of how American politics worked.

Elites

Well before C. Wright Mills published *The Power Elite* in 1956, there were Marxists who insisted that American politics was dominated by a "ruling class" drawn from and accountable only to the country's capitalist class.[23] But where Marxist critiques of American politics had languished on the shelves, Mills's *Power Elite* became a best-seller and inspired a host of disciples. Mills, a populist and progressive from Texas and a well-known sociologist at Columbia University, argued that American politics was ruled by an "intricate of set of overlapping cliques" that occupied the "command posts" of the great economic, military, and political institutions.[24] He called these "self-conscious members of a social class" the "power elite." "In so far as national events are decided, the power elite are those who decide them," Mills wrote.[25]

Mills's analysis, if taken purely at face value, was neither surprising nor controversial. While not denying that upstarts could enter the higher circles, Mills was arguing that most of the country's top military, economic, and political leaders knew each other at least vaguely and that most of them came from the same social class. He stopped short of drawing any precise conclusions about the country's direction from this sociological account. Unlike the Marxists, Mills did not argue that one group—the economic leaders—was primary in such a way that it dictated what political and military leaders did.[26] He was content to demonstrate who was in the country's leadership, while insinuating—to the consternation of his critics—that something more was involved.

Mills's followers took his analysis in two different directions. E. Digby Baltzell, a University of Pennsylvania sociologist who studied with Mills, wrote two classic portrayals of what he called the "establishment."[27] An upper-class Tory himself, Baltzell argued that an establishment was desirable, but only if it functioned as what Thomas Jefferson called a "natural aristocracy." His concern was that the American establishment had hardened into a "caste" that kept out Jews, Catholics, and blacks. In contrast to Baltzell, University of California sociologist G. William Domhoff put a populist or Marxist spin on Mills's thesis. In *Who Rules America?*, Domhoff argued that within Mills's power elite, the "corporate rich" and their interests should be accorded primary status.[28] "Contrary to Mills, we wish to suggest that the corporate elite . . . form the controlling core of the power elite. The interests and unity of the power elite are thus determined primarily by the interests of the corporate rich," Domhoff explained.[29]

Domhoff, like Baltzell, moved the empirical analysis of politics forward. Domhoff described how Mills's power elite actually influenced legislation and politics through forming policy groups, think tanks, and foundations. But Baltzell's work was more subtle. He understood that the American establishment was a unique historical creation that couldn't be fitted into conventional Marxist or sociological categories. It had its own ethos and worldview, and it performed certain functions within American society that other national elites did not necessarily perform within their countries. Baltzell also did not view the establishment as all-powerful, but as sharing power with voters and ordinary interest groups. Domhoff, on the other hand, labored under the same illusion as the pluralists he attacked. He thought he could establish an overarching theory of politics in which one aspect—the political activity by elites—eclipsed the rest.

There have been elites in the country since well before the nation's founding. Their descendants, swelled by the ranks of the self-made, still commute between high positions in the private sector and the upper echelon of the White House and the Departments of the Treasury, State, and Defense. Many have been lawyers, but now they are also likely to be investment bankers, corporate executives, or professors. Entry into this elite has certainly eased since Baltzell wrote *The Protestant Establishment.* Now what matters most is not a prep school diploma and the proper social pedigree, but graduation from a select group of graduate law and business schools. Jews and Catholics have broken into the upper circles. In 1916, Boston's Brahmins took umbrage at Wilson's appointment of Louis Brandeis to the Supreme Court. Eighty years later, there was virtually no reaction to Bill Clinton's consecutive appointment of two Jewish judges, Ruth Bader Ginzburg and Stephen Breyer, to the high court.

This elite or establishment, as Baltzell understood it, is not simply a collection of powerful businessmen and politicians, but has always stood for and been judged by certain standards of political behavior. There is a tradition that stretches from Samuel Adams, George Washington, and Thomas Jefferson through Theodore Roosevelt and Henry Cabot Lodge down to Henry Stimson, Dean Acheson, and John McCloy. These men placed public service above private gain and sought as public servants to represent the interests of the nation rather than those of a particular class, region, or industry. Washington, Jefferson had said, sought to cultivate a perfect "disinterestedness."[30] It was embodied in Alexander Hamilton's portrayal of the lawyer, professor, and minister in *The Federalist Papers:*

> Will not the man of the learned profession, who will feel a neutrality to the rivalships between the different branches of industry, be likely to prove an impartial arbiter between them, ready to promote either, so far as it shall appear to him conducive to the general interests of society?[31]

This concept of public service fell into disfavor among Jacksonian Democrats, who identified it with antidemocratic Federalists, but it was revived in the late nineteenth century by Theodore Roosevelt, Henry Cabot Lodge, and Brooks and Henry Adams. It was then carried forward by Brandeis and his protégé Felix Frankfurter and by *New Republic* founders Herbert Croly and Walter Lippmann. When Frankfurter praised the New Deal, it was because it had put "more intelligent and more purposeful and more disinterested men in the service of the government than there has been for at least half a century."[32]

There was a clear connection between Hamilton's "impartial arbiter" and Frankfurter's "disinterested man," but Frankfurter's concept also included elements that were peculiar to twentieth-century progressivism. For Frankfurter or Theodore Roosevelt, disinterestedness meant being able to stand above the conflict between business and labor and to help devise approaches that would reconcile the two to a larger national interest. Brandeis argued that the lawyer should hold a "position of independence, between the wealthy and the people, prepared to curb the excesses of either."[33] Banker George Perkins, a partner in J. P. Morgan and Co., who became active in policy groups and served as an advisor to Theodore Roosevelt, described himself as looking upon industrial life "from the point of view of an intelligent, well-posted and fair arbitrator."[34] In practice, this put Brandeis, Perkins, and Roosevelt in direct conflict much more often with business proponents of laissez-faire individualism than with labor.

In the twentieth century, disinterestedness was also tied to faith in social science. Croly, Lippmann, John Dewey, and Thorstein Veblen believed that the way to a disinterested social policy was through the application of social science to national problems. Social science not only provided answers; it also provided the basis for the disinterested temperament. "If the scientific temper were as much a part of us as the faltering ethics we now absorb in our childhood, then we might hope to face our problems with something like assurance," Lippmann wrote in 1914.[35] The same faith in social science underlay the decision of St. Louis businessman Robert Brookings to found the Institute for Government Research in 1916, which later became the Brookings Institution, or of economist Wesley Mitchell to start the National Bureau of Economic Research in 1920.

Finally, many of the members of the new twentieth-century political and intellectual elite were committed in some form to the Protestant social gospel—the belief that Christians had a responsibility to create a new kingdom of God on earth through social action on behalf of the working class and the poor. Unlike those Protestants who, threatened by Darwin's theory of evolution, would embrace the "Fundamentals" and reject science as an instrument of knowledge, Walter Rauschenbush, Washington Gladden, and other ministers saw social science as a useful tool in achieving the kingdom. When Richard Ely, Simon Patten, and Edwin Seligman formed the American Economics Association in 1885 to combat William Graham Sumner's laissez-faire school of thought, they were joined by thirty-three ministers. Together they attempted to unite, in their words, "the efforts of church, state and science."[36] Ely founded an American Institute of Christian Sociology, and his student John Commons, a founder of the American Association for Labor Legislation, would link reform, social science, and the Protestant mission in a book, *Social Reform and the Church.*

Of course, not all progressive elites nor their descendants subscribed to the precise terms of the Protestant social gospel, but what they believed was consistent with the social gospel. Pious business leaders were Presbyterians, Baptists, or Episcopalians who believed that their role on earth was not to accumulate riches as an end in itself, but to advance the greater glory of God by enhancing his earthly kingdom. They became philanthropists and advocates of public service. Andrew Carnegie was a disciple of Herbert Spencer, but he also remained a Presbyterian who believed that by doing good works for mankind he could demonstrate his fitness for salvation.[37] Some intellectuals like Lippmann were agnostics and atheists who were equally dedicated to public service and human betterment. Their socialism and progressivism presaged the transition from a more explicitly religious to a secular version of the gospel that would gradually occur over the twentieth century.

Taken together, the commitment to public service, the ideal of disinterestedness, the insistence on standing above class and party—and later race, the faith in social science, and the adherence to the Protestant social gospel became the basis of a new American elite that played a leading role in the development of democratic reform during the Progressive Era, the New Deal, and the 1960s. By seeking to reconcile capital and labor, rich and poor, elites were led inevitably toward attempting to reconcile popular democracy with the economic inequality created by the new corporations. The debate between Roosevelt and Wilson, Croly and Brandeis, and the New Nationalism and the New Freedom in

1912 was not over whether, but how, to square democracy with the new corporations.

While elites themselves predated the Revolution, elite organizations didn't really appear until the twentieth century. They were not mega-interest groups for the corporate rich, which is how Domhoff portrays them. Like the elites who founded and served in them, they aspired to be above class, party, and interest. They saw their role as conciliatory, as bringing classes and interests together rather than siding with one against the other. Although their membership was predominately drawn from the upper class, most of them made a point of including labor leaders; later, they also included environmentalists, consumer activists, and civil rights leaders.

The first elite organizations were formed at the same time as the great national interest groups. They began in the wake of the depression of 1893 and in the wake of the class violence and political turmoil of the 1890s, which appeared to pose a long-term threat to the nation's political and economic stability. The National Civic Federation, the first and most important pre–World War I organization, was founded auspiciously in 1900.[38] Its career demonstrates clearly the difference between an elite organization and an interest group. The federation sought to bring together business, labor, and the public in a tripartite structure designed to develop approaches that would transcend particular interests. It was founded by former newspaper editor Ralph Easley, who in the wake of the Pullman strike in 1894 had created the Chicago Civic Federation.[39] Its first chairman was Cleveland industrialist Mark Hanna, who became notorious as William McKinley's moneyman in 1896, but who, after McKinley's assassination in 1901, devoted himself to persuading his fellow industrialists to negotiate with labor unions. He wrote in 1901, "We must get right down to the belief that life is a matter of mutual interest between labor and capital. . . . There will always be neutral ground where conflicting interests can meet and confer and adjust themselves—a sort of Hague tribunal, if you please, in the everyday affairs of life."[40] He conceived of the National Civic Federation in that light. Hanna denied that he was acting simply on behalf of his class. Herbert Croly, his biographer, wrote of him:

> "Class consciousness" of any kind was precisely the kind of consciousness which an American like Mark Hanna did not have. There welled up in him a spring of the old instinctive homogeneity of feeling characteristic of the pioneer American. His whole attitude toward labor and his program of conciliation are, indeed, the product of an innocent faith that his country was radically different economically and socially from Europe, and that no fundamental antagonism of economic interest existed among different classes of Americans.[41]

The membership of the Civic Federation included George Perkins, Elbert Gary of U.S. Steel, and other bankers and businessmen, but it also included prominent politicians, university presidents, lawyers, including Brandeis, and several labor leaders, including AFL president Samuel Gompers and John Mitchell of the United Mine Workers (who was co-chair of its Trade Agreements Department). Easley wanted the civic federation to make "possible the commingling in unconscious equality and in conscious cooperation" of representatives of "billions of capital, millions of wage earners, of scholarship and letters, of the bar, the press, the platform and the church."[42] It established commissions to promote legislation on regulating public utilities and on child labor. It also got involved in the discussions over the regulation of national banking, which culminated in the Federal Reserve Act.[43] It even sought to settle strikes. Although it continued to meet and function after World War I, it had little role to play in the 1920s—an epoch thoroughly dominated by business and its interest groups. But it spawned many imitators, including the Twentieth Century Fund, the Committee for Economic Development, and the Ford Foundation.

The domestic-oriented elite organizations that were established from 1900 to 1930 saw themselves as being above class and narrow interest. The Russell Sage Foundation was founded with a bequest from the widow of multimillionaire Russell Sage to use social science to promote "the improvement of social living conditions in the United States of America."[44] The Rockefeller Foundation was founded to "promote the well-being of mankind through the world" by seeking "to cure evils at their source."[45] The National Bureau of Economic Research (NBER) sought to "conduct economic research effectively on a factual basis. . . . In these days of conflicting economic opinions and skillful propaganda, the interests of economic knowledge can best be served by the presentation and analysis of data, objectively collected and interpreted. Unless some guarantee of impartiality can be given, results will be viewed with distrust by many."[46] The foundation's by-laws required that the "directors be chosen to provide a balanced representation of the different viewpoints from which significant groups within the country survey its economic and social problems."[47] Of the nine directors in 1936, two were from labor unions and a third was an economist identified closely with labor. In the 1940s, an AFL economist was the vice president of NBER.

When philanthropist Robert Brookings founded what became the Brookings Institution, he said he wanted an institute that was "free from any political or pecuniary interest" to "collect, interpret and lay before the country in a coherent form the fundamental economic facts."[48] The institution's first director, Robert Moulton, was a classical economist who was wary of unions and government economic intervention, but when coal operators complained about a Brookings study calling for their nationalization, Moulton informed them, "We are concerned only in finding out what will promote the *general welfare.*"[49]

In the early twentieth century, these elite policy groups and foundations were joined by new kinds of newspapers and magazines whose editors envisaged their role in a similar manner. In the nineteenth century, some editors, publishers, and writers had certainly been part of the political establishment, but the publications themselves were instruments of partisan warfare. That began to change in the same years that the other elite groups were founded. When Ochs purchased the *New York Times,* he declared that

> It will be my earnest aim that the *New York Times* give the news, all the news, in concise and attractive form, and give it as early, if not earlier, than it can be learned through any other reliable medium; to give the news impartially, without fear or favor, regardless of any

> party sect or interest involved; to make the columns of the *New York Times* a forum for the consideration of all questions of public importance, and to that end to invite intelligent discussions from all shades of opinion.[50]

News was to be separate from editorial judgment, and editorial judgment, while favoring distinct policy alternatives, was to be free of partisan attachments. The *Times,* Ochs declared, would be a "nonpartisan newspaper—unless it be, if possible, to intensify its devotion to the cause of sound money and tariff reform, opposition to wastefulness and peculation in administering the public affairs and in its advocacy of the lowest tax consistent with good government, and no more government than is absolutely necessary to protect society, maintain individual vested rights and assure the free exercise of a sound conscience."[51]

Under Croly's editorship, *The New Republic* also sought to maintain a posture of disinterestedness. Unlike Ochs's *New York Times,* it didn't maintain a distinction between fact and opinion. The magazine's "primary purpose," Croly wrote Willard Straight in 1913, "will not be to record facts, but to give certain ideals and opinions a higher value in American public opinion."[52] But it tried to present its opinions in the same spirit as Ochs presented news: disinterestedly, without the taint of partisanship. That led quickly to a break between the magazine and Croly's political patron Theodore Roosevelt. When Croly and the magazine criticized Roosevelt, he charged them with "personal disloyalty." Croly wrote Roosevelt in response that "we all of us considered it merely the same kind of criticism which candid friends continually pass upon one another, and we had no idea that any question of loyalty or disloyalty could be raised by it." But then he added tellingly, "The *New Republic* has never pretended to be a party organ, and its whole future success in life depends upon the impression which it makes upon its readers of being able to think disinterestedly and independently."[53]

In 1935, two years after buying the *Washington Post,* financier Eugene Meyer explained how he saw the role of the elite media:

> The first mission of a newspaper is to tell the truth as nearly as the truth can be ascertained. The newspaper shall tell *all* the truth so far

> as it can learn it, concerning the important affairs of America and the world. As a disseminator of news, the paper shall observe the decencies that are obligatory upon a private gentleman. What it prints shall be fit reading for the young as well as the old. The newspaper's duty is to its readers and to the public at large and not to private interests of its owners. In the pursuit of truth, the newspaper shall be prepared to make sacrifices of its material fortunes, if such a course be necessary for the public good. The newspaper shall not be the ally of any special interest, but shall be fair and free and wholesome in its outlook on public affairs and public men.[54]

Many of the same people served in the leadership of these policy groups, foundations, and publications. In the 1950s, corporate lawyer and former official John McCloy came to be called the chairman of the board of the American establishment from having served as chairman of the Council on Foreign Relations and the Ford Foundation at the same time. The omnipresence of people like McCloy could be taken as evidence of conspiracy; but it was more clearly evidence that the members of these different groups held a common view of their purpose and their place. They weren't just leaders, but certain kinds of leaders.

Some of these organizations and their leaders significantly influenced what government did. The National Civic Federation was a force in the Roosevelt, Taft, and Wilson administrations. The Brookings Institution helped guide the Kennedy administration's domestic and international trade policies. The Ford Foundation was enormously important in securing environmental legislation in the early 1970s. But the elite policy groups rarely acted in isolation, often sharing power with popular political movements. And at other times, these organizations actually found themselves isolated from the powers-that-be, branded as outcasts and dissidents. They were far from being part of a "ruling class." The free-market Brookings floundered during the New Deal. The Ford Foundation and the *New York Times* came under withering attack in the 1970s. Perhaps the best example of this purely contingent relationship between elite organizations and governmental power is the Council on Foreign Relations.

The worldview of the council founders was a variant of progressivism and of the social gospel. Just as domestic reformers had been guided by the social gospel, the foreign policy elites believed that the United States had a responsibility to extend its idea of a democracy and capitalism globally—to combat both old-world imperialism and, later, Soviet Communism. Well before Henry Luce predicted an "American century," Progressive Era leaders were talking about "the United States of the world," in which "the American spirit becomes predominant."[55] The elites' view contrasted sharply with what would be called isolationism. The isolationists, citing George Washington and Thomas Jefferson, believed that the development of American democracy depended upon its avoidance of "entangling" overseas alliances. By contrast, the progressive elites believed that American democracy and prosperity depended upon America's actively extending its model overseas. One of the first organizations to clearly embody this outlook was the Council on Foreign Relations.

The council was established in 1921 primarily by men who followed Woodrow Wilson to Paris, but who felt afterward that in signing the punitive treaty at Versailles, the president had betrayed the promise of internationalism contained in the Fourteen Points. They included Morgan banker Thomas Lamont, professors Archibald Cary Coolidge of Harvard and Robert Shotwell of Columbia, and Isaiah Bowman, the director of the American Geographical Society. The *Saturday Review* described them as representing "the revolt of the peacemakers against the peace."[56] They joined forces with former Roosevelt Secretary of State Elihu Root, who had been holding a regular dinner under the name of the Council on Foreign Relations. Together they formed an organization called the Council on Foreign Relations and a journal called *Foreign Affairs.*

The organization was meant to transcend party and interest. Its honorary president was the Republican Root, and its first president was former West Virginia governor and ambassador to Britain John W. Davis, who in 1924 was the Democratic nominee for president. Coolidge, the first editor of *Foreign Affairs,* warned his assistant Hamilton Fish Armstrong that "if I became identified with Democratic politics, he would take to the stump for the Republicans regardless of his personal opinions in order to maintain the review's neutrality."[57] Many of its 200 early members were bankers and lawyers, but its work was primarily shaped by professors and intellectuals like Coolidge, Bowman, and Armstrong. After World War II, it would actively seek out representatives of labor, religious, civil rights, and other organizations. Two disciples of Mills and Domhoff, who sought to demonstrate that the council represented the "capitalist class," nevertheless acknowledged that as of 1973, only 40 percent of council members were businessmen, bankers, or lawyers.[58]

The council did not take official positions, but like the National Civic Federation, embraced a general set of ideas within which disagreements took place. Council members favored the removal of international trade barriers, the drastic reduction or elimination of war debts, and the creation of international treaties to secure peace. Members also backed the diplomatic recognition of Soviet Russia. These stances put the council at odds with the Republican administrations of the 1920s. In these years, the council functioned, if anything, as a center of dissent against the prevailing foreign policy rather than as an arm of the ruling class.

The council began to attain great influence in the late 1930s. In September 1939, after war broke out in Europe, Armstrong, who had succeeded Coolidge as the editor of *Foreign Affairs,* met with U.S. State Department officials to set up secret council research on war and peace. Council members also poured into the State and War Departments. Council member John McCloy recalled that when he served as personnel chief to council member and Secretary of War Henry Stimson at the beginning of World War II, whenever they needed to fill a position, "we thumbed through the roll of Council members and put through a call to New York."[59] The council continued to play this preeminent role well into the 1950s, but by the late 1960s it had become paralyzed by internal division over the Vietnam War. And no sooner had it begun to overcome these differences than it faced the hostility of a conservative Republican administration in Washington. It would never recover the position of preeminence it had held from 1939 through the mid-1960s.

Whether or not the elites and elite organizations like the council played a leading political role depended on how much support they enjoyed among their primary constituency of lawyers, investment bankers, and corporate officials and on how receptive interest groups, parties, and politicians were to the mediating role these elites sought to play. During the Progressive Era, the New Deal, and the immediate decades after World War II, elites and elite organizations enjoyed enormous influence. During those periods they played an important role in uniting diverse and conflicting interests behind a single idea of the national interest. But during the 1920s and during the last quarter of the twentieth century, elites and elite organizations were eclipsed and coopted by business organizations and lobbies. They have largely ceased to play a mediating or leadership role in American political life. What this suggests is that, far from being a threat to democracy, elites and elite organizations have been essential to its success.

The Role of Government

Elites, interest groups, and political parties have moved the country, and made history, through their influence over what government does. Their degree of influence over government has depended in turn on what Americans believe the role of government to be. Hamilton, Madison, and other founding fathers saw government as the guardian of elite values. Government represented the public or the national interest against the particular interests of the states and of individuals and groups within the states. Madison distinguished between a republican and a direct democratic model of government. The republican model, he wrote, is to "refine and enlarge the public views by passing them through a chosen body of citizens whose wisdom may best discern the true interest of their country, and whose patriotism and love of justice, will be least likely to sacrifice it to temporary and partial considerations."[60]

What guaranteed the republican character of government were the legislators themselves—whom Hamilton and Madison assumed would be chosen from the ranks of "gentlemen"—and the process of deliberation and reflection by which decisions were made. This view of government was repudiated by the Jacksonians, and was then revived by progressives, but without the connotations of caste and class. Wrote Woodrow Wilson in 1887, "Self-government does not consist in having a hand in everything, any more than housekeeping consists necessarily in cooking dinner with one's hands. The cook must be trusted with a large discretion as to the management of the fires and the ovens."[61] Wilson cheered the creation of a civil service that was removed from "the hurry and strife of politics" and that was staffed by "men definitely prepared for standing liberal tests as to technical knowledge."[62] Wilson, Theodore and Franklin Roosevelt, and other progressives and New Dealers shared a view of the government as the expression of the national and public interest. It was a repository of the elites' commitment to disinterested public service, social science, and the reconciliation of classes and interests.

This progressive view of government recognized that one important factor in governmental decisions would be group interests, but that the function of government was to arbitrate and ultimately choose among them. The philosopher John Dewey expressed this conception of government discriminating among "associations" in *The Public and Its Problems:*

> When a state is a good state, when the officers of the public genuinely serve the public interests . . . it renders the desirable associations solider and more coherent; indirectly, it clarifies their aims and purges their activities. It places a discount upon injurious groupings and renders their tenure of life precarious.[63]

The first challenge to this view of government came from the Jacksonians, who repudiated not only the Federalists' model of government by gentlemen, but also the idea of government as an autonomous realm above party and interest. They replaced the Federalist model of government by disinterested gentlemen with a "spoils system." Victorious parties swept out the defeated party's government workers and replaced them with their own loyalists, who, it was presumed, would carry out the dictates of their party. The Jacksonians also rejected the Federalist view that government required men of special knowledge and experience. Jackson declared in his first message to Congress, "The duties of all public officers are, or at least admit to being made, so plain and simple that men of intelligence may readily qualify themselves for their performance; and I cannot but believe that more is lost by the long continuance of men in office than is generally to be gained by their experience."[64]

The Jacksonian spoils system did not survive the Pendleton Act of 1883, but the basic Jacksonian view of government has endured in the conservative rejection of government and in the popular distrust of experts and civil servants—who were given the title of "bureaucrats." Herbert Hoover revived it in the 1920s under the idea of "rugged individualism" and it became the leading ideology of anti–New Deal Republicans and later of Reagan Republicans who invoked it to justify proposals that would abolish cabinet departments and regulatory agencies. Under Jackson and Martin Van Buren, it had been an argument for democratizing government and redistributing power downward. Under Coolidge and Reagan, it was an argument against the government promoting political equality by regulating large corporations on behalf of the public.

After World War II, political scientists argued that government should act predominately as a referee among contending groups. Amherst political scientist Earl Latham wrote, "The legislature referees the group struggle, ratifies the victories of the successful coalitions, and records the terms of the surrenders, compromises and conquests in the form of statutes."[65] This understanding was embodied in the Administration Procedure Act of 1946, which removed discretion over the enforcement of government regulations from government administrators. According to Robert Reich, who served on the Carter administration's Federal Trade Commission and later as Secretary of Labor in the Clinton administration, the 1946 act meant that the administrator's role was "not to discover the public interest directly, only to find it indirectly by identifying programs or solutions that accommodated most groups."[66]

High government officials saw themselves as following pluralist rules, insisting that they were "honest brokers." Presidents sought to find cabinet officials who could negotiate among contending interest groups rather than articulate clear views of their own. These officials have become, wrote political scientist Hugh Heclo, "policy politicians, able to move among the various networks, recognized as knowledgeable about the substance of issues concerning these networks, but not irretrievably identified with highly controversial positions. . . . Their mushiness . . . makes them acceptable."[67]

While a cousin of pluralism, the view of government as a referee became a rallying cry for business lobbies concerned about government regulation of labor relations and the environment. By making government a passive arbiter in the contest among interest groups, it favored those groups who could command the greatest financial resources on behalf of their cause. James Landis, who headed the Securities and Exchange Commission during the Franklin Roosevelt administration, recognized the conservative character of this view of government:

> To restrict governmental intervention, in the determination of claims, to the position of an umpire deciding the merits upon the basis of the record as established by the parties, presumes the existence of an equality in the way of the respective power of the litigants to get at the facts. . . . In some spheres the absence of equal economic power generally is so prevalent that the umpire theory of administering law is almost certain to fail.[68]

To Landis, failure meant the failure to promote political equality among business, labor, and consumers, but this is exactly what drew many business lobbyists to this theory of government.

The republican view of government as the repository of elite values was, of course, the ideology of the antidemocratic Federalists, but in the twentieth century, it became, ironically, the rallying cry for progressives and liberals who wanted government to throw its weight behind the public and behind labor and consumers to balance the power of the great corporations. It was seen as integral to maintaining rather than subverting democratic pluralism. By contrast, the referee theory of government became the instrument of a more conservative pluralism that sought to insure the supremacy of business over other interest groups.

The Three Realms

American politics in the twentieth century is not simply a giant polling booth, nor a contest of special interest groups and organized movements, nor a product of an elite politburo, but a combination of all three. Just as different political periods are distinguished by their prevailing view of government, they have also been marked by the relative importance of the different realms of political activity. Thus, interest groups played a dominant role in the 1920s and 1980s, and elites did not, while elites played a significant role in the Progressive Era and the 1960s. Voters were quiescent in the 1920s, but very active during the New Deal.

Within these different eras, interest groups were sometimes able to join hands with political organizations and parties to form political *movements.* The progressive movement, the liberal movement of the 1930s, the new left of the 1960s, and the conservative movement of the 1980s combined interest groups and political organizations. They reached into the government itself. They also attracted elites and elite organizations. The National Civic Federation was a bulwark of the progressive movement, just as the Ford Foundation was a key ally of the new left. To the participants in these movements, the end of a political era was signaled by the end of the movement itself and its reversion to an interest group. In the early 1970s, many in the new left began to complain of the "death of the movement," just as the conservatives of the late 1980s began to lament the "conservative crack-up."

How, then, to understand the promise of American democracy? In the purely electoral view of democracy, what makes an era more or less democratic is the active participation of voters, but that is clearly not a sufficient criterion. Turnout averaged a whopping 79.8 percent in the 1880, 1884, and 1888 presidential elections, even though the political system, by every other measure, was in disrepair.[69] These elections were public entertainment. The parties rarely discussed issues. Instead, they dwelt on what were called "moral" differences between the candidates. Like the 1996 election, the 1884 election was ostensibly about "character." Henry Adams wrote of the election in a letter to an English friend:

"We are here plunged in politics funnier than words can express. . . . Every one takes part. We are all doing our best, and swearing at each other like demons. But the amusing thing is that *no one talks about real interests.*"[70]

The post–Civil War governments largely reflected the growing economic inequality within the country; they were controlled by powerful businessmen who could buy legislators and their votes. The great practical insight of twentieth-century pluralists was that to achieve a genuine and effective democracy, workers and consumers had to organize powerful interest groups of their own that could challenge those of business. Moreover, to affect policy, these groups had to go beyond conventional lobbying. They had to win political support, build coalitions, and create political movements. This is what the progressives, the New Deal liberals, and the new left of the 1960s did.

The full realization of democracy also required elites and elite organizations. In the Progressive Era and the 1930s, elites have stood for the accommodation of all interests and against the unchecked reign of wealth and property. In the 1960s, they came to stand for racial reconciliation and protection of the environment. The elites and elite policy groups advocated the development of policy based on fact and knowledge. They nourished public trust in government by defending and explaining complex decisions that the ordinary voter did not have time to study. And they have carried forward a tradition of disinterested public service against the venality and corruption that interest groups have often encouraged in political life. Of course, elites and elite institutions have not always functioned in this manner. They have sometimes become arrogant and irresponsible or have been co-opted by the business lobbies and political factions that they were supposed to co-opt. But the periodic failure of elites and elite organizations should not obscure their fundamental importance to American democracy.

The conditions for the flowering of American democracy lie in the full functioning of all three realms of the American political system—in a fully mobilized electoral system free of corruption, in an equal contest of interest groups and organized movements, in the effective performance of elites and elite organizations, and in a government that is more than a referee among interest groups or a reflection of polling numbers or election results. This democratic ideal has emerged gradually out of the three key reform eras in twentieth-century American politics—the Progressive Era, the New Deal, and the 1960s—and it remains the ideal with which we must measure the present and find it wanting.

[2]

The Development of Democratic Pluralism

Democracy is not a fixed ideal that has exactly the same meaning in the Athens of Pericles, the London of Disraeli, and the Washington of Jackson or the Roosevelts. Its meaning has differed with the social and economic setting in which politics takes place. There are two great dividing lines in the history of American democracy: the first was the abolition of slavery in the South after the Civil War, and the second was the rise in the late nineteenth and early twentieth century of corporate capitalism. The emergence of the large corporation and its domination of the economic landscape sets the twentieth century off from the nineteenth, and fixes the parameters in which our own quest for democracy has taken place.

The initial American vision of democracy was based upon the predominance of small-property ownership. In 1831, when Alexis de Tocqueville set sail for America, four of five free Americans who worked owned property. Americans saw politics and political democracy as a means of protecting that rough equality through preventing the rise of state-sponsored monopolies. They viewed the state not as a protective institution, but as an instrument of monopoly. The "true strength" of government, Jackson declared in his 1832 veto of the charter of the Bank of the United States, "consists in leaving individuals and state as much as possible to themselves."[1]

That vision of democracy was undermined by the rise of the large corporation. As America industrialized in the late nineteenth century, the joint-stock corporation eclipsed the individual proprietorship. Through being able to raise capital without threat of liability for losses, it made possible businesses on a scale that dwarfed those in Tocqueville's day. An initial wave of mergers in the 1870s consolidated the railroads. Another wave at the century's end dealt a final blow to Tocqueville's America. In 1893, there were twelve great companies with capitalization of less than half a billion dollars. By 1904, there were 318 giant companies, and U.S. Steel alone was capitalized for $1.4 billion.[2] The top 4 percent of companies produced 57 percent of the total industrial output.[3]

The growth of the corporation led to a small group of managers overseeing thousands of workers, many of whom were immigrants. It created a rigid class system of a kind that Tocqueville had foreseen, but had discounted:

> I am of the opinion, on the whole, that the American manufacturing aristocracy which is growing up under our eyes, is one of the harshest which ever existed in the world, but at the same time, it is one of the most confined and least dangerous. Nevertheless the friends of democracy should keep their eyes anxiously fixed in this direction; for if ever a permanent inequality of conditions and aristocracy again penetrate into the world, it may be predicted that this is the channel by which they will enter.[4]

By 1900, the channel had become a raging torrent. There were more workers in manufacturing, transportation, communications, and public utilities than in agriculture, and America, like Europe, appeared headed toward a two-class society divided between a small bourgeoisie and a large, unruly proletariat.

Tocqueville, and the Jacksonians, viewed political equality as an outgrowth of economic equality, but by the late nineteenth century, growing economic inequality was undermining political equality. Political equality had become merely an abstraction. In fact, who was elected and what elected officials did were increasingly dictated by the industrialists and bankers who financed and sometimes bribed the politicians. (Civil service reform in 1883, which prohibited federal workers from contributing money and time to campaigns, had the perverse effect of making politicians more dependent on business for cash and campaign workers.) By controlling politicians and also judges, business was able to bend laws and regulations to its own purposes. Economic inequality had spawned political inequality.

Corporate leaders and sympathetic economists insisted that the new economic institutions were merely fulfilling the promise of the market and warned that the imposition of state regulation could undermine prosperity and freedom. But beginning in the 1870s, farmers, small businessmen, workers, and intellectuals fought back against the new corporate system. Grangers, Knights of Labor, members of the Greenback Party, and Populists campaigned to regulate or even break up the new corporations. These movements didn't see the federal government as an instrument of monopoly and tyranny, but as a means of curbing private monopolies. They saw the corporations as the enemy. Senator John Sherman, the sponsor but not the author of the Sherman Anti-Trust Act in 1890, quipped, "They had monopolies and mortmains of old, but never before such giants as in our day."[5]

The movements of the late nineteenth century demanded a host of reforms from government, including the setting of railroad rates, the establishment of an eight-hour work day, the abolition of child labor and of night work for children and women, the setting of a minimum wage, the supervision of collective bargaining, and the provision of cheap credit. In some Midwestern and Western states, they actually got some of what they wanted, but business was able to stop them in the courts. The courts adopted a principle of "corporate individualism," according to which it defined corporations as "persons" and exempted them from regulations.[6] Nationally, Populists and other reformers were totally stymied by business's control of the Senate (dubbed the "millionaires' club" in the late nineteenth century), the Supreme Court, and the White House. The stage was set, however, for a series of reform battles—extending over the first four decades of the twentieth century—that would attempt to resolve the looming contradiction between corporate capitalism and America's democratic ideals. The Progressive Era would etch in the outlines of a solution, which business and the Republicans would then attempt to erase during the 1920s, only to have the outline redrawn and filled in during the New Deal of the 1930s. The result would be a new vision of democracy that depended on the power of organized workers and consumers, working often through the government, to contest the new power of the corporations and their managers. This new vision would be democratic pluralism.

The Progressive Era

The two great reform eras of the early twentieth century would both be precipitated by severe economic depressions that unsettled the existing configuration of political power and gave rise to new political movements. The Progressive Era dates from the depression of the 1890s and the political reaction to it. This depression saw the emergence of nationally organized interest groups and elite policy organizations and the predominance of what was called the "labor question" in American politics.

Like most severe economic downturns, it was unexpected. On the eve of leaving office in early 1893, President Benjamin Harrison told Congress, "There has never been a time in our history when work was so abundant, or when wages were as high, whether measured by the currency in which they are paid, or by their power to supply the necessities and comforts of life."[7] But that May, a financial panic occurred, and by the end of the year 500 banks and over 16,000 businesses had gone under and unemployment was about 20 percent. The economy picked up in 1895, but then plunged again the next year. It did not fully recover until 1901.

Before the depression, there had already been serious signs of political unrest. In the 1892 presidential race, the Populist Party, formed out of Southern and Western Farmers' Alliances, polled over a million votes—about 9 percent of the total—and won twenty-two electoral votes, more than any third party since 1860. The American Federation of Labor was organized in 1886 and by 1893 had increased its membership from 140,000 to 275,000 workers.[8] In 1892, AFL unions went on strike against Carnegie Steel at Homestead near Pittsburgh. The depression brought still greater unrest. In 1894 alone, about 750,000 workers were out on strike. The most important strikes were by railroad workers. In 1893,

Eugene V. Debs organized the American Railway Union out of the feuding craft unions. Within a year, it had 150,000 members and had struck successfully against James J. Hill's Great Northern Railway. Debs then led a strike against the Pullman Company, a strike that was finally broken with a government injunction.

In the 1894 Congressional elections, the Populists garnered a million and a half votes, or 11.2 percent of the total.[9] Populist Congressmen introduced reform bills in the House of Representatives. In Ohio, Populist Party supporter Jacob S. Coxey, a small businessman from Ohio, organized a march on Washington to demand federal relief for the unemployed. While Coxey's Army ended up with only 500 marchers by the time it arrived in the capital, it was greeted by 15,000 cheering onlookers.

By the end of the depression, the Populists had been absorbed into William Jennings Bryan's Democratic Party, and Debs's American Railway Union had been destroyed by its defeat at Pullman, but labor and the left drew conclusions about the need for organization and national political action out of the experience. Debs helped found the American Socialist Party in 1901. It grew from 10,000 to 118,000 members by 1912, when it elected 1,200 public officials and published over 300 magazines and newspapers. In 1912, Debs got 6 percent of the vote for the presidency even though Theodore Roosevelt ran that year as the candidate of the Progressive Party.[10] In 1905, dissident trade unionists including Debs and Big Bill Haywood founded the International Workers of the World (IWW). The IWW's largest single group was the Western Federation of Miners. By 1906, the AFL, prodded and embarrassed by its city and state labor councils, had begun to take positions on national politics and to support candidates and lobby for national legislation.[11]

Business was equally active in the years following the 1893 depression. It undertook massive consolidation at the beginning of the century with the hope of stabilizing production and preventing overcapacity. Businesses also worked closely with Congress and the White House to pass banking, tariff, and trust legislation that, they hoped, would make panics less likely. At the same time, business leaders organized politically in response to the depression and the growth of labor and the Populist, and later, socialist left. They feared that as capitalism suffered deeper crises, workers would become more organized. The parties would be divided by classes, and the country would be engulfed by class war. Socialists themselves, imbued with Marx's prophecies, did nothing to allay these fears. Wrote socialist Upton Sinclair in an open letter to multimillionaire Vincent Astor, "I tell you that this country is moving today with the speed of an avalanche into one of the most terrific cataclysms in the history of mankind."[12]

Businesses organized lobbies that would unequivocally stand up for their interests against labor. The National Association of Manufacturers (NAM) was founded in 1895 at a meeting in Cleveland at which William McKinley, then the governor of Ohio, was present. It was initially intended as a lobby for trade protection, but in 1903, its leaders were ousted by three Midwestern manufacturers, David M. Parry, John Kirby, Jr., and James W. Van Cleave, who focused on combating the spread of unions. In 1906, the organization's leaders accused the National Civic Federation of being "part and parcel" of the AFL and an exponent of "the most virulent form of socialism, *closed shop unionism.*"[13] The NAM got deeply involved in Republican politics, backing Taft in 1912 when Roosevelt bolted the party.

The NAM was soon joined by other business organizations. At the urging of President Taft and his Secretary of Commerce and Labor, the U.S. Chamber of Commerce was formed in 1912 out of local chambers of commerce. By 1913, according to the Department of Commerce and Labor, there were 240 regional and national trade associations. The Chamber itself was more politically diverse and its Washington office more inclined to seek a modus vivendi with the administration in power than the NAM, but in 1914, the Chamber lined up with the NAM and other business organizations to oppose an AFL proposal to exempt labor unions from monopoly injunctions under the Sherman Anti-Trust Act—the kind of injunction that had destroyed Debs's American Railway Union.

Business enjoyed considerable influence in these years. Standard Oil kept Ohio Senator Joseph Foraker on a retainer. Senators Nelson Aldrich of Rhode Island and Orville Platt of Connecticut allowed bankers from the Morgan and Co. and Kuhn, Loeb and Co. to draft their bills. U.S. Steel received regular intelligence from Pennsylvania Senators Donald Cameron and Matthew Quay. Taft and his cabinet solicited the NAM's advice on appointments. But the major legislation passed during the Roosevelt, Taft, and Wilson administrations represented a compromise between these business groups and labor and the left. That reflected the relative power of the competing groups, but it was also the result of intervention by an entirely different kind of organization: the elite policy group.

Some business leaders like Ohio industrialist Mark Hanna, Boston department store magnate Edward Filene, and Morgan and Co. partner George Perkins found common cause with the progressives who sought to craft what Woodrow Wilson called a "middle ground" between socialism and corporate individualism.[14] They opposed both the intransigence of the NAM and the revolutionary objectives of the Socialists and the IWW. They sought to eliminate or transcend class differences by accommodating what was most reasonable in the demands of the opposing classes. Theodore Roosevelt and Wilson, both of whom were intellectuals as well as politicians, exemplified two sides of the movement—Roosevelt was far less wary than Wilson of using governmental power—but they shared these objectives.[15] Roosevelt told journalist Jacob Riis in 1904:

> "I am for labor," or "I am for capital," substitutes something else for the immutable laws of righteousness. The one and the other would let the class man in, and letting him in is the one thing that will most quickly eat out the heart of the Republic.[16]

And Wilson declared in 1916:

> What I have tried to do is to get rid of any class division in the country, not only, but of any class consciousness and feeling. The worst thing that could happen to America would be that she should be divided into groups and camps in which there were men and women who thought that they were at odds with one another.[17]

What united the progressive economists, politicians like Roosevelt and Wilson, businessmen like Hanna and Perkins, social reformers like Jane Addams, and social gospel theologians like Rauschenbush was a belief in the power of government—whether as an expression of expert knowledge or popular will—to overcome the inequity and irrationality that was endemic to a pure market capitalism. They saw democracy as a social system in which the government itself would attempt to mitigate economic inequality. Wilson and Roosevelt—or Roosevelt and Debs—disagreed about the extent to which government could or should intervene in the market, but they shared this conception of positive government.

The clearest statements of the progressive faith were Herbert Croly's book *The Promise of American Life* and Roosevelt's speeches for the Progressive Party, which Croly helped to write. Croly argued that the older Jeffersonian and Jacksonian view of democracy and government, which had been meant to sustain an egalitarian society, had unwittingly encouraged the growth of trusts and robber barons. Unfettered competition had spawned industrial concentration and consolidation. In this way, the older faith "in individual freedom has resulted in a morally and socially undesirable distribution of wealth," he wrote. To keep the promise of American life, "the national government must step in and discriminate; not on behalf of liberty and the special individual, but on behalf of equality and the average man."*

The progressive movement found important allies in elite organizations. These included national policy groups such as the National Civic Federation and the American Alliance for Labor and Democracy, local and regional groups such as Edward Filene's Cooperative League, and foundations such as Russell Sage, Rockefeller, and Carnegie. And they

*Tocqueville also warned that Jacksonian democracy could eventually bequeath its opposite:

> As the conditions of men constituting the nation became more and more equal, the demand for manufactured commodities becomes more general and extensive. . . . Hence there are every day more men of great opulence and education who devote their wealth and knowledge to manufactures and who seek, by opening large establishments and by a strict division of labor, to meet the fresh demands which are made on all sides. Thus in proportion as the mass of the nation turns to democracy, that particular class which is engaged in manufactures becomes more artistic. Men grow more alike in the one, more different in the other; and inequality increases in the less numerous class in the same ratio in which it decreases in the community. Hence it would appear, on searching to the bottom, that aristocracy should naturally spring out of the bosom of democracy. (*Democracy in America,* New York, 1945, vol. 2, p. 170.)

included many local and state organizations, often founded by upper-class women, such as the Child Labor Committees, Consumers' Leagues, Charities Aid Societies, and church organizations. In the end, this larger progressive movement won out. It stood between the specter of European revolutionary socialism and the social Darwinism of the selfish rich.

Wilson's career demonstrates the triumph of progressivism. Before he became governor of New Jersey and president of the United States, Wilson's views on democracy and government sometimes sounded closer to those of the NAM than to the progressives. In a 1907 essay in the *Atlantic Monthly,* Wilson condemned any kind of government regulation of the economy as "socialistic."[18] He was also hostile to labor unions and supported the use of injunctions against strikes. But faced with political pressure from below and the arguments of progressives in Congress, Wilson established a record as president that put him clearly in the progressive camp. He compromised on the Clayton Anti-Trust Act, forbidding the use of labor injunctions except when "necessary to prevent irreparable injury to property." He signed bills—uniformly opposed by the NAM—providing workers' compensation for federal employees, making child labor illegal, and establishing an eight-hour day for railway workers. During World War I, he put into practice the Civic Federation's tripartite model of government, establishing government boards that included business, labor, and academic representatives to oversee the war effort.

The Progressive Era came close to what the pluralists called "balanced government." In the battle among interest groups, business held the upper hand, but its power was checked by elites and their organizations and by progressive, socialist, and populist political movements. The result affirmed a spirit of accommodation and class cooperation. As World War I came to a close, Herbert Croly and other progressives believed that these pluralist principles, which Wilson put into practice during the war, would govern America's future. But the end of the war brought instead the beginning of a very different era—one that repudiated the underlying tenets of the Progressive Era and changed the political balance of power in the country.

The Age of Mellon

The 1920s were one of the most inventive and interesting periods in American history. They saw the rapid growth of industry and manufacturing, highlighted by Henry Ford's Model T, the birth of consumer capitalism and the installment plan, and the growth of a national market for popular entertainment. But it was a much less positive time for American politics and democracy. The popular movements and elite organizations of the Progressive Era receded, as business leaders and organizations reclaimed control of the political system. Politics sustained economic growth, but in its blind subservience also hampered it, and contributed to its destruction in the Depression.

The conclusion of the Progressive Era was precipitated by business's sharp reaction to the specter of class war and the looming threat of revolution. While the IWW was destroyed by wartime repression, the AFL grew dramatically during the war, thanks to government-supervised bargaining agreements. In two years, its membership doubled from two million to four million.[19] The Socialist Party, which opposed the war and had its mails confiscated, its rallies disrupted, and its leader jailed, still held its own in the 1918 elections, electing 32 state legislators, compared to 20 in 1912 and 33 in 1914.[20] The Russian Revolution, which had climaxed with the Bolshevik takeover in October 1917, also roused revolutionary hopes. The Soviet leadership had organized the Communist Third International in March 1919 to spread the revolution. Karl Radek, its executive secretary, declared that the money the Comintern sent to Germany was "as nothing compared to the funds transmitted to New York for the purpose of spreading bolshevism in the United States."[21] William F. Dunne, a Socialist Party member who was elected to the Montana state legislature in 1918, contended that revolution was on the horizon. "Unemployment will increase, there'll be starvation, and some day the banks will fail and the people will come pouring out on the streets and the revolution will start."[22]

Most of the AFL leaders were opposed to the Russian Revolution, but some of them were impressed by the British Labor Party, which after the war drafted an ambitious plan to nationalize industry. In 1919, railway unions adopted a program, called the Plumb Plan, to nationalize the railroads, which the AFL endorsed. That year, too, workers went on strike in the textiles, clothing, food, transportation, steel, and coal industries. In January, after 35,000 Seattle dockworkers went out on strike for higher wages and a shorter workweek, the Central Labor Council declared a general strike on their behalf. In September, Boston policemen went out on strike after nineteen policemen had been fired for belonging to a union. Two days later, steelworkers, who were working twelve-hour days and seven-day weeks for an average of $28, struck. Soon afterward, 394,000 miners went out on strike.

Businesses responded to these strikes by standing firm. They won the support of city, state, and national officials, including Wilson's Attorney General A. Mitchell Palmer, who linked the strikes to the Russian Revolution. Seattle's general strike lasted five days until the mayor, charging a Communist plot, crushed it. When Massachusetts Governor Calvin Coolidge urged intransigence against the police strikers, Boston's mayor successfully replaced the entire police force. In October 1919, with the war over and 365,000 steelworkers out on strike, Wilson called for a National Industrial Conference to enshrine the collaborative principles of collective bargaining that had been practiced during the war. He appointed seventeen representatives of employers, including Elbert H. Gary, chairman of U.S. Steel, and nineteen representatives of unions. But when the labor representatives asked for the government to arbitrate the strike, Gary balked. When the labor representatives called for collective bargaining to become the peacetime norm between unions and management, the employers also balked. The conference broke up without reaching any agreement. With Palmer branding the strikers as reds, the steel owners held out for two months until the strikers returned to work without gaining any of their demands.

Business's reaction to the strike wave in 1919 established a precedent for the next decade. The NAM's strategy of attempting to block and destroy unions became widely accepted. Businesses organized local and national groups to back what they called the "American Plan." They branded collective bargaining as "un-American" and sought to establish company unions and to force workers to sign "yellow dog" contracts agreeing not to join a union. Hundreds of American Plan groups sprouted up in the early 1920s—forty-six in Illinois alone. The companies used force and subterfuge, when necessary, to prevent unionization. They blacklisted potential union organizers, they sent spies into shops and factories—according to one estimate there were 200,000 spies employed by 1928—and hired firms that specialized in busting picket lines. One organization, the National Metal Trades Association, was set up after the war expressly to break strikes.[23]

During the Progressive Era, business and businessmen had sometimes been looked upon with disfavor. To win public acclaim, corporations began employing public relations specialists. The first American "PR" agent was Ivy Lee, a former journalist who convinced the anthracite coal operators in 1906, after they had lost a strike, that they needed his services. Lee was subsequently hired to burnish the reputations of the Rockefellers after soldiers killed wives and children of striking miners during the 1914 Ludlow massacre. But it was the experience of World War I that convinced many business leaders that public relations could work. Former journalist George Creel, whom Wilson hired to run the government's Committee on Public Information during World War I, succeeded brilliantly in turning the public against the "Hun." Afterward, every company had to hire a PR man. Said businessman Roger Babson in 1921, "The war taught us the power of propaganda. Now when we have anything to sell to the American people, we know how to sell it. We have the school, the pulpit and the press."[24]

Every large bank and corporation hired a PR man to put out company newsletters and manage press relations. Companies began using polling techniques to test public opinion; businesses bought radio stations, endowed university chairs, and pressured schools to fire teachers they deemed subversive.[25] The guru of the new public relations men was Edward Bernays, a nephew of Freud, who worked for Creel during the war. Wrote Bernays in *Propaganda,* "As civilization has become more complex, the technical means have been invented and developed by which opinion may be regimented."[26]

B. J. Mullaney, a utility company official, explained the reason for public relations in testimony before Congress.

> When a destructive bill is pending in a legislature, it has to be dealt with in a way to get results. I am not debating that. But to depend, year after year, upon the usual political expedients for stopping hostile legislation is shortsightedness. In the long run isn't it better and surer to lay a groundwork with the people back home who have the votes, so that proposals of this character are not popular with them, rather than depend upon stopping such proposals when they get up to the legislature or commission?[27]

In the 1920s, businesses also began to establish offices in Washington, and trade associations, which had been located in New York City or Chicago, moved their headquarters to Washington. According to E. Pendelton Herring, businesses came to Washington because it was the "seat of government," and because it was also "the chief center of news. . . . There in one concentrated area, the ear of the entire nation can be reached."[28] All in all, the 1920s marked a zenith in business's influence over government. Wrote journalist William Allen White, "Businessmen crowded into the White House until the luncheon guest-list looked sometimes like a chart of interlocking directorates of high finance."[29]

Business's program was to defeat labor and to roll back the regulations that had been adopted in the Progressive Era. E. Hofer, a publicist whom business organizations hired to disseminate editorials and news to newspapers around the country, said that his highest priorities were "to reduce the volume of legislation that interferes with business and industry" and "to minimize and counteract political regulation or business that is hurtful."[30] Warren Harding put business's agenda succinctly in the 1920 campaign. What was wanted was "less government in business and more business in government."[31]

Under pressure from business, Harding appointed Pittsburgh banker and industrialist Andrew Mellon, one of the richest men in America and a major contributor to the Republican Party in Pennsylvania, as Secretary of the Treasury. The prim and dour Treasury Secretary became the leading member of the Harding, Coolidge, and Hoover administrations. Much more than Hoover, a former progressive who still retained the older commitment to a society that accommodated labor, Mellon was a representative of his class and narrow business interest. He single-mindedly went about reducing the tax burden on business and the wealthy, which he claimed was imperiling investment. His efforts initially encountered sharp resistance from progressives in Congress when he tried to undo Wilson's progressive tax code, but in 1926 he finally succeeded in revamping it. He drastically reduced tax rates for the wealthy, cut the estate tax in half, eliminated the gift tax, and reduced taxes on corporations. In 1928, he got Congress to cut corporate taxes again. After the crash of 1929, Democrats discovered that Mellon had been secretly granting tax credits and subsidies to many of the largest corporations, including those in which he and his family had significant holdings. He had even gotten the commissioner of Internal Revenue to provide him with a memo about how he could legally evade taxes.[32] He then hired the author of the memo to advise himself and his family. Heeding Mellon, the government also curbed spending on health and welfare and public works, while services to business, shipping subsidies, and law enforcement rose.[33] "The government is just a business and should be run on business principles," he declared.[34]

Business also won the battle for public opinion. One of the best-selling books of the 1920s was advertising man Bruce Barton's *The Man Nobody Knows,* a portrayal of Jesus as a businessman and the apostles as his salesmen. "He picked twelve men from the bottom ranks of business and forged them into an organization that conquered the world," Barton wrote. He described Jesus's parables as "the most powerful advertisements of all time."[35] Political scientists adjusted their view of business and its representatives. While they had earlier described lobbyists as representatives of "the interests"—a term carrying the same thrust as "the syndicate" or "the mob"—they now called them "legislative agents."[36]

In winning over the public, business succeeded in redefining democracy. Business and its Republican allies envisioned the captain of industry as a "rugged individualist" and government as the enemy of prosperity and equality. Corporate capitalism, if left to its own devices, would eliminate class differences. "We are reaching the position," Calvin Coolidge declared, "where the property class and the employed class are not one but identical."[37] Harding, Coolidge, and Hoover rejected the progressive view of the state. "It does not at all follow because abuses exist," Coolidge said, "it is the concern of the federal government to attempt their reform."[38] Government intervention, Hoover warned, "would increase rather than decrease abuse and corruption. It would stifle initiative and invention. It would undermine the development of leadership. It would cramp and cripple the mental and spiritual energies of our people."[39]

Business was so successful in pressing its case partly because it was far more united than it had been during the Progressive Era. The threat of Bolshevism and the strike wave of 1919 had united large and small employers. The NAM and the National Civic Federation no longer were at odds. During the 1920s, Civic Federation director Ralph Easley became obsessed with the menace of Bolshevism to the exclusion of all other interests. The federation's most active committee was its Department on the Study of Revolutionary Movements, which championed legislation to prevent Communist infiltration.[40] Much of the old progressive movement became transmuted into civic boosterism. The child labor and good government associations of the 1910s were replaced by business service clubs, which cheered the new individualism. The Rotary Club, founded in 1905, had 150,000 members by 1930. The Kiwanis Clubs grew from 205 in 1920 to 1,800 in 1929. The Lion's Club was founded in 1917; by 1930, there were 1,200 chapters.[41]

Business also benefited from having deceptively weak opponents. By 1920, the American socialist left had virtually disintegrated. It blamed its fall on the Palmer raids, which resulted in the deportation of several hundred foreign-born Soviet sympathizers, but the real culprit was the mindless revolutionary fervor created by the Russian Revolution. In 1919, about half the Socialists quit the old party, which they denounced as "right-wing," to form two new pro-Bolshevik Communist parties, a Communist Party dominated by recent immigrants, many of whom did not speak English, and a smaller Communist Labor Party led by John Reed and other native-born leftists. The Communists called for immediate insurrection.* When Palmer initiated his "red scare," both parties

*When Socialist Party and Marxist theoretician Leonard Boudin attended the Communist Labor Party convention, he left in disgust. "I did not leave a party of crooks to join a party of lunatics!" he is reported to have said. See Theodore Draper, *The Roots of American Communism,* New York, 1957, p. 180.

went underground in imitation of the Bolsheviks. At the beginning of 1919, the Socialist Party had boasted 106,000 members. By the year's end, the three parties—Communist, Communist Labor, and Socialist—had only 36,000 among them. The socialist left would never fully recover from this disastrous split.[42] What was politically viable (and not merely revolutionary fantasy) in the socialist movement would become part of the old progressive movement, which would attempt unsuccessfully to stage a comeback in 1924 when Robert M. La Follette ran for president on a third-party ticket. The progressive movement would not revive until the 1930s.

The labor movement fared almost as poorly as the socialist left. Union membership peaked at 5,047,800 in 1920. It fell to 3,622,000 in 1923 and to 3,442,600 in 1930—from 19.4 percent of the nonagricultural workforce in 1920 to only 10.2 percent in 1930.[43] Business intransigence took its toll, but so did the inability and unwillingness of the AFL's leadership to adapt to an economy and workforce different from that of the late nineteenth century, when the AFL began. Except for the miners, the AFL was organized primarily along craft lines—such as cigar makers (from whom Samuel Gompers came), carpenters, horseshoers, and plumbers (from whom later AFL-CIO leader George Meany came). Even though modern industries had eliminated many crafts, replacing the craftsman's tool with a machine and the craft worker with the assembly line worker, the AFL was unwilling to organize by industry. (When the AFL tried to organize the steelworkers in 1919, they had to appoint an unwieldy committee to oversee the twenty-four craft unions that claimed members in the steel factories.) As a result, during the 1920s, the federation held its own in construction and the remaining crafts, but lost the few members it had gained during the war in the great auto, steel, rubber, electrical utility, and chemical industries.

Business also benefited from the peculiar economy of the 1920s. After an initial panic and recession in 1920, the economy enjoyed rapid gains in output and productivity. National income rose 21 percent between 1923 and 1929.[44] The gains were sufficiently dramatic to defuse protest and anger against employers, but they were not dramatic nor secure enough to sustain the kind of confidence that buoyed protest militancy in the 1960s. Wages never kept pace with salaries and dividends. The highest

1 percent of income recipients increased their share of national income 19 percent from 1923 to 1929.[45] According to a Brookings study, unemployment was surprisingly high, due in part to automation on farms and in factories—up to 13 percent in 1924, 1925, and 1928.[46] As a result, there were pockets of progressive, socialist, and populist resistance to the reign of business, but for the most part, workers simply ignored politics. In all, the Age of Mellon represented a triumph of business over labor and over politics itself.

Voter turnout dropped precipitously—from 61.8 percent in 1916 to 48.9 percent in 1924, due only in part to woman suffrage.[47] There was a prevailing cynicism about politics and about government. In lectures given in 1929, Felix Frankfurter reflected, "Perhaps the dominant feeling about government today is distrust." Americans believed that "ineptitude and inadequacy are the chief characteristics of government."[48] Where the electorate was mobilized, it was at the margins over social issues. Wrote Walter Lippmann in 1927:

> There are no parties, there are no leaders, there are no issues. . . . The questions which really engage the emotion of the masses of the people are of a quite different order. They manifest themselves in the controversies over prohibition, the Ku Klux Klan, Romanism, Fundamentalism, immigration. These, rather than the tariff, taxation, credit and corporate control, are the issues which divide the American people.[49]

The elite organizations fared as poorly as labor and the left. During the Progressive Era, they had served as respected intermediaries between the classes, but business groups made clear from the beginning that their services were not required. John D. Rockefeller, Jr., humbled by the calumny heaped upon his name after the Ludlow massacre, established an Industrial Relations Department at the Rockefeller Foundation, headed by former Canadian Labor Minister Mackenzie King. But when Rockefeller urged U.S. Steel's Henry Clay Frick and Judge Elbert Gary to consider collective bargaining or employee representation during the 1919 steel strike, he found them "utterly opposed" to "representation of any kind."[50] Herbert Hoover was rebuked when he called a meeting with industrialists at New York's Metropolitan Club to urge them to "establish liaison" with Gompers and the AFL.[51]

Elite organizations by no means disappeared, but these groups had little effect on the policy during the Age of Mellon. The pursuit of the national interest became reduced to the enactment of business's American Plan. In *The New Republic,* Herbert Croly lamented that "Americanism itself [has] finally [become] popularly confused with a combination of optimism, fatalism, and conservatism."[52] During the 1920s, the ideal of the disinterested public servant was displaced by the image of the businessman as savior. Croly's former colleague Walter Lippmann looked upon this new governing class with scorn:

> Our rulers today consist of random collections of successful men and their wives. . . . They give orders. They have to be consulted. They can more or less effectively speak for, and lead some part of, the population. But none of them is seated on a certain throne, and all of them are forever concerned as to how they may keep from being toppled off. They do not know how they happen to be where they are, although they often explain what are the secrets of success. They have been educated to achieve success; few of them have been educated to exercise power. Nor do they count with any confidence upon retaining their power, nor in handing it on to their sons. They live, therefore from day to day, and they govern by ear.[53]

America, of course, paid a large price for the unwillingness of its leaders to see beyond their balance sheets. Mellon's economic policies favored profits and dividends over wages and encouraged both the industrial overcapacity and the speculative frenzy that led up to the stock market crash of 1929. American foreign policy during the 1920s also contributed to, or at least did little to stem, the gathering storm in Europe.

The New Deal

The stock market crashed in October 1929. By 1932, unemployment had climbed to 24.1 percent.[54] There were 660,000 unemployed in Chicago and a million in New York City. In Cleveland, 50 percent were out of work, in Akron and Toledo 80 percent.[55] Manufacturing output was 54 percent of what it had been before the crash. Treasury Secretary Andrew Mellon declared the crash a blessing. "It will purge the rottenness out of the systems. People will work harder, live a more moral life," the tribune of the rich declared.[56] But the initial victims of the purge were Mellon and his allies.

The crash and the Depression destroyed in one stroke the edifice of wisdom and invincibility that businessmen had erected for themselves. Wrote Gerald Johnson in 1932, "It will be many a long day before Americans of the middle class will listen with anything approaching the reverence they felt in 1928 whenever a magnate of business speaks."[57] Many Americans took a harsher view. At Congressional hearings, Senator Burton Wheeler told Charles Mitchell of the National City Bank, "The best way to restore confidence in the banks would be to take these crooked presidents out of the banks and treat them the same way as we treated Al Capone when he failed to pay his income tax."[58]

The crash itself was the immediate result of the speculative frenzy of the late 1920s, which took place amid a national and world economy that was already beginning to slow. But there were deeper factors at work that turned the crash into a full-fledged depression. The boom of the 1920s had been based on rapid increases in productivity that had occurred because of the replacement of steam by electricity and the introduction of scientific management. This created the danger of more goods being produced than workers had the income to purchase—what John Maynard Keynes would call a problem of effective demand. The danger was realized by the late 1920s as a growing proportion of income went to profits rather than to wages and to purchasing stocks and real estate rather than consumer goods.

In this sense, the Depression gave the lie to the widespread assumption that the success of capitalism depended on the sacrifice and even misery of the working class. It suggested that policies that improved workers' ability to purchase goods—and their standard of living—could also improve the overall economy. Stuart Chase, a journalist and not a professional economist, was a prophet of the new order. Writing in 1932, Chase argued the Depression was caused by a malfunction in the distribution, not the production, of goods. The only answer to depressions, Chase maintained, was "a dependable supply of purchasing power."[59] Such an argument—which would be made in more sophisticated form by Keynes and become widely accepted by economists and business leaders—would have been ridiculed in the Age of Mellon.

The onset of the Depression also fueled a heated rejection of Hoover and business's rugged individualism. Historian Charles Beard wrote in 1931, "The cold truth is that the individualist creed of everybody for himself and the devil take the hindmost is principally responsible for the distress in which Western civilization finds itself."[60] In an article in *The Nation,* economist Ernest Gruening, later a senator from Alaska, reaffirmed what Croly and Theodore Roosevelt had argued about the government and the corporation. Gruening wrote that in order to create a "self-governing democracy, the people will proceed from control of the political state, and by means of it, to control also of the now uncontrollable economic super-power, a conquest essential if we would make 'life, liberty, and the pursuit of happiness' other than a travesty."[61] After he was reelected in 1936, Roosevelt made a similar argument. "The power of a few to manage the economic life of the Nation must be diffused among the many or be transferred to the public and its democratically responsible government."[62]

The rejection of business and their Republican backers registered at the polls. In the 1930 election, Democrats picked up 49 House seats and 8 Senate seats. In 1932, a coalition of progressive Democrats and Republicans passed the Norris–La Guardia Act forbidding the use of the injunction against strikes and outlawing the yellow dog contract. That year, veterans also staged a "Bonus Army" march in Washington, but political activism was slow to take hold, as the Depression's initial impact was shock and despair. The transformation of politics only began in earnest after Franklin Roosevelt's landslide victory for the presidency in November 1932.

The 1932 elections—and even more so the 1934 Congressional elections—gave a coalition of progressive Democrats and Republicans major influence over Congress. These legislators—Republicans like Hiram Johnson, Robert La Follette, Jr., and George Norris, and Democrats like Robert Wagner, Sam Rayburn, and Hugo Black—included both the heirs to pre–World War I progressivism and a large number of urban progressives elected from districts created by Congressional reapportionment in 1930.[63] These politicians became closely linked to the growing industrial labor movement. In 1934 and 1935, a number of populist and socialist movements also threatened to challenge the Roosevelt administration from the left. In 1934, Louisiana Senator Huey Long founded an organization called "Share Our Wealth." By February 1935, Long claimed more than 27,000 clubs and a mailing list of 7.5 million. A poll by the Democratic National Committee showed that if he ran for president on a third-party ticket in 1936, he would win between three and four million votes.[64]

In 1934, the labor movement, inspired by the National Recovery Act, which called on employers to establish unions (without stipulating whether or not they would be company unions), awoke from its decade-long slumber. There were 1,856 strikes involving 1,470,000 workers.[65] Strikes engulfed Toledo, Minneapolis, and San Francisco. Garment workers, coal miners, truck drivers, and West Coast longshoremen scored significant gains, but other workers in steel, textiles, and rubber were defeated, partly because of the indifference of the AFL leadership, which rejected pleas to organize on industrial rather than craft lines.

The Depression also revived the elite networks and organizations that had flourished in the Progressive Era but floundered in the 1920s. The Russell Sage Foundation, the American Association for Labor Legislation, the Taylor Society, founded by industrial engineer Frederick Taylor, and the Twentieth Century Fund, established by Edward Filene and manufacturer Henry Dennison, encouraged social scientists to meet with businessmen and with labor leaders to develop programs that would arrest the Depression, partly through improving the workers' lot.* Much of the major legislation in Roosevelt's first term—from the Na-

*In his autobiography, *A Life in Our Times* (Boston, 1981), John Kenneth Galbraith recalled being hired by Dennison, a paper product manufacturer, in 1936 as a tutor and co-author of a study on employment in the Depression. Galbraith, who had not yet read Keynes, recounted how he viewed with incredulity Dennison's insistence that the Depression was caused by the working class having too little to spend and the upper classes too much to save. When he finally read Keynes, "I discovered that Keynes was with Dennison and not with me" (p. 65).

tional Industrial Recovery Act to the Social Security Act—came out of studies from these groups. Many of the intellectuals who assumed key policy positions had worked closely with these groups.*

Another important elite network was organized around Harvard Law professor Felix Frankfurter.[66] After graduating first in his class at Harvard Law School in 1906, Frankfurter had joined a prestigious Wall Street law firm. Bored by corporate law, he had gone to work under U.S. attorney Henry Stimson, even at a considerable loss in salary. Frankfurter followed Stimson to Washington when Taft made him Secretary of War. In Washington, he made the acquaintance of Brandeis, who helped get him an appointment at Harvard Law School. Like Brandeis, he was a progressive deeply interested in the "labor question." He was close not merely to Brandeis and Oliver Wendell Holmes, Jr., but also to Croly and the editors of *The New Republic.* When he served during World War I as chairman of the War Labor Policies Board, he became friendly with Assistant Secretary of the Navy Franklin Roosevelt.

At Harvard, Frankfurter encouraged his students to take on social causes and enter public service. He disdained the lawyer as businessman, and championed the cause of public administration. "The difficulties of our social-economic problems will not abate with time," Frankfurter wrote just after the stock market crash. "One may be confident that they will become more complicated. They will make increasing demands upon training intelligence. If government is to be equal to its responsibilities, it must draw more and more on men of skill and wisdom for public administration."[67]

Once Roosevelt became president, Frankfurter operated as a kind of personnel agent for the New Deal, acting not merely to advance his own standing and pet causes, but also to further the ideal of disinterestedness.

*These intellectuals included brain trusters Rexford Tugwell and Adolf Berle, Jr., Secretary of Labor Frances Perkins, and William Leiserson, future chairman of the National Labor Relations Board. Sidney Hillman, the president of the Amalgamated Clothing Workers and a key ally of John L. Lewis in the AFL, was close to Filene, Leiserson, and the Twentieth Century Fund. Bruce Bliven, who would succeed Croly as editor of *The New Republic,* was on the board of the Twentieth Century Fund. See Steven Fraser, *Labor Will Rule: Sidney Hillman and the Rise of American Labor,* New York, 1991, p. 130.

"He has a passion for good, disinterested, inconspicuous work in government," the columnist Joseph Alsop observed.[68] Many of the Roosevelt administration's key bills were written by Frankfurter's students and protégés, whom he helped get jobs with the administration. These included Benjamin Cohen and Thomas Corcoran, who wrote the laws creating the Securities and Exchange Commission and regulating utility holding companies and who became key White House advisors; James Landis, who became SEC commissioner; State Department official Dean Acheson; White House official James Rowe; Tennessee Valley Authority director David Lilienthal; Labor Department counsel Charles Wyzanski; and State Department official Herbert Feis. These men didn't necessarily agree about every administration policy, but they shared Frankfurter's ideal of public service and his opinion of the failure of business rule during the 1920s. One administration critic described Frankfurter's recruits as "boys with their hair ablaze," but Frankfurter defended them as "public servants of higher grade."[69]

Business organizations were divided over how to respond to the New Deal. The NAM was one of the few to maintain its old stance. NAM president John Edgerton blamed the Depression squarely on the workers. If workers "do not practice the habits of thrift and conservation . . . is our economic system . . . to blame?" he asked in 1930.[70] The NAM opposed Social Security as the "ultimate socialistic control of life and industry."[71] A few businessmen like Filene and Dennison worked with the elite organizations and with the Business Advisory Council, which the Roosevelt administration established in June 1933 to provide advice from, but also to marshal support among sympathetic business leaders. The council included GE's Gerard Swope; Walter Teagle of Standard Oil; Pierre S. Du Pont, board chairman of E. I. Du Pont de Nemours & Co.; and Alfred P. Sloan, chairman of General Motors. It backed the administration's early efforts, but many of the members resigned during the "second hundred days" of 1935 to join the NAM and Du Pont's Liberty League in unequivocal opposition.

By 1935, there was a unique political situation: business and businessmen lacked decisive influence, even a veto, over policy; and an assortment of labor leaders, socialists, populists (led by Long and his movement), and progressive politicians and social scientists (with a smattering of businessmen) were demanding dramatic change. That was the basis for Roosevelt's climactic "second hundred days" in 1935.[72] Roosevelt's legislation that year established a high-water mark of progressivism. It included the Social Security Act, which eventually became the centerpiece of a new welfare capitalism; the Wagner Act, which granted workers the right to join unions without obstruction from employers; a wealth tax that increased estate, gift, and capital gains taxes and levied an excess profits tax; a Public Utility Holding Company Act that ended the utility empires of the 1920s; and major new spending programs, including the Rural Electrification Administration and the Public Works Administration.

The New Deal initiatives furthered the integration of government and economy that had begun during the Progressive Era. The reforms made the government, and not merely the courts or militia, a witting party to the relations between business and labor. The Wagner Act was based on the central contention of the new economics: that whatever prevented workers from improving their standard of living contributed to the Depression itself. "The inequality of bargaining power," the act stated, "substantially burdens and affects the flow of commerce and tends to aggravate recurrent business depressions." But it was also based on an explicitly pluralist view of democracy. By making it more difficult for employers to impede workers' organization, the Wagner Act sought to redress the "inequality of bargaining power between employees who do not possess full freedom of association . . . and employers who are organized in the corporate or other forces of association."

Jefferson and Jackson had seen government itself as a threat to liberty and equality. Citizens could meet that threat through their participation in politics. But the rise of corporate capitalism had undermined the power of the individual citizen to affect history. The ordinary worker, forced to sell his labor power to a large company, was no match for the managers and financiers of the new capitalism. The Wagner Act was the first piece of legislation to acknowledge that economic and political equality depended upon workers organizing to counter the power of the corporations and their managers. Democracy depended on the countervailing power of groups, without which democracy would be a sham.

But the Wagner Act did more than acknowledge the power of

groups in politics. It made government responsible for ensuring that the power of business would be challenged, or perhaps even matched, by that of labor. The pluralist theory of government—as spelled out by Bentley and his disciples—was a theory of might is right. The democratic pluralism of the New Deal was entirely different: its premise was that a society in which the power of business overwhelmed that of labor was wrong and that it was the responsibility of government to counter the power of business with that of labor—and by extension, the ordinary American.

The legislation of the second hundred days also expanded the scope of government and the meaning of democracy. It implicated the national government in the broader welfare of American workers. It became responsible, along with employers, for Americans' standard of living. In its initial form, Social Security was a carefully wrought insurance scheme that merely transferred income from workers to retirees, but by replacing private with government insurance, the Roosevelt administration opened up the question of government's greater responsibilities. Equally, the New Deal's initial relief programs were targeted at the emergency created by the Depression, but they, too, created a presumption that the government would now seek to prevent large-scale unemployment. In this way, the second hundred days didn't merely shift the balance of power between business and labor; they also broadened the terrain on which the two sides would contest for power, income, and benefits.

The immediate political effects of legislation were dramatic. The Wagner Act speeded changes already taking place in the labor movement. In November 1935, John L. Lewis, the leader of the United Mine Workers, led a walkout of the fledgling industrial unions from the AFL, establishing the Congress of Industrial Organizations as a rival federation. The CIO formed Labor's Non Partisan League to mobilize union members behind Roosevelt's reelection. In spite of almost united business opposition, Roosevelt won by another landslide, and Democrats and progressive Republicans increased their margins in both the Senate and the House of Representatives. Union organizers from both the CIO and the AFL unleashed another strike wave. From September 1936 to May 1937, 484,711 workers were involved in sit-down strikes, where workers would take over the factories. Roosevelt and Democratic governors like Michigan's Frank Murphy refused to heed the companies' requests for troops to reclaim their factories. In February 1937, General Motors, the biggest prize of all, fell to the United Auto Workers. At the height of the New Deal, progressive politics and a revived labor movement proved a match for business and set the agenda for the elite organizations.

The legislation of the second hundred days created a long-term constituency for Democrats, progressives, and liberals. Programs like Social Security and rural electrification became symbols of progressive and liberal commitment to Americans' well-being. Even during the backlash to the New Deal in the late 1930s and to the welfare state in the 1980s, politicians who attempted to overturn these programs risked almost certain defeat in the polls. As a result of the New Deal, American politics shifted decisively away from the underlying assumptions about the limits of government that prevailed during the Age of Mellon. It would be another four decades before these new assumptions would be effectively challenged.

[3]

The Great American Celebration

In 1939, as Roosevelt's New Deal had clearly begun to lose its momentum, historian Arthur M. Schlesinger introduced a theory to explain why American politics had undergone such sharp changes in direction, and where it was now headed. Schlesinger, whose son would also become a famous historian, divided American political history into periodic cycles similar to business cycles. He saw alternating periods of conservatism and liberalism, rightward and leftward politics, and governmental passivity and activity: "A period of concern for the rights of the few has been followed by one of concern for the wrongs of the many. Emphasis on the welfare of property has given way to emphasis on human welfare."[1]

Schlesinger naturally labeled the Progressive Era (1901–18) "liberal," the 1920s (1918–31) "conservative," and the New Deal (1932–) "liberal." On this basis, he predicted that a "conservative" era would begin in the mid-1940s.* Schlesinger turned out to be half-right—a new political era did begin sometime in the 1940s—but it defied the cyclic alternation between left and right, liberal and conservative, that had characterized twentieth-century politics until then. It represented a turn away from

*In a revised version of the essay, published in 1949, Schlesinger posited a twelfth, conservative era beginning in 1947 and ending in 1962, and a liberal one that would last until 1978, followed by another conservative one. See Arthur M. Schlesinger, *Paths to the Present,* New York, 1949.

New Deal's democratic pluralism, but not back toward the corporate individualism of the 1920s. Instead the politics of the Truman and Eisenhower years was characterized by the preponderance of powerful interest groups *and* of elites. They saw the emergence in practice of what James Landis had called the "umpire theory" and Earl Latham had tabbed the "referee theory" of government, in which government acted not as a guarantor of democratic pluralism but merely as an arbitrator among interest groups.

The End of the New Deal

The collapse of the New Deal occurred very suddenly and took the Roosevelt administration unawares. In November 1936, flush with another landslide victory, Roosevelt and his advisors believed that they had beaten the Depression—that month, business activity climbed to pre-Depression levels for the first time. They thought that they could build on the reforms launched during the second hundred days. Roosevelt boasted to Harold Ickes that he now had a "free hand" to reshape the country.[2] His main obstacle appeared to be the Supreme Court, which had thrown out the Agricultural Adjustment Act and the National Industrial Recovery Act. To create a New Deal majority on the court, Roosevelt proposed a law that would allow the president to add new judges when aging judges refused to retire. Roosevelt also sought to complete another part of his original agenda—to transform the Democratic Party by purging conservative Southern Democrats and attracting Midwestern Republican progressives.[3]

Within the administration, power had shifted by 1937 to the staffers who were called the "New Dealers" because of their eagerness to build on the second hundred days. Roosevelt's more conservative brain trusters such as Raymond Moley had been replaced by Ickes and by disciples of Frankfurter like Corcoran, Cohen, and Landis.[4] They foresaw the expansion of the New Deal's regulatory agencies to create a new kind of public administration that would uphold the public interest against the threat of business domination. James Landis, who headed the Securities and Exchange Commission and later the Civil Aeronautics Board, argued that in order to police and regulate industry, government had to create an "administrative process" that allowed experts to make decisions about particular industries. Landis's model and that of the New Dealers was not the attenuated interest group pluralism that would later characterize administrative decision, but democratic pluralism. It was the republican rather than the referee theory of government.

During the same time, both the AFL and the CIO continued to expand their membership, widening the New Deal's most important base of support. That winter, the CIO organized U.S. Steel and its subsidiaries. In the late spring, the Steelworkers' Organizing Committee declared a strike at "little steel"—Bethlehem, Republic, Youngstown, and Inland Steel. The movement that included insurgent labor, Southern and Western populists and progressives, the business community, and universities appeared to be unstoppable. Yet sometime that summer of 1937, the New Deal lost its momentum.

Roosevelt's failure to extend the New Deal during his second term is often blamed on his attempt to pack the court, which split the progressive coalition. (Brandeis himself opposed the move.) But the most important factor was the economy itself. Confident of the economy's buoyancy, Roosevelt had heeded the advice of his Treasury Secretary Henry Morgenthau and slashed public expenditures to balance the budget. That summer, as the administration's budget cuts began to take effect, the economy began to slump, and in October the stock market crashed. From the summer through the spring of 1938, industrial production fell 40 percent, and 6 million workers lost their jobs. Unemployment climbed back to 19 percent.[5]

With the economy faltering, businesses became increasingly unwilling to meet union demands. The "little steel" companies refused to recognize the Steelworkers' Organizing Committee. Company officials encouraged local police to fire on workers and their families. In July 1937, the strike ended in defeat for the CIO. Other companies took a similar hard line. From 1938 to 1940, CIO membership actually declined from 4 million to 3.6 million. The new federation was also hampered by continuing jurisdictional disputes with the AFL, which carried over into what legislation they backed and which candidates they supported.

Where the public had blamed the crash of 1929 on business and Wall

Street, many Americans blamed this slide on the administration. Employed Americans, who had identified with the unemployed in 1932 and 1934, now viewed public expenditures for the unemployed as a drain on their own income. Middle-class professionals and property owners were alarmed by the wave of sit-down strikes. The populist movements of the mid-1930s had already turned anti-Semitic and racist. Midwestern Republicans who had backed the New Deal fretted about whether Roosevelt would drag the country into a war in Europe—a concern that would become even more pronounced in 1940.[6]

The change in the political climate registered clearly in the 1938 elections. In the Democratic primaries, progressive challengers, backed by Roosevelt, failed to unseat conservative incumbents in Georgia, Alabama, and Maryland. In the general election, the Republicans didn't lose a single seat, while Democrats lost 81 seats in the House, 8 in the Senate, and a net of 13 governorships. In Ohio, Republican Robert Taft, who would become the leader of anti–New Deal forces in Congress, won a Senate seat, while several prominent New Deal governors, including Michigan's Murphy, lost. The Democrats continued to enjoy a majority in each house, but a coalition of conservative Southern Democrats and Republicans now held a veto over the administration's legislative agenda.

From November 1938 through American entry into the world war in December 1941, these Southern Democrats and Republicans, backed by the NAM, the Liberty League, and business leaders alarmed by the spread of industrial unionism, blocked the expansion of the New Deal. Roosevelt and his Democratic supporters would not be able to pass a single new piece of reform legislation for the remainder of his time in office. Roosevelt's opponents also began to chip away at the edifice of democratic reform that he had already erected. With Roosevelt still enormously popular, they didn't attack him directly, but instead went after New Deal agencies by charging that they were being run by Communists—a charge given some credence by the smattering of Communists within the administration. The most important agency was the National Labor Relations Board (NLRB), or as *Fortune* termed it, the "G—— D—— Labor Board."[7]

In 1938 the House had established a Committee for the Investigation of Un-American Activities, chaired by Texan Martin Dies. The committee's liberal sponsors had believed it would be used to root out Nazi sympathizers, but Dies used it instead to attack the NLRB and the CIO. The next year, Republicans and Southern Democrats also established a special Committee to Investigate the National Labor Relations Board.[8] They introduced legislation to limit the agency's scope and powers. Roosevelt temporarily headed off these measures by replacing board members who viewed the NLRB as an instrument of social justice with appointees who saw it purely as a forum for resolving disputes.[9]

Truman and Taft-Hartley

During World War II and its immediate aftermath, American political history—the cycle of reform leading to reaction—appeared to be repeating itself. It was 1917–21 all over again. War brought national unity. Under the supervision of Roosevelt appointees, business leaders joined labor officials and liberal academics on government war-planning agencies. Just as during World War I, business and labor both prospered under this arrangement. Businesses operated at full capacity for the first time since the October 1929 crash, while the AFL and CIO gained new members by trading off higher wages and the right to strike for union recognition and the closed shop. Union membership climbed from 10.5 million at the beginning of the war to 14.75 million at the end. Roosevelt's business foes from the NAM and the Liberty League kept a grudging silence, while the U.S. Chamber of Commerce, under a new president, Eric Johnston, adopted a conciliatory stance toward labor. Johnston, who advocated a "new capitalism," described collective bargaining as "an established and useful reality."[10]

Like the post–World War I socialists and labor organizers, labor and the liberal movement had their hopes unduly inflated by the war experience. They hatched plans to revive the New Deal and to expand their own political base. With almost one-third of American workers belonging to a union, they believed they had an opportunity to become the dominant influence in American politics. The liberals focused on a bill that committed the government to ensuring full employment. The proposal, inspired by the Economic Bill of Rights that Roosevelt had advocated in his last State of the Union address, was introduced in the Senate by James E. Murray of Montana in January 1945. The CIO's Political Action Committee, the Union for Democratic Action (later Americans for Democratic Action), and the National Farmers Union strongly backed it.[11]

The unions sought to win back the share of profits they had given up during World War II and prevent backsliding. The war's end brought the biggest wave of strikes since 1919—the result partly of workers suffering from a 30 percent decline in their wages as overtime was phased out. In November 1945, 320,000 autoworkers went out on strike, followed soon after by workers in steel, rubber, meatpacking, oil refining, and electrical appliances. Strikes shut down Rochester, Oakland, and Pittsburgh. The CIO also began a major organizing drive in the South, dubbed Operation Dixie.

But just as after World War I, the strikes encountered stiff resistance, and Operation Dixie proved a failure.[12] As the Cold War began, the coalition that united liberals, labor, and the left also began to fray. In 1947, the movement virtually split into two, with liberal anti-Communists congregated in the Americans for Democratic Action and Cold War critics and outright Communists in the Progressive Citizens for America. In 1948, the PCA would become the vehicle for Henry Wallace's third-party challenge to Harry Truman. Buoyed initially by illusions of omnipotence, the broader liberal movement seemed to be coming apart just as the progressive movement had disintegrated after World War I and the Russian Revolution.

American business emerged from the war stronger than ever. Most Americans recognized that the efforts of the nation's industry—highlighted by the rapid conversion of the auto industry to war production—had been instrumental in the Allied victory. With war's end, business leaders were once again accorded respect, even if the public still feared and distrusted them.[13] Corporations expanded their operations in Washington. New legal firms that specialized in lobbying began to sprout up around Washington's K Street—some of them, like Arnold & Porter, staffed by veterans of the New Deal. New trade associations opened their doors, such as the National Association of Electric Companies. Business mounted a major public relations effort, led by the newly created Advertising Council.[14]

Some businesses and business organizations reacted to the postwar strike wave just as businesses had reacted to the strike wave after World War I. At the Chamber of Commerce, local chamber leaders forced the ouster of the conciliatory Eric Johnston. Together, the Chamber and the NAM declared war on labor.[15] In the eighteen months after the armistice, House Republicans and conservative Democrats, working with these business groups, introduced seventy-three bills designed to repeal the Wagner Act. In November 1946, voters, fearful of Communism, impatient with meat shortages, and concerned that they would be prevented from enjoying prosperity by incendiary labor disputes and a seemingly inept administration, rewarded Republicans with the majority in Congress they had been denied since 1932. Republicans gained a 51-to-45 margin in the Senate and a 246-to-188 edge in the House. It looked as if the United States was about repeat the experience of the early 1920s, when militant business leaders and their Republican allies, bent on restoring the status quo ante, took control of the country. But it didn't happen.

One reason that 1946 did not turn out to be 1919 was the enduring legacy of the New Deal. While the Progressive Era's democratic reform achievements had occurred primarily on the state and local levels, the New Deal had made the federal government responsible for the welfare of its citizens—for their employment and for their security in old age. Even if voters did not support the extension of the New Deal, they backed what it had accomplished. In 1948, Truman defeated his Republican opponent Tom Dewey by painting him as an opponent of Social Security and other New Deal programs. Another reason why this period was different was that while the liberal movement faltered, it did not collapse. Anti-Communist liberals who backed Truman carried the day against the pro-Soviet left in the Democratic Party and in the labor movement. The labor movement didn't disintegrate as it had in the 1920s. Spurred by competition between the two federations, unions kept organizing. They won more bargaining elections than they lost, and while the movement failed to expand in the South, it continued to command about a third of the workforce right up through the 1955 merger of the AFL and the CIO.

The role of elites was also decisive. The survival and success of liberal anti-Communism depended on the support it received from elites and elite organizations. As the Cold War with the Soviet Union began, elite organizations, seeking to marshal a national consensus, made a special effort to include labor leaders and liberals in their deliberations and to encourage the spread of liberal anti-Communism. In 1946, the Council on Foreign Relations recruited top labor officials from both the CIO and the AFL, including the staff director of the CIO's International Affairs Department and the executive director of the AFL's Free Trade Union Committee.[16] By recruiting labor leaders and liberals, the elite organizations deflected attempts by the NAM and Republicans to discredit unions and liberal organizations by tying them to their former pro-Soviet allies.

A significant segment of business leaders also opposed the efforts of the NAM and Republicans to repeal the Wagner Act and Social Security and to abolish the New Deal regulatory agencies. These leaders were products of a structure of business that had changed dramatically from the early 1920s. In the 1920s, the new corporations still had to share power with thousands of small and medium-sized enterprises, but by 1950, the economy was thoroughly dominated by several hundred firms and banks. The 200 largest nonfinancial corporations accounted for 40.3 percent of the total value produced.[17] Many of these corporations had been unionized during the 1930s or World War II, and had learned to live with, and even benefit from, long-term negotiated contracts with their workforce. Their executives had accepted the basic premise of the New Deal. They had worked with Roosevelt's Business Advisory Council and opposed the anti-union, antigovernment thrust of the NAM, many of whose leaders would later join the far-right John Birch Society.[18] As the debate over legislation began, they attempted to forge a middle ground between the New Deal liberals and the NAM in much the same way as the leaders of the National Civic Federation had earlier blazed a path between socialists and laissez-faire capitalists.

The organization that summed up this new sentiment among business leaders was the Committee on Economic Development (CED), which was founded in Washington during World War II. In September 1942, Paul Hoffman and William Benton, a vice president of the University of

Chicago, established the CED. Hoffman, the Lee Iacocca of the 1930s, had successfully pulled Studebaker, a mid-sized auto maker, out of bankruptcy in 1934. He was one of the first businessman lionized by Henry Luce in his new magazine *Fortune*. Benton was a successful advertising man—the cofounder with Chester Bowles of Benton and Bowles—who retired from business in 1936 at age thirty-six to become vice president of the University of Chicago, which was being run by his college classmate Robert Hutchins. Hutchins, a key figure in his own right, recruited Hoffman, who had attended the University of Chicago, to become a trustee. Benton and Hoffman met at Chicago and hatched plans for the CED.[19]

Many of the CED's founding 200 members were from the Roosevelt administration's Business Advisory Council. Its purpose was to develop plans for the postwar economy that would prevent the recurrence of another depression. While composed of businessmen and academics, it defined itself in the tradition of elite organizations like the National Civic Federation and the Twentieth Century Fund. Its mission, its charter said, was to carry out research "without regard to and independently of the special interests of any group in the body politic, either political, social, or economic."[20] Hoffman and Benton were far more similar to Hanna, Perkins, and other progressives than to the businessmen who belonged to the NAM or the Liberty League. Hoffman told the group's founders that it was "very important that we as a group think of ourselves not as 'right,' 'left,' 'conservative' or 'radical' but as 'responsible.' "[21] "Responsible" meant for Hoffman what "disinterested" meant to the progressives.

Hoffman was a Republican who backed Wendell Willkie in 1940, while Benton was a Roosevelt Democrat, but both men shared the progressive view of business and labor. Hoffman began negotiating with an AFL union in 1934 and signed a contract with the United Auto Workers in 1936 without a strike. He was guided as a manager by what he called "enlightened self-interest." Hoffman, who supported the Wagner Act, believed in the employer who "deals frankly with his employees, pays the highest wages, and promotes the self-interest of the workingman." He declared that the "personal dignity of the workman and his individual right to plan his own life certainly encompass the privilege of belonging to a union and dealing collectively with an employer."[22] Hoffman applied the same principles to the economy as a whole.

Hoffman and Benton fell under the influence of Beardsley Ruml, a social scientist turned businessman. Ruml typified the progressive commitment to using social science in the interest of accommodating business and labor. He got a Ph.D. from the University of Chicago in psychometry in 1917. At age twenty-seven he became the director of the $74 million Laura Spelman Rockefeller Memorial Fund. The fund had previously specialized in medical research, but he turned it toward social science. In 1930, he went back to the University of Chicago as a dean of social science and professor of education. But in 1934 he joined W. H. Macy's as its treasurer, and in 1937 became a director of the Federal Reserve Bank of New York. An ardent Keynesian, he was responsible the next year for wooing Roosevelt away from the balanced budget. He would be the key intellectual in the CED and a bridge between the CED and other elite organizations, such as the Twentieth Century Fund.

The CED attracted the more thoughtful corporate executives of the 1940s, including General Motors' Charles Wilson, General Electric's Philip Reed, and Kodak's Marion Folsom. It also commanded the support of major figures in the media and advertising, including Luce and Raymond Rubicam of Young and Rubicam. The CED supported tax cuts and spending to stimulate the postwar economy. It backed government planning to prevent unemployment. It supported foreign aid to help other countries buy American exports. And as the battle over the new era resumed after the war, it opposed efforts by the NAM and other business conservatives to repeal the New Deal and cripple the labor movement.

The first big battle occurred over the progressives' full-employment bill. It probably would have been defeated outright had not Hoffman, appearing in August 1945 before the Senate Banking and Currency Committee, lent critical but qualified support to the measure. Hoffman praised the bill, but contended that the commitment to "full employment" was unrealistic, preferring a "coordinated and progressive program of measures designed to meet the responsibilities of the federal government for a more stable and prosperous society."[23] Hoffman recommended that the bill establish economic oversight committees in the executive and legislative branches to ensure that government met this responsibility. Hoffman and the CED accepted the idea that the government was responsible for ensuring prosperity, but they rejected giving administrators the power and the discretion to adopt whatever programs were needed to achieve it.

The Senate passed a bill that committed the government to "continuing full employment," but the bill was soon bottled up in a five-man House committee, with two of its members backing the Senate bill and two members against any bill. The swing vote was that of Mississippi Democrat Will Whittington. Whittington used the CED's approach, laid out in a draft, to forge a compromise that passed the House and became the Employment Act of 1946. It established the Council of Economic Advisors in the White House and the Joint Economic Committee of Congress and required them to report annually on government efforts to "promote maximum employment, production, and purchasing power." The Employment Act gave government administrators an advisory role in establishing how it should exercise that responsibility. The final determination would be made through the interplay of interest groups and elites, in which the CED and similar organizations hoped to exercise preponderant influence.

The battle then shifted to bills designed to curb the NLRB and labor. In June 1946, Congress passed a measure that would have severely limited the right to strike, but its supporters could not override Truman's veto. After the Republicans captured Congress in November 1946, they began drawing up a new labor bill. In April the House passed a measure that the NAM reportedly helped to write.[24] It would have barred the CIO from bargaining industry-wide, which the NAM's small and medium-sized firms believed put them at a disadvantage. It would have also repealed the Norris–La Guardia Act's ban on employer injunctions against strikes and would have created an "employer bill of rights."[25] In effect, it would have destroyed the CIO unions and put the labor movement back to where it had been in 1929.

But the corporate executives in the CED and in the American Management Association favored on an industry-wide basis bargaining rather than having to reach hundreds of separate contracts. Under pressure from the business elite and needing Democratic votes to override a veto, the Republicans in Congress had to back down from their attempt to repeal the Wagner Act. They removed the most provocative provisions from the Taft-Hartley Act, which passed over Truman's veto in June 1947.

Union leaders, who branded Taft-Hartley a "slave labor law," particularly took umbrage at a provision in the act that had been insisted on by Southern Democrats. It allowed states to pass right-to-work laws forbidding unions to require that new employees join the union. But its effect was not so much to cripple existing unions as to make it difficult for the labor movement to expand out of its Northern industrial and its old AFL craft base. The main thing Taft-Hartley did was to complete the transformation of the NLRB from a tribune of social justice to a dispute settlement board. It subjected NLRB decisions to judicial review and appeals and it turned NLRB members into referees of labor-management disputes. It put the class struggle between labor and business in the hands of Washington lawyers and lobbyists.[26]

Just as the Wagner Act summed up the New Deal's view of government and democracy, Taft-Hartley summed up a crucial ingredient in the new postwar pluralism. Under the pluralist assumption that business, labor, and other interest groups could contend for themselves on the federal terrain, it shifted the locus of governmental power away from the agencies themselves to the competition among the interest groups and their members and lobbyists. Like the Employment Act, Taft-Hartley rejected the activist republican view of government that Croly had advocated during the Progressive Era and that had prevailed during Roosevelt's first term in favor of the conception of the state as referee among contesting interest groups.

This view of pluralism had been most clearly expressed in a piece of legislation that had passed in 1946 with little public notice, but that anticipated the final version of Taft-Hartley. In the 1930s, the NAM and the New Deal's most strident opponents favored abolishing the regulatory agencies created during the Progressive Era and the New Deal, but corporate leaders had again sought a middle way. They wanted to limit the prerogatives of agency administrators without eliminating the SEC, FCC, and other federal agencies. Corporate lawyers from Washington, including Covington & Burlington's Dean Acheson who represented the electrical power industry, sought to rewrite the rules governing agency decisions. They worked through the American Bar Association, which in

1940 recommended a new set of rules that would have made regulatory decisions subject to judicial review. The bill passed Congress, but Roosevelt vetoed it.

In 1946 the American Bar Association and the corporate lobbyists finally got their way. Congress passed, and Truman, fearing an override, signed, the Administrative Procedure Act. While it had little immediate effect, it helped to undermine the democratic pluralism of the New Deal and to establish the referee theory, or what Landis had called the "umpire theory" of administration. The new act forced regulators to hold extensive hearings prior to making rulings and subjected their rulings to court review to determine whether they were "reasonable."[27] It turned the regulatory agencies themselves into mini-courts in which the different affected interests vied for the regulators' attention. The act was a boon to Washington's lawyers and lobbyists.[28] It removed power from the government and placed it in their hands. Government decisions became, in effect, the outcome of a contest among interest groups.

While domestic politics was shaped by the contest between business and labor, foreign policy was largely dominated by elites and elite organizations. They set the agenda for discussion, advocated a course of action, and then convinced major interest groups and the public of its wisdom. The most important groups were the Council on Foreign Relations (CFR) and the CED. Council leaders, who were the heirs of Wilson's internationalism, had been early advocates of American intervention against Hitler; after the war, they argued for the importance of free trade, foreign aid, and international financial institutions in preventing the recurrence of a depression. In 1946 the council organized a group on reconstruction in Europe, with David Rockefeller as its secretary, that helped come up with the outlines for what became the Marshall Plan. In 1947, it produced along with the Twentieth Century Fund a very influential study, *Rebuilding the World Economy,* that argued that only through free trade and foreign aid could foreign countries acquire the currency to buy American goods. But unlike the CED, the council did not function generally as an advocate for very specific policies. The organization's most prominent individuals took specific positions, but the council leadership was held together by a broader consensus on certain key ideas.

The outlook of the Council on Foreign Relations and other elite groups was by no means strictly economic. Reflecting their Wilsonian roots, they argued that creating economic prosperity was essential to containing Communism and nurturing democracy in Western Europe and the Far East. They took the lead in combatting Republican isolationists who opposed foreign aid American participation in NATO and other international alliances. While the Republicans like Senate Majority Leader Robert Taft insisted that America could sustain its prosperity without relying on growing foreign trade, the foreign policy elites argued that the future of American capitalism and democracy were inextricably bound up with that of other advanced industrial nations.[29]

The council conveyed these ideas to a generation of bankers, lawyers, academics, and industrialists through its publications, through numerous study groups, and through satellite organizations set up around the country. Between 1938 and 1946, it established twenty-one Foreign Relations Committees in such cities as Birmingham, Boise, Detroit, Seattle, St. Louis, Tulsa, and Los Angeles. Eisenhower himself was educated at a council study group on aid to Europe. Journalist Joseph Kraft, a member of the group, said afterward, "Whatever General Eisenhower knows about economics, he learned at the study group meetings."[30]

The CED's leadership, like that of the council, was adamant about the importance of free trade and foreign aid to postwar prosperity. Ralph Flanders, a Vermont industrialist and later senator, wrote in a 1945 CED study, "A restrictive course by America toward foreign trade is contrary to American interest. It will be followed by restrictions abroad. The United States has a major interest in the expansion of world commerce."[31] A CED research group helped formulate the initial American proposals for the World Bank and the International Monetary Fund. The CED also helped to shape the Marshall Plan. In 1947, the Truman administration set up a committee chaired by Secretary of Commerce Averill Harriman to develop a plan for European aid. Five of the nine businessmen on the committee were CED trustees, including Hoffman himself. The CED also came up with a plan for administering the aid through a new government agency. After the plan was adopted, Truman appointed Hoffman the administrator of the Economic Cooperation Administration.

In foreign policy, the government functioned as the preserve of the elites. Dean Acheson, Paul Nitze, George Marshall, and other foreign policy leaders who shaped post–World War II foreign policy did not see themselves as responding to a popular electoral mandate or to pressure from interest groups. Instead, they conceived themselves as actively defining the national interest for both the populace at large and the interest groups. Was this fundamentally undemocratic? Only if one assumes that they were defying a clearly defined majority, or even a significant minority, that favored a different course of action. And that was not the case.

In the mid-1950s, most Americans shared the basic foreign policy ideas of the council and the CED. Left-wing opposition to the Cold War was confined to a few little-read journals; criticism from the right, calling for the "rollback" and not merely "containment" of Communism, was noisier, but no more influential. The CIO and AFL both backed the CED's free-trade philosophy. The overall consensus on foreign policy allowed the elite organizations, working closely with government officials, to fill in the actual details. They were not subverting the public will, but acting upon it in an area where the public had extended them its proxy.

The Age of Agreement

The real losers in the new postwar pluralism were not so much the liberals and labor unions that had prospered during the New Deal as the Republican proponents of laissez-faire capitalism and isolationism. After Truman's victory in 1948 and the Democratic recapture of Congress, embittered Republican conservatives, unsure of their popular appeal, turned back to a strategy of investigations in order to discredit the Democrats. Led by Wisconsin Senator Joseph McCarthy, they charged prominent Democratic officials with being Communists or Communist sympathizers. But McCarthy's crusade, which began as an attempt at self-promotion and partisan attack, ended up destroying McCarthy himself and jeopardizing the Republican Party. Led by former CED leader Ralph Flanders, half of Senate Republicans joined Democrats in voting to censure the Wisconsin senator.

The Eisenhower years affirmed the approach to domestic and foreign policy that was forged in the late 1940s. In domestic policy, much of what was done reflected the power of interest groups, but the dominance of business was tempered by the continuing labor and liberal organizations and by the determination of organizations like the CED to seek balance. The CED itself was well represented in the administration. CED founder Paul Hoffman chaired the Advisory Committee of Citizens for Eisenhower, and Eisenhower named CED officials to his top domestic policy posts, including Secretary and Undersecretary of the Treasury and Secretary of Health, Education, and Welfare. Two of Eisenhower's most important advisors, his brother Milton and law school dean Arthur Larson, whom he appointed chairman of the United States Information Agency, were the heirs to Perkins, Brandeis, and Frankfurter. They saw the administration as mediating between labor and business rather than taking the side of either. Larson captured this philosophy in his 1956 book, *A Republican Looks at His Party:*

> It is the genius of the Eisenhower administration's achievement that it has merged and brought into balance all the positive forces in our country. It is not against any of them. It realizes that they sometimes conflict, but it has found a way to encourage them to work together to a common benefit.[32]

Larson defined the way that the Republican Eisenhower administration saw itself as an instrument of interest group pluralism.

These views were reflected in what the administration did. In 1952, Eisenhower won by a landslide and Republicans won back Congress, but "Old Guard" Republicans discovered to their dismay that Eisenhower had no intention of repudiating the New Deal. Eisenhower was willing to live with those New Deal measures that didn't threaten corporations, such as the minimum wage and Social Security. In 1954, Eisenhower backed the greatest expansion of the Social Security system since 1935. In 1956, he asked for and got from Congress a 33 percent increase in the minimum wage. Labor and liberal attempts to remove the right-to-work provision from Taft-Hartley failed, but conservative attempts to enact right-to-work laws also failed—most notably in a fiercely fought 1958 referendum in California.

In their battles over legislation, interest groups and elites both appealed to the public, but the public of the 1950s was remarkably quiescent. Americans took an interest in politics during the decade, but, as David Riesman put it in *The Lonely Crowd,* they saw politics "in most of its large-scale forms as if they were spectators."[33] In this sense, the fifties were the perfect model for the most extreme forms of pluralist theory—those that stressed that interest group interaction was the sole determinant of what government did. Many Americans of the fifties believed that what happened in Washington was largely shaped by interest groups and elites, but unlike Americans of today, they had a far more benign view of both. They saw the large organizations that occupied city blocks in the capital—the AFL-CIO (the product of a merger in 1955), the Chamber of Commerce, and the American Farm Bureau—as representative bodies that had a genuine constituency outside the capital.

This view of interest groups and lobbies was echoed in major political works of the time. The classic statement was that of political scientist V. O. Key, whose *Politics, Parties, and Pressure Groups* became the standard text in university government courses. "The view that pressure groups are pathological growths in the body politic is . . . more picturesque than accurate," Key warned. "It is a safer assumption that the group system developed to fill gaps in the political system." Likewise, Key rejected the negative view of the lobbyist. "The explanation of the development of this system of specialized segments of society probably rests in part on the shortcomings of geographical representation in a highly differentiated society," he wrote.[34]

The public also viewed elites favorably. After the anti-Communist scare of the early fifties abated—in which conservative Republicans labeled any liberal institution or individual pro-Communist—the public held a generally high opinion of the large foundations and of national leaders like Hoffman (who was touted as a presidential candidate in 1952) and the Dulles brothers. One clear indication that the public wasn't worried about an alien establishment was the election of Nelson Rockefeller as New York's governor in 1958 and his emergence as a Republican presidential aspirant. Earlier in the century, it would have been inconceivable for a Rockefeller or a Morgan to have run successfully for popular office.

By the late 1950s, some of the best-known pluralist theorists had begun to acknowledge that American democracy required both countervailing interest groups and elites. In 1959, David B. Truman, one of the leaders of the pluralist school, incorporated elites into his analysis. Defining elites as "those who occupy leading positions within the groups constituting the intervening structure of American society," Truman argued that democracy depended on the "consensus of elites."[35] To that extent, the political scientists had grasped the essence of American democracy in the 1950s.

This political system of the fifties was certainly far from perfect, not only when measured against the democratic ideal, but even when compared to the claims of pluralists like Dahl. Many Americans could not claim any real connection to the large interest groups of Washington or to the elite organizations that claimed to speak for the national interest. Quipped political scientist E. E. Schattschneider, "The flaw in the pluralist heaven is that the heavenly chorus sings with a strong upper-class accent."[36] As the civil rights movement would demonstrate, the South was a bastion of racial and political reaction, which also lagged behind the rest of the country in its industry and standard of living. Yet from 1948 through the early 1960s, most Americans accepted the political status quo. Arthur Larson was not mistaken when he wrote in 1956, "We have greater agreement than ever before in history on fundamental issues."[37]

One reason Americans were so satisfied with their own situation—C. Wright Mills called the fifties "the great American celebration"—was that they compared the United States to Soviet Russia. Placed against the Soviet system, American democracy appeared even to its harshest critics to be the embodiment of freedom. Even more important, however, was the comparison of the America of the 1950s with the America of the 1930s. Most Americans still remembered the poverty and insecurity of the Depression. Since 1939, Americans' income and standard of living had risen steadily. Home ownership rose from 40 to 66 percent and disposable income rose three and a half times between 1939 and 1955.[38] Median family income went from $19,500 in 1947 to $26,800 in 1959 (in 1997 dollars). And disparities in wealth decreased. The percentage of Americans living in poverty went from 32 to 22 percent in the same period.[39] Recessions were frequent in the 1950s, but were shallow and of short duration. Only by the decade's end did Americans begin to wonder whether the economic growth could be accelerated.

In the 1950s, Americans considered "the labor question" to have been answered. *Harper's* editor Frederick Lewis Allen wrote in *The Big Change,* his appraisal of America from 1900 to 1950:

> At the turn of the century America seemed in danger of becoming a land in which the millionaires had more and more and the rest had less and less, and where a few financiers had a stranglehold, not only on the country's economic apparatus, but on its political apparatus, too.
>
> . . . Through a combination of patchwork revisions of the systems—tax laws, minimum wage laws, subsidies and guarantees and regulations of various sorts, plus labor union pressures and new management attitudes—we . . . repealed the Iron Law of Wages. We had brought about a virtual automatic redistribution of income from the well-to-do to the less well-to-do. . . . That, it seems to me, is the essence of the Great American Discovery.[40]

In 1955, Murray Kempton wrote in a similar spirit of the change that had taken place among Detroit's auto workers:

> . . . today Detroit is quiet; it moves not, nor shakes, nor seems pregnant with violence as it once did. There has come upon it the peace of understanding. An auto worker earns a minimum of $84 a week; he has a pension and a paid vacation and the automatic assurance that his wages will move up and up; he is in short the unexpected inhabitant of an industrial democracy.[41]

The great political questions that had occupied Americans over the first half-century also seemed to be settled. Even before Senator Joseph McCarthy proclaimed that the State Department housed 238 card-carrying Communists, the American Communist movement had lost whatever fleeting influence it had had. There were still Marxists in the universities, but like conservatives, they were curiosities. Historians Richard Hofstadter and Louis Hartz argued that from the beginning America had adhered to what Hartz called a "Lockean liberal" consensus.[42] Political scientist Robert Lane also proclaimed a new "politics of consensus," in which political debate would become "more a discussion of means than ends."[43]

The organization that most clearly exemplified this new consensus was the "think tank." The think tank was dedicated to discovering the best means for given ends. The prototype of this new institution was the RAND Corporation. RAND, which stands for "Research and Development," was set up by the Army in 1945 inside of Douglas Aircraft. It became a separate corporation in 1948 with a $3 million budget and 300 employees. Its funding came primarily from government contracts.[44] RAND's specialty was the use of game theory and cost-benefit analysis to evaluate different military strategies and weapons systems. When President John F. Kennedy took office, his new Secretary of Defense Robert McNamara put RAND veterans in charge of reorganizing the Pentagon. As *Business Week* commented, "Anyone looking for a line on the Kennedy Administration's defense policy soon finds the trail leading to a group of military economists, mathematicians, and statisticians and to Santa Monica's RAND Corporation."[45]

John Kennedy's election in 1960 appeared to represent the final triumph of the new American system. Where Truman was a former haberdasher and Eisenhower a professional soldier, John Kennedy had been raised to be part of America's elite. He had attended Harvard, and was at home with the ideas of the CED and the Council on Foreign Relations. At the same time, he was a Roman Catholic and the first Catholic president. His administration included a new generation of American leaders who saw a higher calling for themselves. These included White House advisor McGeorge Bundy; Secretary of State Dean Rusk, former president of the Rockefeller Foundation; Americans for Democratic Action academics Arthur Schlesinger and John Kenneth Galbraith; as well as two prominent Wall Street investment bankers who were active in the Council on Foreign Relations, Secretary of the Treasury C. Douglas Dillon and Assistant Secretary of State for Economic Affairs George Ball. Kennedy also chose an actual labor lawyer, Arthur Goldberg, as his Secretary of Labor. Sociologist E. Digby Baltzell saw Kennedy's election and the emergence of his family as a vindication of America's mix of pluralism and natural aristocracy. "The Kennedys are, I think, in an excellent position to assimilate the members of a wide variety of contemporary elites into some sort of new and stable establishment."[46]

Kennedy's policies also reflected the priorities of the CED, the Brookings Institution (where his transition team held their meetings), the Council on Foreign Relations, and other elite policy groups. His tax cut was the fruition of Hoffman and Ruml's crusade on behalf of Keynesian deficit spending. His trade bill drastically lowering tariffs reflected the work of the CED and the Commission on Foreign Economic Policy, which Eisenhower had appointed in 1953. It was chaired by Clarence Randall, the former head of Inland Steel, but also included United Steel Workers president David McDonald, whose proposal for trade adjustment for displaced workers became part of Kennedy's bill.

There were some strikes, of course, in the early 1960s, but relations between labor and business leaders were generally amicable. At the beginning of his term, Kennedy appointed an Advisory Committee on Labor-Management Policy made up of top labor leaders, including George Meany and Walter Reuther, and top CEOs, including Henry Ford II and Joseph L. Block of Inland Steel. In May 1962, it issued a cheerful report calling for "development by the parties to collective bargaining of improved methods of reconciling their separate and mutual interests with those of the larger community."[47]

Kennedy himself reflected the faith in the disinterested application of social science that had characterized American elites since the beginning of the century. He told a conference of businessmen held at the Brookings Institution in May 1963, "Most of us are conditioned for many years to have a political viewpoint—Republican or Democratic, liberal, conservative, or moderate. The fact of the matter is that most of the problems . . . that we now face, are technical problems, are administrative problems."[48] This faith, and other assumptions that underlay the great American celebration, would presently be shattered.

[4]

The Legacy of the Sixties

In 1998, Bob Dylan's album *Time Out of Mind* won the Grammy award for the best popular record. The National Organization for Women, the Consumer Federation of America, the Environmental Defense Fund, and other organizations founded in the 1960s were still influential in American politics. On the other hand, a host of grumpy social critics and cultural commentators, from Robert Bork and William Bennett to John Leo and Hilton Kramer, were making a career out of denouncing the evils that the sixties wrought in American life. According to these critics, the "Vietnam syndrome" ruined our foreign policy, and the spirit of permissiveness and "anything goes" corrupted our schools and youth and destroyed the nuclear family. "The revolt was against the entire American culture," Bork declared.[1]

As a political era—one characterized by utopian social experiments, political upheaval, and dramatic reform—the sixties left an indelible mark on the decades that followed. It vastly expanded the scope of what citizens expected from their government—from clean air and water to safe workplaces, reliable products, and medical coverage in their old age. It also signaled a change in what Americans wanted out of their lives. During the sixties, Americans began to worry about the "quality of life" and about their "lifestyle" rather than simply about "making a living." The sixties unleashed conflicts within these new areas of concern—over affirmative action, abortion, homosexuality, drugs, rock lyrics, air pollution, toxic waste dumps, and automobile safety. And it raised questions about the purpose of America and its foreign policy that are still being debated. The sixties have preoccupied late twentieth-century America as much as the Civil War preoccupied late nineteenth-century America.

The difficulty in understanding the sixties comes from the fact that it was much more than a political era. It witnessed tectonic changes in American capitalism and culture—from an older blue-collar industrial social order, rooted in self-sacrifice and the Protestant ethic, to a new postindustrial society consumed by the search for worldly happiness and well-being. These changes originated earlier in the century, but they came fully to light during the sixties and transformed political protest into cultural and social upheaval. These changes, like those in the late nineteenth century, also threw into question the meaning of political democracy and contributed to the sharp reaction that followed.

The Triple Revolution

Like most periods described by the name of a decade, the 1960s don't strictly conform to their time span. You could make a good case that the sixties began in December 1955 when Rosa Parks refused to give up her seat in a segregated Montgomery, Alabama, bus and only ended in August 1974 when Richard Nixon resigned.[2] Probably the best way to understand the sixties is to divide it into two periods. The first period—running from the mid-1950s to 1965—spans the rise of the Southern civil rights movement and of Martin Luther King, Jr., the founding of Students for a Democratic Society (SDS) in 1962, the achievement of a liberal Democratic Congressional majority in 1964, the passage of the civil rights bills and Medicare, and the initiation of the Great Society and the War on Poverty.

The first period looks like a belated continuation of the Progressive Era and the New Deal. A recession in 1958 helped Democrats to increase their margin in the House from 35 to 129 and to replace eight conservative Republican senators. Another recession only two years later helped Kennedy win the White House. By the early 1960s, the Southern civil rights movement enjoyed enormous support in the North, financial backing from the Ford Foundation, the Rockefeller Brothers Fund, the Field Foundation, and the Stern Family Fund, and editorial support from the major political magazines, newspapers, and television networks.[3] In 1964, President Lyndon B. Johnson, facing Barry Goldwater, an opponent identified with Southern segregationists and with a trigger-happy foreign policy, won a landslide victory, and liberal Democrats gained control of Congress for the first time since 1936.

Business leaders, buoyed by prosperity after having endured six recessions in a decade, accepted Johnson and the administration's major legislative initiatives with equanimity. Businesses paid for three-fourths of Lyndon Johnson's 1964 campaign. They didn't oppose Medicare (only the AMA lobbied against it), and they actively backed the Great Society and War on Poverty programs, which they saw, correctly, as creating demand for new private investment.[4] When Johnson's Model Cities program, part of the War on Poverty, faced difficulty in Congress, twenty-two leading corporate executives came to its defense. "Our cities are being submerged by a rising tide of . . . disease and despair, joblessness and hopelessness," they declared. "America needs the demonstration cities act."[5]

There was also cooperation between business and labor within elite policy groups and commissions. In December 1964, Johnson appointed a National Commission on Technology, Automation and Economic Progress. Its members included the UAW's Walter Reuther, Communications Workers of America president Joseph Bierne, IBM chairman Thomas J. Watson, Jr., utility executive Philip Sporn, sociologist Daniel Bell, and Urban League president Whitney Young. The commission issued a report eighteen months later recommending a guaranteed annual income and a massive jobs training program.[6]

It is hard to imagine a report with this kind of conclusion being issued any time except during the mid-1930s, and at that time most business leaders probably would have dissociated themselves from any far-reaching conclusions. During the 1950s, of course, relative harmony also existed between business and labor at the top levels of policy, but business clearly held the upper hand. American pluralism, as Schattschneider quipped, sang with an "upper-class accent."[7] In the early Johnson years, harmony still prevailed, but the voices of the civil rights movement, the AFL-CIO, and liberal Democrats could be heard much more clearly. America was as close as it would ever come to Galbraith's pluralist ideal of countervailing power.

There was not only a creative equilibrium between interest groups, but there was also ferment among voters. In the early sixties, students, who had been relatively quiescent during the fifties—"apathetic" was the most commonly heard description—began to awaken. SDS's Port Huron Statement from 1962 proclaimed the importance of "participatory democracy." "Politics," the manifesto declared, "has the function of bringing people out of isolation and into community."[8] Activity was not limited to the political left. In 1962, student conservatives founded the Young Americans for Freedom. And Goldwater's nomination in 1964 was the work of a draft committee organized by dissident Republicans.

Many of the key leaders of the sixties, including Martin Luther King, Jr., George McGovern, Hubert Humphrey, and Walter Mondale, were raised on the Protestant social gospel's faith in the creation of a kingdom of God in America. King, the major figure of this period, read Christian socialist Walter Rauschenbusch's *Christianity and Social Crisis* at Crozer Theological Seminary and would frequently cite his influence.[9] McGovern's biographer says the future senator "gorged himself" with Rauschenbusch's work while he was at Dakota Wesleyan.[10] The political-economic premise of this optimistic vision, enunciated in Galbraith's *The Affluent Society* and Michael Harrington's *The Other America,* was that American industry, which was becoming highly automated, was capable of producing great abundance but that archaic political and economic arrangements were preventing many Americans from enjoying its fruits. The goal of such programs as Medicare, the Great Society, and the War on Poverty was to allow the poor, the aged, and the disadvantaged to share in this abundance.

The crowning document of the early sixties—one that combined the spirit and the economic thought of the era—was issued in March 1964. A group of thirty-two social scientists, labor officials, businessmen, and political activists delivered to President Johnson a manifesto called "The Triple Revolution." The group itself was a perfect mix of new left and policy elite, new middle class and old upper class. It was convened by W. H. Ferry, the son of the owner of Packard Motors and a protégé of Paul Hoffman and Robert Hutchins. Ferry recruited, among others, Ralph Helstein, the president of the United Packinghouse Workers; socialist Michael Harrington; economist Robert Theobald; civil rights leader Bayard Rustin; scientist Linus Pauling; and Tom Hayden, the author of SDS's 1962 founding manifesto, the Port Huron Statement.

The document declared that "three separate and mutually reinforcing revolutions" were taking place: a "cybernation revolution" that had brought about "a system of almost unlimited productive capacity which requires progressively less human labor," a "weaponry revolution" that has "eliminated war as a method for resolving international conflicts," and a "human rights revolution" that had created a "universal demand for full human rights."[11] "The Triple Revolution" held out the possibility of a "potential abundance of goods and services" that could transform the United States and the world, but the signatories warned that this potential could not be realized without "a fundamental change in the mechanisms employed to insure consumer rights."

From Saving to Consumption

During this first phase of the sixties, there were also signs of a looming redefinition of politics that would differentiate it from early reform epochs. During the Progressive Era, the New Deal, and the fifties, politics pivoted primarily on conflicts between small and big business and between business and labor. The great battles of the first five decades of the twentieth century had been over the trusts, the tariff, the banking system, the abolition of child labor, and government regulation of collective bargaining. No legislative struggle attracted so many lobbyists and was fought as fiercely and had as much impact on presidential politics as that over the Taft-Hartley labor bill in 1947.

Throughout the sixties, these kind of issues would recur. From 1953 to 1976, 5 million public workers joined unions, precipitating battles over union recognition in almost every state.[12] But in the early 1960s, new issues that didn't fit this older mold began to emerge. They extended the scope of conflict between popular democracy and corporate capitalism. Americans became concerned not merely with obtaining lower prices for goods, but with government overseeing the safety, reliability, and quality of goods. President Kennedy announced a "consumer bill of rights" in 1962. In 1963, over the strong objection of the clothing industry, Congress passed landmark legislation requiring flame-resistant fabrics in children's wear. In 1964, Assistant Secretary of Labor Daniel P. Moynihan hired a young Harvard Law graduate, Ralph Nader, to research auto safety. Two years later, amid the furor created by Nader's work, Congress passed the National Traffic and Motor Vehicle Safety Act.

Americans also became concerned about the environment—not merely as a source of renewable resources or as a wildlife preserve, but as the natural setting for human life. In 1962, Rachel Carson's *Silent Spring* became a best-seller. Congress passed its first Clean Air Act in 1963 and its first Clean Water Act in 1965. American women also began to stir as a political force. In 1963, Betty Friedan published *The Feminine Mystique,* and two years later, she and other feminists formed the National Organization for Women. While the older women's movement had focused on suffrage, the new movement reached into the workplace and the home and even into the private lives of men and women.

These new concerns were part of a fundamental change in American culture. During the nineteenth and early twentieth centuries, Americans had still adhered to an ascetic view of life. Under the hold of the Protestant work ethic promulgated by seventeenth-century English emigrants to America, they viewed idleness, leisure, and bodily pleasure as sinful and work and life itself as unpleasant prerequisites to a heavenly reward. This view was reinforced by classical economic theory, which regarded saving and the denial of consumption as the condition of economic growth. This view of life and work began to break down in the 1920s, but the emergence of an entirely different outlook was delayed by the Depression and World War II. By the 1950s, Americans had begun finally to abandon this harsh view of life and work for an ethic of the good life. The good life itself no longer meant a life of virtue that would signify or earn salvation in the afterlife, but a full and happy life on earth.

Americans continued to be religious, but religion itself—typified in Norman Vincent Peale's best-selling *The Power of Positive Thinking*—became a means to securing happiness on earth. They worried about the "quality of life," including the kinds of foods they ate, the clothes they wore, the car they drove, and the air they breathed. They fretted about their "interpersonal relations" and about their "sex lives." These new concerns became reflected eventually in Americans' political concerns and in their ideas of what government could do.

This transformation in American culture was the result of deep-seated changes that had taken place in American capitalism over the century. Changes in morality and religion came to reflect changes in work and in the requirements of the workplace and of economic growth. In the nineteenth and early twentieth centuries, economic growth, and the growth of the working class itself, were driven by the expansion of steel, machine tools, chemicals, and other "capital goods" industries. Workers at McCormick's agricultural machinery plant in Chicago went from 150 in 1850 to 4,000 in 1900 to 15,000 in 1916. Workers' and capitalists' consumption was held down in order to free up funds that could be used to invest in these new capital goods. As Francis Walker, the president of MIT, wrote in his 1889 textbook on economics, "At every step of its progress capital follows one law. It arises solely out of saving. It stands always for self-denial and abstinence."[13] This economic theory, which held that the growth of the industry depended upon restricting capitalists' and workers' consumption, justified a broader ethic of self-sacrifice and personal austerity, of the identification of virtue and unending toil.

As the historian Martin J. Sklar has demonstrated, sometime around the 1920s the dynamic of economic growth changed, and helped to bring about profound changes in Americans' larger conception of themselves.[14] By the 1920s, the modern factory had become so productive that it could now increase its output without increasing its overall employees. During the 1920s, manufacturing output grew 64 percent but the number of workers fell by 300,000.[15] Output per man-hour grew 32 percent from 1923 to 1929.[16] In this new electrically powered economy, capitalism could expand without increasing the number of workers making steel for automobiles or machines for factories. During the 1920s the workers in capital goods industries actually fell by 12 percent. In concrete terms, that meant that in order to expand their production, businesses didn't need to take a growing proportion of profits and invest them in hiring new workers. Economic growth no longer depended strictly upon capitalists' saving and self-denial.*

This new productivity also changed the underlying pattern of growth and consumption. In the nineteenth century, growth was driven by the growth of capital goods industries. Wages in consumer goods production had to be kept down to provide profits to invest in the capital goods industries. When the owners and managers of these capital goods industries hired new workers, these workers created new demand for consumer goods, which reignited the process of capital accumulation. But beginning in the 1920s, the process broke down because the capital goods sector stopped growing. When new workers weren't hired, new demand for consumer goods failed to appear, and the economy began to suffer from a lack of "effective demand." In this sense, keeping wages down hampered rather than facilitated the growth of the new capitalism.

During the 1920s, Edward Filene, Gerard Swope, and other businessmen understood that the fulcrum of the economy had shifted—that in the future, the growth of economy would have to be triggered by new demand for consumer goods and services and that to avoid depressions, employers would have to pay higher wages and induce their workers, through advertising, to spend them on consumer goods. In the hope of fueling profits and suppressing the class struggle, they advocated a different kind of "industrial democracy" centered on a worker's freedom to define his life outside the job. It was a freedom to consume. Workers should be "free to cultivate themselves," Filene wrote. They should seek "a larger share in the mental and spiritual satisfactions" from what they

*By way of analogy, imagine an office in 1985 that produced greeting cards on a minicomputer and printer that cost $50,000 and required several trained technicians to oversee. Seven years later, the company could have taken a small percentage of the money it had put away to replace that machine and bought a new computer and printer for $5,000 that would have produced more greeting cards with much less expensive labor. There would be no new net investment, merely the replacement of an older machine with a new one. If you imagine that process taking place in the economy as a whole, you'll get some idea of the American economy in the 1920s.

receive for their jobs rather than "a larger share in the management of the enterprise which furnishes that job."[17] Their views were echoed by AFL economist Roy Dickinson. Writing in *Printer's Ink* in 1921, Dickinson warned that "lower wages reduce purchasing power; men on starvation wages do not buy phonographs, clothes, shoes, etc."[18]

But the efforts to increase consumption through advertising and the installment plan during the 1920s proved insufficient. In the 1930s and 1940s, the government got into the business of encouraging demand for consumer and capital goods through public works spending, welfare payments, and later guaranteed loans programs and military spending. After World War II, businesses also took up the cause of consumer demand in earnest. They adopted a new ethic of consumption. Prodded by unions, they paid higher wages. They also devoted growing parts of their budget to advertising, which was aimed at persuading Americans to spend rather than to save. Advertising budgets doubled between 1951 and 1962. Businesses and banks also introduced the installment plan and consumer loans and later credit cards as inducements to buy rather than save. But more important, businesses vastly expanded into realms that had been either unexplored or previously reserved for upper-class luxuries. In search of profit, businesses sold leisure and mental and physical health to the working class; they marketed not merely edible food, but gourmet delights and prepackaged and frozen food. They sold fashion and not merely clothes. They produced entertainment for the home.[19]

To sell these new goods and services, businesses, abetted by popular entertainment, encouraged a new conception of what Americans should want and should want to be. They promoted the idea of a new American who differed dramatically from the older American of the Protestant ethic and the work ethic. For this new American, the goal of life was not salvation in the afterlife but happiness in this life. The goal of work was a comfortable and pleasurable life for yourself and your family. The satisfaction of bodily pleasures, through sex, sports, social activity, entertainment, and eating, was an integral part of happiness. Leisure was a reward for having worked, and the enjoyment of leisure was an important part of happiness. The older life had been based on saving and self-denial; the new was based on spending and on self-fulfillment—on achieving the "good life."

In the sixties, Americans began to look for the right "lifestyle." The older American had inherited his identity; the new American chose his identity, constructed his appearance (through diet, fashion, and cosmetics), created a personality (through school and even psychotherapy), and selected a career. One achieved happiness by choosing the right lifestyle. Without being consciously profane, businesses transformed religion itself by replacing the older Protestant ethic's quest for salvation through virtue with a new search for happiness.

The origins of what came to be called the sixties counterculture lay at the interstices of this new American culture of leisure and consumption that business helped to promote. The counterculture was a product of the new culture and at the same time was a critique of and a counter to it. It accepted a broader definition of happiness, but it rejected Filene's suggestion that workers seek their freedom entirely in consumption rather than work. It held out for meaningful work, but not as defined by the nineteenth or early twentieth centuries. When Paul Goodman, writing in *Growing Up Absurd* in 1960, complained that "there are not enough worthy jobs in our economy for average boys and adolescents to grow up toward," he was not complaining about the lack of jobs at General Motors or on Wall Street.[20]

The counterculture also rejected TV dinners and cars with tailfins that the advertisers urged Americans to buy, but it did so on behalf of more discriminating standards of its own. The critique of consumerism—articulated in the 1950s by Vance Packard's *The Waste Makers* and *The Hidden Persuaders*—led directly to the formation of the modern consumer and environmental movements. And the rejection of sex symbols and stereotypes did not lead to a celebration of abstinence, but to a wider exploration into sexual pleasure and to a reevaluation of homosexuality and heterosexuality. In the early sixties all these concerns became the subject not merely of books and small artistic cults, but of political manifestos and platforms and embryonic social movements.

The movements of the sixties initially took root among college students and recent college graduates—a group that had previously had little impact on real change. Students who entered college in 1960 had been born after the Depression—they had been, in the words of SDS's Port

Huron Statement, "bred in at least modest comfort." Living in a time of unprecedented prosperity, they could afford not to worry about whether they would be able to get a job. They were raised to think about the "quality of life" rather than the iron law of wages, even to scorn some elements of what was then called "materialism." By the 1960s, they had also become a major social group, capable on their own of disrupting society and upsetting its politics. The workforce of the sixties was entirely different from that of 1930. If the archetypal worker in the old economy was a steelworker, miner, farmer, or machinist, the typical worker in the new economy was a school teacher, physical therapist, accountant, dancer, designer, short-order cook, grocery clerk, bus driver, waitress, hospital orderly, or janitor. By 1970, 65 percent of Americans were engaged in producing services rather than goods.

White-Collar Service Occupational Categories
(percentage of total workforce in selected years)[21]

OCCUPATIONAL CATEGORY	1900	1920	1930	1960	1974
Professional and technical	4.3	5.4	6.8	10.8	14.4
Managers, officials, and proprietors	5.8	6.6	7.4	10.2	10.4
Clerical	3.0	8.0	8.9	14.5	17.5
Sales	4.5	4.9	6.3	6.5	6.3
Total of all workers	17.6	24.9	29.4	42.0	48.6

As preparation for work, a majority of young Americans now attended college. In 1900, 5 percent of 18-to-21-year-olds attended college; by 1970, 51.8 percent did.[22] By the end of the sixties, about 12 million Americans were in college, compared to about 21 million who worked in manufacturing and about 3.5 million who worked on farms. If everyone who worked at or around a college is included, then there were more Americans engaged in higher education in 1970 than were engaged in manufacturing. So when students agitated in the sixties and shut down university towns, what they were doing was not isolated from the society at large.

The new left groups of the early sixties attacked the new consumer economy, but they, too, implicitly used the new standards and ideals it had fostered. SDS's Port Huron Statement condemned the "idolatrous worship of things," but called for "finding a meaning in life that is personally authentic"—a formulation that would have made no sense to an industrial worker in 1909. In Berkeley, the free speech movement of 1964—aimed at reclaiming the rights of students to distribute political literature on campus—gave way the next year to the filthy speech movement, aimed at defending students against literary and sexual censorship. Over the next decade, these two movements—political and cultural—would develop in tandem.

Visions of Armageddon

The second period of the sixties began with the Watts riot and President Johnson's escalation of the Vietnam War in 1965. These events signified and helped to precipitate a darker, more frenzied and violent period of protest. The escalation of the war threw into question the purpose of American foreign policy. Students who entered college in the 1960s had been imbued with the idea that America's mission was to create a democratic world after its own image. But in Vietnam, the United States appeared to be backing a corrupt dictatorship, which, at our urging, had ignored the 1954 Geneva agreements to hold elections in Vietnam. The seeming contradiction between U.S. intervention and American ideals, Johnson's dishonesty and betrayal, and the rising list of casualties on both sides of the war inspired a growing rage against Johnson and the government. The antiwar movement split into a moderate wing that sought a negotiated withdrawal and a violent pro–North Vietnamese wing that threatened to "bring the war home." As the conviction grew that U.S. intervention was not an unfortunate blunder but reflected the priorities of American corporations and the country's power elite, many antiwar militants began to see the United States itself as the enemy. SDS, the leading student organization, imagined itself by 1969 to be the vanguard of a violent revolution *against* the United States.

The first ghetto riots took place in the summer of 1964 and then grew in size and strength over the next three summers. In the Watts riot of 1965, 1,072 people were injured, 34 were killed, 977 buildings were damaged, and 4,000 people were arrested. In July 1967, there were 103 disorders, including five full-scale riots. In Detroit, 43 persons were killed and 7,200 were arrested. Some 700 buildings were burned and 412 were totally destroyed. The riots were spontaneous, but they were invariably triggered by black perceptions of unequal treatment, particularly at the hands of white police forces.[23]

At the same time that the riots began, Martin Luther King, Jr., attempted to take the civil rights movement northward to Chicago. King never saw political and civil equality as ends in themselves, but as part of a longer struggle for full social and economic equality. King wanted to desegregate housing in the North (which was the key to de facto school segregation), improve city services for blacks, and gain higher wages and better jobs for blacks. He failed abysmally in Chicago. The combination of the ghetto riots and King's failure contributed to the radicalization of the black movement. By 1968, when King was assassinated in Memphis while trying to support striking black garbagemen, much of the black movement had turned toward insurrectionary violence. They saw the Northern ghettos as Third World colonies that had to be liberated from their white imperialist oppressors.

Both the radical antiwar and the black power movements espoused what they called "revolutionary politics." They saw themselves in the tradition of Marx, Lenin, Mao, Fanon, Castro, and even Stalin, but by the late sixties they had become unwitting participants in a much older American tradition of Protestant millennialism. As historian William G. McLoughlin argued in *Revivals, Awakenings and Reform,* the sixties were part of a religious revival comparable to the great awakenings of the mid-eighteenth century and early nineteenth centuries.[24] At such times, the seeming discord between older ideals and new realities had inspired intense self-examination, the proliferation of new sects and schisms, and alternating visions of doom and salvation. In the early awakenings, the content was explicitly Christian and biblical. The awakening of the sixties was primarily secular, but the inner form remained the same—like a melody played with different instruments. While the first phase of the sixties saw the revival as a form of postmillennial Protestant social gospel—the view that the world would end *after* the glorious millennium—the second phase saw "premillennial" visions of the apocalypse and Armageddon occurring *before* the millennium.

The emergence of this premillennial vision was provoked by the war's escalation and the combination of rage and guilt (guilt at complicity in the slaughter of seeming innocents) that it inspired; the repeated visions of violence and destruction in Vietnam and in American cities, which reinforced an image of change as conflagration; the assassinations of John and Robert Kennedy and of Martin Luther King, Jr., and Malcolm X; the Republican advances in 1966 and Nixon's election in November 1968, which discouraged new left activists who had believed that they could achieve majority support for their revolutionary aspirations; and the apparent success of the North Vietnamese in the war and the onset of China's Cultural Revolution, which suggested that revolution in the United States would only occur after a global revolution against American imperialism had succeeded.

Radicals of the late sixties dreamed not of their country's salvation but of its destruction. If socialism or the "good life" were to come to the United States, it would only be after Armageddon—after a victorious armed struggle that would lay waste to the country. The Black Panthers referred to the United States as "Babylon." When the Weatherman group took over SDS in 1969, it changed the name of SDS's newspaper, *New Left Notes,* to *Fire.* The new revolutionaries steeled themselves for a life of sacrifice, and eventually death in the service of world revolution. Huey Newton, the cofounder of the Black Panther Party, described its program as "revolutionary suicide." New left sociologist Hal Jacobs, echoing the spirit of Weatherman, wrote in the movement magazine *Leviathan,* "Perhaps the best we can hope for is that in the course of the struggle we can develop human social relations among ourselves, while being engulfed by death and destruction."[25]

The vision of the Weathermen or the Panthers perfectly matched that of the Millerites—the precursors of today's Seventh Day Adventists. They were preparing themselves to be saved in the face of an imminent Armageddon. Even their organization resembled that of earlier Christian sects.

The Weathermen abandoned any pretense of building a mass movement. Instead, they sought to establish "revolutionary Marxist-Leninist-Maoist collective formations" that, through "criticism-self-criticism," would convert their members to true revolutionaries.[26] Under their leadership, SDS, which at one point boasted a hundred thousand members, dwindled to several hundred aspiring visible saints.

During the late sixties, many of the people in the new left, even those who rejected the violence of the Weathermen, got caught up in the debate over class struggle, imperialism, racism, and revolution as if it were a genuine discussion, based on reasonable, if debatable, assessments of world conditions. But others sensed that something was deeply wrong. In his 1968 campaign as the Democratic antiwar candidate, Eugene McCarthy continually frustrated his own followers by counseling calm and "reasoned judgment." Said McCarthy, "It is not a time for storming the walls, but for beginning a long march."[27] Paul Goodman, whose writings had inspired the new left, sensed in 1969 that the political movement had turned unworldly even while it pretended to speak of world revolution:

> If we start from the premise that the young are in a religious crisis, that they doubt there is really a nature of things and they are sure there is no world for themselves, many details of their present behavior become clearer. Alienation is a powerful motivation, of unrest, fantasy, and feckless action. It can lead . . . to religious innovation, new sacraments to give life meaning. But it is a poor basis for politics, including revolutionary politics.[28]

At the time, however, these voices were often ignored. For many leaders of the new left the question wasn't whether it made any sense at all to talk of revolution, but when the revolution would come and who would be on what side of the barricades.

This turn toward violence and revolutionary fantasy alienated many Americans and led to the rise of Ronald Reagan in California and to George Wallace's surprisingly strong showing in the 1968 presidential election. It also contributed to the victory in 1968 of Richard Nixon, who ran a subtle "law and order" campaign to exploit the unpopularity of the would-be revolutionaries. Yet these movements taken as a whole, in their moderate and radical wings, still wielded enormous influence over the nation's political and legislative agenda. By the early 1970s, they had helped force the Nixon administration to withdraw from Vietnam and had provoked Congress and the administration into pouring money into cities and into adopting a strategy of affirmative action in hiring and federal contracts. During Nixon's first term, spending on Johnson's Great Society programs and on welfare and food stamps dramatically increased, while spending on the military went down.

The movements themselves, which extended from Weatherman and the Panthers at one extreme to the Mobilization Against the War and the Urban League at the other, were deeply split, but still enjoyed wide, and even growing, support in the late sixties and early seventies. While the radicals and revolutionaries provided a useful foil to conservatives like Reagan, they also posed a constant threat of disruption. The major riots stopped by 1969, but the threat of riots persisted—both in actual fact and in the rhetoric and behavior of the black activists.[29] In the summer of 1970 alone, city officials reported that black and Chicano militants made more than 500 attacks on police, resulting in the deaths of twenty policemen. The antiwar movement also became increasingly violent. During the fall semester of 1970, 140 bombings occurred. At Rutgers, by no means a center of antiwar activism, classes had to be vacated 175 times because of bomb threats.[30]

Finally, these movements had either the support or the sympathy of policy elites. Some members of the foreign policy elite, acting partly out of conviction and partly out of fear of further disruption, favored immediate negotiation with the North Vietnamese and later unilateral withdrawal from Vietnam. They were part of the moderate antiwar movement. By 1968, these included the *New York Times* editorial board and prominent members of the Council on Foreign Relations. After Acheson, McCloy, McGeorge Bundy, Clark Clifford, Averill Harriman, and other "wise men," who had unfailingly counseled Johnson to hang tough in Vietnam, advised him to make peace and withdraw, General Maxwell Taylor, Johnson's ambassador to South Vietnam, lamented that "my Council on Foreign Relations friends are living in the cloud of the *New York Times*."[31]

Foundations and policy groups responded to the antiwar movement and to the riots and the black power movement the same way elite organizations in the early 1900s had responded to the threat of socialist revolution. They sought to tame or co-opt the movements by helping the moderate, or less radical, elements achieve their objectives. In some cases, they worked directly with the militants. The Ford Foundation, the wealthiest and most powerful of all the foundations, with assets four times greater than the Rockefeller Foundation's, was particularly important. When Henry Ford died in 1947, he had bequeathed 90 percent of his stock to the foundation, which by the end of 1968 had assets totaling $3.7 billion.[32] But the foundation initially suffered from confusion about its aims. In 1950, Henry Ford II and the foundation's board appointed Paul Hoffman the president and Hoffman brought in the controversial Robert Hutchins, but the two were forced out three years later—Hoffman because he was spending most of his time working for the Eisenhower campaign and Hutchins because he wanted to use the foundation to confront Senator Joseph McCarthy.[33] The Ford Foundation fell into the hands of two successive timid and inconsequential presidents, who devoted most of the foundation's resources to funding hospitals, medical schools, and universities. In the early sixties the foundation's board began demanding that it address current issues, particularly civil rights, and when its president continued to dither, Henry Ford II and foundation board chairman John McCloy brought in former Kennedy national security advisor McGeorge Bundy as the new president.

Bundy, the son of a prominent Boston lawyer who had served under Stimson and McCloy at the War Department, exemplified the ethic of the American elite. He was a Republican who had served in a Democratic administration. Like Stimson, whose memoirs he co-authored, he considered himself above considerations of class and faction. He made a former trade union leader the head of the foundation's powerful National Affairs division and appointed the first black to the foundation's board. And he threw the foundation into the midst of the struggle for racial equality. In 1967 the foundation gave large grants to the Congress of Racial Equality in Cleveland; New York groups advocating community control of schools; La Raza, the Mexican American Legal Defense Fund; and the Mexican American Youth Organization, which was supporting striking farmworkers. Some of these grants got the foundation embroiled in controversy. Its money to CORE ended up funding a voter registration drive that helped elect Carl Stokes as Cleveland's first black mayor, which had Republicans in Congress charging that the foundation had violated its tax-exempt status by engaging in electoral politics. In New York City, Bundy sold Mayor John Lindsay on a plan that put local blacks in charge of their own schools that ended up pitting the city's blacks against the predominately Jewish teachers' union.[34]

Other foundations followed Ford's lead in funding civil rights and even black power efforts. These included the Rockefeller Brothers Fund, the Rockefeller Foundation, the Carnegie Corporation, and the smaller Mott, Stern, Taconic, and Field foundations. The Committee on Economic Development, which was eclipsed in the sixties as an economic policy maker, began focusing its efforts on what it called "social blight" in 1967. Its recommendations echoed those of the earlier Johnson commission, including a guaranteed annual income and jobs training. Like the foundations, the CED's objective was to accommodate rather than reject the demands of black militants.

There was a certain irony in this tacit alliance of militants with the policy elite and foundations. By the late sixties, C. Wright Mills's theory of the power elite had become popular on campus and among left-wing activists. William Domhoff's book *Who Rules America?* and a sequel, *The Higher Circles,* were best-sellers. As these theories had predicted, what the average American wanted and voted for was not necessarily reflected in what government did. But during the late sixties, the new left had little to complain of. While the electoral arena registered a growing backlash against the civil rights and antiwar movements—evidenced most dramatically in George Wallace's candidacy in 1968 and Richard Nixon's landslide victory in 1972 over George McGovern—*these* popular sentiments were not necessarily reflected in what government did. Instead, new left interest groups and movements, aided by foundations and elite policy groups and editorial boards, had enormous influence over government decisions from 1968 to 1972.

Nader and the New Movements

While the later sixties are remembered mainly for the violent antiwar and black power movements, their most enduring legacy was the environmental, consumer, and women's movements. These movements largely continued the spirit of the earlier part of the sixties. The women's and gay movements took their cue from the earlier civil rights organizations, just as environmental groups mimicked the moderate antiwar movement. (Earth Day in 1970 was modeled on the antiwar teach-ins.) Like the antiwar movement, these new movements were usually led by students or recent college or law school graduates. The National Organization for Women (NOW), founded in 1964, had 200 chapters by the early 1970s and had been joined in its efforts by the National Women's Political Caucus, the National Association for the Repeal of Abortion Laws (NARAL), and hundreds of small local and national women's organizations. The movement enjoyed remarkable success in shaping the era's political agenda. In 1972, the year *Ms.* magazine was founded, Congress approved the Equal Rights Amendment to the Constitution, strengthened and broadened the scope of the Equal Economic Opportunity Commission, and included a provision in the new Higher Education Act ensuring equal treatment of men and women. In 1973 the Supreme Court granted women the right to abortion.[35]

The consumer and environmental movements enjoyed equally spectacular success. Organizations like the Sierra Club, the Wilderness Society, and the Audubon Society expanded their purview and quadrupled their membership from 1960 to 1969. They were also joined by new groups, including Environmental Action, the Environmental Defense Fund, and Friends of the Earth.[36] The Consumer Federation of America, a coalition of 140 state and local groups, was founded in 1967, and the Consumers Union, which had published a magazine since 1936, established a Washington office in 1969. These groups got the Nixon administration and Congress to adopt a raft of reforms, from establishing the Environmental Protection Agency and the Consumer Product Safety Commission to major revisions of the Clean Air and Clean Water Acts.

* * *

The key individual behind these movements was Ralph Nader. The son of Lebanese immigrants who settled in Winstead, Connecticut, Nader graduated from Princeton and Harvard Law School. He was a classic progressive who defined his role as being above party and faction. Very much in the tradition of Brandeis, whom he read and admired as a teenager, he saw his mission as using the law to further the public interest. Like Brandeis, he sought to defend popular democracy against the unchecked power of large corporations and banks. "I thought of myself as a lawyer for unrepresented and unorganized constituencies," Nader explained.[37] But where Brandeis was interested in the rights of organized labor and the establishment of industrial democracy, Nader was single-mindedly devoted to defending the rights of the consumer against the large corporation.

Nader didn't dissociate himself from the other parts of the new left, but he saw himself as broadening its horizon. "I extended it into the corporate accountability issue," he recalls. "Into corporate crime and corporate fraud. Long ago I knew that the issue was corporate power."[38] Nader's views reflected the transformation of democratic ideals in the twentieth century. He accepted the corporation as a given, but vigorously endeavored to hold it publicly accountable on a broad range of activity. He rejected the late nineteenth-century and modern conservative view that the corporation was an individual who, like the early entrepreneur, should be allowed to maximize his profits without government interference.

In 1965, Nader published *Unsafe at Any Speed,* an exposé of General Motors' laxity in building cars that could withstand collisions. When GM got caught hiring a private investigator to shadow him, Nader became famous and his book a best-seller.[39] Over the next five years he used his fame and rising income—he began receiving fifty speaking invitations a week at $2,500 a speech—to help build a consumer movement.[40] Nader understood the growing role of television in politics: how even a lone individual could bring about far-reaching changes by creating incidents that dramatized injustice or hypocrisy. He became, in his own term, a "civic celebrity." In 1974 a *U.S. News and World Report* survey found Nader to be the fourth-most influential American.

Nader also started hiring young lawyers, called "Nader's raiders," in 1968, and founded his first campus-based Public Interest Research Group (PIRG) in 1970. By the mid-1970s he had founded the Center for Responsive Law, Congress Watch, the Public Citizens Litigation Group, the Health Research Group, the Corporate Accountability Project, the Tax Reform Research Group, the Center for Auto Safety, and the Airline Consumer Action Project. Nader's and the other consumer organizations played an important role in the passage of new legislation, including the Wholesale Poultry Products Act, the Wholesale Meat Act, the Radiation Control Act, the Natural Gas Pipeline Safety Act, the Coal Mine Health and Safety Act, and the Occupational Health and Safety Act.

If Nader was the key individual, the key institution behind the environmental and consumer movement was the ubiquitous Ford Foundation. In 1967, a Long Island lawyer, Victor Yannacone, influenced by Rachel Carson's *Silent Spring,* won a suit against DDT spraying in a local marsh and pond. Yannacone decided to found a group that would sue business and government to force their compliance with environmental laws. He asked for funding from the Audubon Society, but was turned down—perhaps because of the society's ties to chemical companies.[41] But the Ford Foundation provided the startup money for the Environmental Defense Fund. It also gave generous grants to the Sierra Club Legal Defense Fund and the Los Angeles–based Center for Law in the Public Interest. Ford put up the money for the environmental movement's foray into consumer and environmental public interest law. By 1972, Ford was providing 86 percent of the grants to environmental and consumer public interest firms.[42] Without Ford's generous assistance, these movements would have been far less visible and successful.

Unlike the later antiwar and black power movements, the environmental and consumer movements inspired enormous popular support rather than fear and opposition. Republican and Democratic politicians vied to sponsor environmental and consumer legislation. In 1970, Nixon and Edmund Muskie, who was planning to run for president in 1972, got into a bidding war for the movement's support, with each championing successfully tougher revisions to the Clean Air Act. The environmental and consumer movements also enjoyed significant support from elite organizations. In addition to receiving grants from Ford, they also received money from the Rockefeller, Stern, Field, and Carnegie foundations. And they also had the leading newspapers and magazines on their side.

Businesses were initially sympathetic because of the buoyant economy. From February 1961 to September 1969, the country enjoyed the longest continuous boom on record. The economy grew by 4.5 percent a year, compared to 3.2 percent in the 1950s.[43] Secure in their standing, only fifty corporations had registered lobbyists stationed in Washington in the early 1960s.[44] Then, in the mid-1960s, as the country's mood darkened, the public's opinion of business began to fall precipitously. In a National Opinion Research Corporation survey, those expressing "a great deal of confidence" in the people running "major companies" fell from 55 percent in 1966 to 27 percent in 1971.[45] In another study, those agreeing that "the profits of large companies help make things better for everyone" fell from 67 percent in 1966 to 51 percent in 1971.[46] Students echoed these sentiments. In 1969, pollster Daniel Yankelovich found that 99 percent of college students thought that "business is too concerned with profits and not with public responsibility."

Instead of attacking their critics, businesses, as David Vogel recounts in *Fluctuating Fortunes,* sought to accommodate the demands of the consumer and environmental movements by stressing social responsibility. While the auto and tobacco companies took umbrage at regulations targeted at them, business as a whole thought it could adapt the new environmental and consumer legislation to its own ends just as it had done earlier with the Interstate Commerce Commission (dubbed by a Nader study the "Interstate Commerce Omission") and the Federal Trade Commission. By backing national regulation, it hoped it could prevent a chaotic patchwork of different state regulations and create a single board that it could control. A *Fortune* survey in February 1970 found 53 percent of *Fortune* 500 executives in favor of a national regulatory agency and 57 percent believing that the federal government should "step up regulatory activities." In a spirit of social responsibility, 85 percent of the executives thought that the environment should be protected even if that meant "reducing profits."[47]

But the executives soon discovered that they were sanctioning a major expansion of government regulation of corporations. The new regulatory bodies, housed in the executive branch and more immediately responsible to elected officials and voters, proved to be guardians of the public interest rather than tools of the corporations they were supposed to regulate. They forced corporations to be accountable to more than their own stockholders. They represented a return to the activist state and the democratic pluralism of the New Deal.

The success of the environmental, consumer, and women's movements, along with that of the antiwar and civil rights movements, permanently altered the nature of politics by extending democratic principles to a range of activities and concerns that had previously been thought to be outside the purview of government and public policy. These ranged from police brutality against blacks to sexual harassment on the job to auto safety to toxic waste dumps. Like the New Deal, these movements established legislative precedents that it would be difficult for later political generations to repudiate or ignore. Americans would continue to support auto safety legislation, OSHA, and the Clean Air and Water Acts. Conservatives as well as liberals would come to accept the Civil Rights Act of 1964 and the Voting Rights Acts of 1965.

Many of the theories of pluralism had assumed a passive citizenry who would be represented by large organizations that, like the members of a corporate board of directors, would vote their proxy in determining the course of government. These political organizations would most closely resemble the AFL-CIO, the Chamber of Commerce, the American Farm Bureau, and other behemoths of the 1950s. But the experience of the sixties undercut these theories. The students and other citizens who participated in civil rights and antiwar demonstrations or in Earth Day were anything but passive, and the movements of the sixties displayed a far more diverse model of political organization—blending large and small, and featuring the "civic celebrity" like Nader who could dramatize the movement's cause not only through public speaking but also on television. The organizations themselves could vanish and reappear in different guise and name without the movement itself losing its force and power.

What underlay this model of pluralism as participatory democracy was the social commitment of the protestors and demonstrators. Like the progressives at the turn of the century and labor organizers of the 1930s, the student protestors saw themselves as trying to create a higher good. In this sense, they were strikingly different from the narcissistic, self-absorbed generation that would follow. As surveys from the late 1960s showed, all students of that era, and not simply protestors, displayed an idealism about their lives and their objectives. The kind of beliefs that thirty years before had inspired Frankfurter's Harvard law students had filtered downward to the state universities and junior colleges.

Beginning in 1966, the UCLA Cooperative Institutional Research Program conducted annual surveys of the attitudes of American college freshmen. That first year, for instance, they found that 57.8 percent of incoming freshmen thought it was essential to "keep up to date with political affairs," 68.5 percent to "help others who are in difficulty," and only 43.5 percent to "be very well-off financially."[48] When Yankelovich conducted a survey for CBS in 1969, he found similar results. He asked college students what values were important to them. Eighteen percent said money was "very important," 51 percent said "service to others" was "very important."[49]

Utopian Visions

In the second phase of the sixties, the counterculture spread from Berkeley, Madison, Ann Arbor, and Cambridge to almost every high school and college in America. Teenagers from pampered suburban homes who had never read Allen Ginsberg or Nelson Algren nevertheless denounced the "rat race" and the "neon wilderness." In extensive polls and interviews conducted from 1968 to 1974, Yankelovich concluded that "from 1968 to the present, there has been a steady upward progression in the percentage of college students who:

> Welcome more acceptance of sexual freedom.
> Reject materialism for its own sake.
> Stress privacy as a personal value.
> Reject patriotism, religion and the additional view of a "clean, moral life" as important personal values.

Find the present prohibition against marijuana unacceptable.
Are ready to let people live as they want—whether it involves premarital sexual relations, homosexuality, etc. without regarding such behavior as a matter of morality.
Question and doubt such traditional American views as putting duty before pleasure, saving money regularly, etc.[50]

Like the other movements of the sixties, the counterculture had its theorists and its own secular version of millennialism. It was, basically, a utopian version of the new capitalism. It could be found in hundreds of alternative newspapers, in sociologist Theodore Roszak's *The Making of a Counter Culture,* in ecologist Murray Bookchin's pamphlets and *Post-Scarcity Anarchism,* and in Yale Law School professor Charles Reich's best-selling 1970 book, *The Greening of America.*

This postmillennial vision was different from that of Galbraith, Harrington, the Port Huron Statement, and "The Triple Revolution." "The Triple Revolution" called, in effect, for extending the New Deal so as to solve once and for all the problems of poverty and inequality. The authors didn't see the very nature of existence transformed, but rather the extension to all classes of the comfort and security enjoyed by the upper and middle classes. They retained a progressive belief in the power of social science and technology to solve problems. Postmillennialists of the late sixties foresaw a change in human nature and human arrangements that would subordinate work to play and science to art. Work, Charles Reich wrote, would become an "erotic experience, or a play experience."[51] The instrument of change would not be a political movement, but the change in consciousness that had already begun among college students.

Bookchin saw the change occurring as students created "liberated communities."[52] Reich saw the essence of change in the new "freedom of choosing a life style."* He argued that the change had been and would be

*For those who question whether the sixties rank as one of the great awakenings, it is instructive to compare Reich's writings with those of Jonathan Edwards in the 1750s. Edwards's language may seem more stilted, but the message is astonishingly similar:

the inevitable result of capitalism—what he called the "machine." As capitalism became capable of producing more goods than it could sell, it was forced to devise ways to expand people's needs and wants. It had to transform people themselves, moving them from the work ethic of "Consciousness II" to the lifestyle ethic of "Consciousness III." Wrote Reich:

> Consciousness III is produced by the machine itself. It is the product of the machine's success, not its failure. . . . It cannot repress and at the same time sell more products, more "freedom to consume." It cannot repress while all of its productive and advertising machinery is emphasizing a new and more liberated way of life—and needs to do so in order to sell its products.[53]

Consciousness III would not eliminate technology, but make it the servant of a new liberated lifestyle:

> Since machines can produce enough food and shelter for all, why should not man end the antagonism derived from scarcity and base his society on love for his fellow man? If machines can take care of our material wants, why should not man develop the aesthetic and spiritual side of his nature?[54]

In sharp contrast to Galbraith, Harrington, and the thinkers of the early sixties, both the new left revolutionaries and the countercultural theorists displayed a skepticism about science and social science. It came

---

> Tis probable that the world shall be more like Heaven in the millennium in this respect: that contemplation and spiritual employments, and those things that more directly concern the mind and religion, will be more the saint's ordinary business than now. There will be so many contrivances and inventions to facilitate and expedite their necessary secular business that they shall have more time for more noble exercise, and that they will have better contrivances for assisting one another through the whole earth by more expedite, easy and safe communication between distant regions than now. . . . And so the country about the poles need no longer be hid to us, but the whole earth may be as one community, one body in Christ.

Quoted in C. C. Goen, "Jonathan Edwards: A New Departure in Eschatology," *Church History,* March 1959.

initially from identifying science with the work of RAND and the other defense think tanks, which had dutifully subordinated their technical expertise to the ends of war and destruction. Paul Goodman recounted his experience when he taught a class in 1967 at the New School for Social Research in New York City. He invited a physician, engineer, journalist, architect, and scholar of the humanities to talk to the students about their professions. Goodman described the students' reaction:

> To my surprise, the class unanimously rejected my guests. Heatedly and rudely, they called them finks, mystifiers or deluded. They showed that every profession was co-opted and corrupted by the System . . . that professional peer groups were only conspiracies to make money.[55]

In *The Making of a Counter Culture,* historian Theodore Roszak offered a philosophical argument for rejecting the verities of science and social science. He described the counterculture as

> a movement which has turned from objective consciousness as if from a place inhabited by plague—and in the moment of that turning, one can just begin to see an entire episode of our cultural history, the great age of science and technology which began with the Enlightenment, standing revealed in all its quaintly arbitrary, often absurd, and all too painfully, unbalanced aspects.[56]

To their credit, Reich, Roszak, and other new left utopians understood that America had inexorably turned a corner from an older industrial ethic and way of life. They also grasped the inability of the political system of the 1950s—centered on trusted elites and large Washington interest groups—to come to terms with the civil rights movement, the ghetto riots, and the war in Vietnam. But new left utopians did not bequeath to Americans the means with which to meet these challenges. Their rejection of science and social science threatened the foundations of deliberative democracy. It encouraged a politics of protest unfettered by reason. It fueled a distrust of governmental authority at the same time as it demanded the extension of that authority to new realms of consumer and environmental protection. Wrote Daniel Bell, "Radicals are becoming increasingly suspicious of government and planning (as benefiting only the planners and the bureaucrats), even though their first reaction to any issue is to call for more 'government.' "[57]

The utopians rejected compromise and conciliation. They identified the preservation of the status quo with decay and decline and they identified political and social change with revolutionary turmoil and upheaval. This perversion of politics would persist not only among the extremes of the left, but among political conservatives such as Newt Gingrich who would claim to be the enemies of all things that the sixties represented.

The End of the Sixties

The end of the spirit of the 1960s was precipitated, first, by an economic slowdown, which began in 1969. This slowdown, later aggravated by the energy crisis of 1973, put a damper on the counterculture. Students became focused on preparing for jobs and careers rather than on discovering the meaning of life. The new attitude of the 1970s would later be captured in Christopher Lasch's 1979 book *The Culture of Narcissism* and in Tom Wolfe's essay "The Me Decade and the Third Great Awakening."[58] The second event was Nixon's signing of a peace accord with North Vietnam in January 1973. The war's end (from an American standpoint) not only put an end to the antiwar movement, but removed a major source of political mobilization and energy. The fervor of the antiwar movement had rippled outward to the consumer and environmental movements. Once the war was over, these movements began to contract into collections of Washington-based pressure groups whose constituencies were the recipients of direct-mail funding appeals.

But the sixties were also put to rest by the furious counterreaction they provoked. Business leaders who had acquiesced in legislation to protect the environment, the consumer, and the worker's health and safety would become convinced that the cost of carrying out these regulations threatened their very existence. Largely apolitical, they would begin organizing political action committees and funding think tanks. Whites would react harshly against affirmative action and busing for minorities and to the rhetorical militancy of the black power movement. They would become deeply alienated from the liberal movements and the Democratic Party and become amenable to appeals from political conservatives. And many middle-class Americans would take umbrage at the libertinism of the counterculture—from sexual and gay liberation to enthusiasm for drugs. By the end of the 1970s, these different strains of counterreaction would cohere into a massive movement that would dominate American politics for years to come.

[5]

Business and the Rise of K Street

In the decades after World War II, many businessmen and -women steered clear of politics. They voted, and sometimes contributed to candidates, but they rarely participated in political movements or policy groups. Among those that did, the small businessman and the head of a family-owned enterprise were most likely to join the Chamber of Commerce and to oppose most kinds of government economic intervention. Some corporate executives and investment bankers joined the NAM or the Liberty League, but others worked with policy groups such as the Committee on Economic Development, which saw the government as having a role in tempering the business cycle and in limiting the inequities or addressing the externalities of unregulated capitalism. They were an important group within the American elite.

These business leaders initially acquiesced in and in some cases actively supported the consumer and environmental movements of the sixties. They served on the boards of the Ford Foundation and the Brookings Institution. They looked kindly on collective bargaining and were comfortable serving with labor leaders on policy groups and commissions. Some of them, like Ford CEO Robert McNamara and investment bankers Douglas Dillon and George Ball, were appointed to cabinet positions. But in the 1970s, many of these corporate leaders and bankers abandoned their commitment to disinterested public service and to a politics that transcended class. They turned against union organizers, environmentalists, and consumer activists with the same resolve that an older generation of business leaders had turned against the AFL, the IWW, and the Socialist Party. They set up lobbies in Washington. They ran "advertorials" attacking their political opponents. They established political action committees that bankrolled hundreds of candidates. And in the process, they turned American politics decisively away from democratic reform.

What precipitated this momentous change was the economic downturn that began in the late 1960s and that foreshadowed a protracted slowdown that persisted well into the 1990s. That slump altered business leaders' views of themselves and their enterprises as profoundly as it changed students' views of the future. In the sixties, Ralph Nader had been a thorn to General Motors, but a hero to many other Americans, including businessmen. In the seventies, business leaders demonized him. Businesses had acquiesced in wage demands from labor unions, while labor unions had not conducted a major strike since 1959. Now they vigorously resisted, setting off a new class struggle. Labor relations became as parlous as they had been forty years before.

The New Class Struggle

The history of capitalism has been characterized not only by short-term cycles of recession and recovery, but also by longer periods of boom and slowdown in which recessions and recoveries have taken place. In 1969, the United States began to slip into a recession. From 1962 to 1968, the economy had grown at 4.6 percent a year. It grew only 2.4 percent in 1969, and then fell 0.3 percent in 1970. This recession proved in turn to be the beginning of a longer downturn. Over the next decades, the nation and other advanced industrial economies grew much more slowly than they had in the previous decades. From 1960 to 1973, America's gross domestic product (GDP) had risen 4 percent annually; it would increase only 2.6 percent annually between 1973 to 1979 and 2.2 percent annually between 1979 and 1995.[1]

What precipitated this longer downturn was growing competition among the major industrial nations, which drove down corporate profit rates—from an average of nearly 10 percent in after-tax profits in 1965 to less than 6 percent in the late 1970s—and led to chronic overcapacity in such key industries as steel, automobiles, machine tools, textiles, chemicals, and shipbuilding.[2] In the past, the world's economies had overcome this kind of overcapacity through the "creative destruction" of a depression that eliminated uncompetitive firms, but after World War II, the United States, Western Europe, and Japan had committed themselves to economic strategies that were intended to prevent sharp downturns. These included government protection of large banks and corporations from bankruptcy. That strategy succeeded in taming the business cycle, but it also prolonged the long slump that began in the late 1960s. From 1973 to 1996, world trade expanded only 3.9 percent annually compared to 7.1 percent annually between 1960 and 1973.

American businessmen got their first inkling that the world economy was changing when, during the 1960s, European and Japanese firms became capable of competing in autos, steel, textiles, and electronics. During the Vietnam War, foreign companies took advantage of rising American demand for goods to capture American markets. From 1965 to 1967 Japanese trade with the United States grew 100 percent.[3] As inflation accelerated in the late 1960s, American businesses found their products being ignored in favor of cheaper foreign goods. In 1971, the nation ran its first trade deficit since 1893.

That same year, the United States also abandoned the gold standard. As long as American goods were in demand, other countries had no incentive to cash in for gold the dollar holdings they had amassed from American overseas investments or military expenditures. Rising prices and trade deficits, however, prompted countries to began demanding gold. Finally, in August 1971, Nixon abandoned the Bretton Woods Agreement, which had fixed the value of the dollar at $35 for an ounce of gold, and forced the value of the yen and deutsche mark to rise against the dollar.[4] Even though the revaluation of the yen and deutsche mark benefited American exporters, Nixon's decision heightened business leaders' anxiety about their own future.

These changes in the international economy put pressure on American business to lower costs by resisting wage increases at home. Firms that had accepted unionization as a fait accompli now resisted union bargaining elections. In 1965, when unions filed petitions to be recognized with the NLRB, 42 percent of companies immediately complied; by 1973, only 16 percent did.[5] Large companies also responded to the downturn by transferring operations to low-wage areas abroad. This threat alone of the runaway shop—made credible by its growing incidence—weakened labor's bargaining position. Writing in *Foreign Policy* in 1997, Harvard economist Dani Rodrik argued that this new globalization had created an "asymmetry":

> Employers can move abroad, but employees cannot. There is no substantive difference between American workers being driven from their jobs by their fellow *domestic* workers who agree to work 12-hour days, earn less than the minimum wage, or be fired if they join a union—all of which are illegal under U.S. law—and their being similarly disadvantaged by *foreign* workers doing the same.[6]

Business's newfound concerns about profits and unions provoked a counterreaction. Labor unions became more militant. At General Electric, a coalition of unions went out on strike in October 1969 and stayed on the picket line through the winter. The next year, 250,000 postal workers went on strike, followed by 400,000 General Motors workers. In each of these strikes, unions were able to win concessions.

To business leaders, these strikes raised a political specter. Business leaders were disturbed by the support the GE and GM strikers received from new left activists. Earlier in the sixties, militant students had played a major role in United Farm Workers leader Cesar Chavez's grape boycott, but Chavez's campaign was linked to civil rights as much as to labor. Now, several hundred thousand students, declaring their newfound solidarity with workers, joined picket lines, held rallies on campuses in support of the strikes, and kept corporate recruiters off of campuses. In February 1970, for instance, 10,000 Boston University students (out of a student body of 17,000) protested the arrival of a GE recruiter on campus.[7] In July 1969, *Nation's Business,* the magazine of the Chamber of Commerce, reported that "Students for a Democratic Society—SDS—is shifting this summer from the campuses it engulfed in violence to a new target: American business and industry." It offered instructions to employers how to stop student militants from infiltrating their shops and offices.[8]

In a special December 1969 issue on the "Seventies," *Business Week* expressed common fears for the future of business:

> In the America of 1969, political and economic power rests with two groups: the corporations and the middle- and upper-bracket income earners. Challenging this power and the way it has been used are at least three identifiable groups: the blacks, the labor unions, and the young. The attacks, retreats, shifting alliances and internal dissension of these groups will make the Seventies one of the tumultuous decades in U.S. history. . . . And the U.S. corporation . . . may well change most of all. As producer, market, and employer, it will be on the firing line throughout the decade. . . . Business will still be business in 1980 but the meaning of the word may have undergone some significant changes.[9]

The rise over the next two or three years of the consumer and environmental movements only stoked these fears. Business leaders, suddenly facing factory inspections and lawsuits, became genuinely alarmed. Murray Weidenbaum, who was an Assistant Secretary of the Treasury in the Nixon administration and would later chair the Council of Economic Advisors in the Reagan administration, recalled the case of the Occupational Safety and Health Act, which passed Congress easily in 1970. "Business ignored the debate," Weidenbaum said. "Then after it was enacted members of Congress started getting more letters on it than on any other subject."[10]

As the economy slowed, business and labor also came to blows over trade and international economic policy. Since World War II, business groups and labor unions had clashed periodically over social legislation, but top corporate leaders and AFL-CIO leaders had worked together in groups like the Council on Foreign Relations to forge a common foreign and international economic policy. In 1962, the AFL-CIO had backed President Kennedy's Trade Expansion Act after the administration had agreed to aid workers who lost their jobs because of imports and pledged to enforce rules against foreign companies "dumping" their products on the U.S. market at prices below their cost of production. But AFL-CIO leaders began to feel that they had been taken advantage of. Between 1962 and 1969, the Tariff Commission rejected all fifteen petitions for trade adjustment assistance for unemployed workers.

By 1969, the AFL-CIO was also becoming concerned not only about low-wage imports of shoes and textiles, but also about an entirely new phenomenon: the American multinational firm that moved its operations abroad in search of lower wages and was now importing goods back into the United States—costing American jobs twice. AFL-CIO economist Elizabeth R. Jager found that from 1966 to 1970, multinational firms' foreign employment had risen 26.5 percent and their American employment 7.6 percent, while their sales of goods back to the United States had increased 130 percent.[11] By 1970, imports from U.S. multinationals accounted for 34 percent of total imports.[12]

In 1971 the federation hired a Washington lawyer to draft a bill restricting the operation of multinationals, and got Senator Vance Hartke of Indiana and Representative James Burke of Massachusetts to sponsor it. The Burke-Hartke bill, as it became called, removed the tax breaks for companies that invested overseas—breaks that entitled them to pay taxes only on income they brought back into the country. The bill also allowed the president to restrict the export of capital when it would threaten jobs in the United States. And it established quotas on imports that competed directly with American-made goods.

Burke-Hartke was a flawed bill, particularly because of its quota on imports. But it opened debate over an entirely new area of public and democratic control of corporate behavior. It was based on the premise that the public had a right to regulate what an American corporation did internationally when American jobs were at stake. The government was already implicitly regulating the international flow of capital on behalf of corporations through its tax and monetary policies. Burke-Hartke wanted it regulated on behalf of the public and national interest. The debate over the Burke-Hartke bill foreshadowed the debates over the North American Free Trade Agreement, the World Trade Organization, and fast-track authorization during the Clinton administration.

The bill thoroughly alarmed business leaders. Businesses poured money into the Emergency Committee for Foreign Trade (ECAT), which had been established in 1967 by David Rockefeller of Chase Manhattan, Arthur Watson of IBM, James Linen of Time Inc., and First National City Bank's George Moore, to defend the multinationals.[13] ECAT ran full-page ads in newspapers warning, "Congress: Please don't declare a world trade war."[14] Rockefeller warned members of the Detroit Economic Club in a May 1972 speech that multinationals were "being hauled before the court of public opinion and indicted."[15] Both the Chamber of Commerce and the NAM made defeat of Burke-Hartke a major priority, and the administration had both the Commerce and the State Departments do studies to invalidate the AFL-CIO's charges. Though Burke-Hartke didn't come up for a vote, both Republican and Democratic politicians endorsed its basic principle—that American multinationals should be regulated so that they acted in the national interest. Declared the GOP in its 1972 platform, "We deplore the practice of locating plants in foreign countries solely to take advantage of low wage rates in order to produce goods primarily for sale in the U.S. We will take action to discourage such unfair and disruptive practices that result in the loss of American jobs."[16]

The national media ignored the controversy over Burke-Hartke, and historians of the Nixon years have invariably passed over it. But more than any single debate, it expressed the basic conflict that the new post–Bretton Woods world economy was creating between business on the one hand and labor and the movements of the sixties on the other. Twenty-five years later politicians and policy makers would be acting as if they discovered something called globalization and the "race to the bottom" caused by international competition, but these issues were clearly raised in 1971. The looming divisions caused by the new international economy would profoundly affect the American political system by undermining the pluralism that had prevailed since the New Deal.

In the early 1970s, labor's hostility to multinational corporations, together with the success of the consumer and environmental movements, the renewed militancy within the labor movement, and the looming threat of an alliance between students and striking workers—all occurring within a protracted economic downturn—prompted business not only to take a harder line in the workplace, but also to alter its basic approach to politics and government. That didn't happen immediately, however. It would take a disparate group of intellectuals, politicians, and lobbyists to put business's fear of anticapitalist revolution into words and to develop a counterrevolutionary strategy.

Powell and Kristol

The two men who played the leading role in articulating business's fear were Lewis D. Powell, a lawyer from Richmond, Virginia, whom Richard Nixon would appoint to the Supreme Court in the fall of 1971, and Irving Kristol, a former leftist and Trotskyist who had become a columnist for the *Wall Street Journal,* the editor of a new journal, *The Public Interest,* and a professor of public policy at New York University. Neither man was known as a spokesman for American business, yet their words would have more influence on business leaders than those of any other politician or writer of the time.

In Richmond, Powell would often complain to his neighbor, businessman and Chamber of Commerce official Eugene B. Sydnor, Jr., about the growing hostility to business. Sydnor asked him to lay out thoughts in a memo for the Chamber. In August 1971, two months before Nixon would nominate him to the high court, Powell wrote a bristling memorandum. "The American economic system," Powell warned,

> is under broad attack. . . . We are not dealing with sporadic or isolated attacks from a relatively few extremists or even from the minority socialist cadre. Rather, the assault on the enterprise system is broadly based and consistently pursued. It is gaining momentum and converts. . . . The overriding first need is for businessmen to recognize that the ultimate issue may be *survival*—survival of what we call the free enterprise system, and all that this means for the strength and prosperity of America and the freedom of our people.

Powell described Ralph Nader as the "single most effective antagonist of American business" and the campus as the "single most dynamic source" of opposition. But he warned that antibusiness sentiments had spread from college students to college faculties, especially in the social sciences, and from faculties to the media, Congressional staffs, and politicians themselves, who "stampede to support almost any legislation related to 'consumerism' or the 'environment.' "

Business leaders, Powell charged, had proved no match for these enemies of the system, and he called on the Chamber and business to organize against the threat to their survival. He advocated not only more energetic lobbying, but business support for efforts to enlighten public thinking—not so much about the businessman and his individual role as about "the system which he administers, and which provides the goods, services, and jobs on which our country depends." Powell urged businesses, among other things, to fund sympathetic professors on campus and to demand "equal time" for outside speakers to present their own point of view, to monitor closely school textbooks and the media, to devote 10 percent of their advertising budget to combating critics of free enterprise ("There should be no hesitation to attack the Naders, the Marcuses and others who openly seek destruction of the system") and to "cultivate assiduously" political power.[17]

Powell's memorandum found an eager readership among the Washington lobbyists and among CEOs at company headquarters. It convinced businessmen that they had to become involved in national politics and in Washington policy making.

As early as 1970, Irving Kristol was warning in the *Wall Street Journal* that unless the new movements were restrained, "we shall move toward some version of state capitalism in which the citizen's individual liberty would be ever more insecure."[18] Two years later, Kristol was painting the followers of Senator George McGovern as socialists who were moving the nation from "the modified version of capitalism we call the 'welfare state' toward an economic system so stringently regulated in detail as to fulfill many of the traditional anti-capitalist aspirations of the left."[19]

When Kristol warned of "state capitalism" and "anti-capitalist aspirations," he was not referring to state ownership of the means of production, but to the regulation of corporations favored by "environmentalism," "ecology," and "consumer protection."[20] Under the guise of resisting socialism, Kristol was in effect reasserting the older priorities of corporate individualism. What he objected to was governmental regulation of corporations on behalf of the public interest.

Adapting Daniel Bell's sketch of a new postindustrial capitalism to his own polemical purposes, Kristol called for a corporate offensive against what he called the "new class." Kristol argued that the growing group of knowledge workers that Bell described had become the locus of "anti-capitalist aspirations of left." These members of the new class occupied key places in foundations like Ford, in think tanks like Brookings, in social science departments at Harvard and Yale, on the editorial boards of the *New York Times* and *Washington Post,* and on Capitol Hill. Most of their research and publications were being funded by the same corporations that they were attacking. Kristol urged that corporations start funding their own thinkers and think tanks: "When you give away your stockholders' money, your philanthropy must serve the longer-term interests of the corporation. Corporate philanthropy should not be, and cannot be, disinterested."[21]

Kristol's recommendations on corporate philanthropy ran directly counter to the historic assumptions that had motivated American elites, but in the midst of the renewed class struggle of the 1970s, they found a receptive audience. Financier William Simon, who, after serving as Ford's Secretary of the Treasury, would head the powerful Olin Foundation, quoted Kristol to justify his own determination "to funnel desperately needed funds to scholars, social scientists, writers and journalists who understand the relationship between political and economic liberty."[22] In the *Harvard Business Review,* Robert H. Malott, the CEO of the FMC Corporation, also cited Kristol in recommending a probusiness approach to philanthropy. "We are too often witness to corporations providing support to groups that are hostile to the competitive enterprise system," Malott warned.[23]

Powell and Kristol's message was echoed by a handful of lobbyists and public officials in Washington. These included Bryce Harlow, Proctor and Gamble's chief representative in Washington and an éminence grise among Washington lobbyists; Nixon's Secretary of Defense Melvin Laird; and Deputy Secretary of the Treasury Charls Walker. Harlow had been a speechwriter for both Eisenhower and Nixon. Laird, an intellectually inclined former Congressman from Wisconsin, had backed Goldwater in 1964 and had championed the rise of a conservative politics in the Republican Party. Walker (whose mother had named him "Charls" so that he wouldn't be called "Charley") had been a lobbyist for the American Bankers Association before joining the Nixon administration and would later become Washington's most powerful tax lobbyist. If Powell and Kristol furnished the intellectual framework, Harlow, Laird, and Walker would provide the organizational savvy and the fundraising connections to launch a new movement.

The Business Roundtable

During the 1920s, businesses sought to win political power and to quash union drives, but most of their organization took place on a local or regional level. The National Metal Trades Association, one of the main groups promoting the "American plan," was primarily an Eastern and Midwestern group confined to one kind of industry. The NAM, based in New York, did not work closely with the Chamber of Commerce, which was based in Washington. Businesses and banks hired publicists and public relations firms, but they didn't band together to influence public opinion through think tanks or policy groups or through funding joint political action committees. From the 1930s through the 1960s, businesses were deeply divided in their approach to government. While organizations like the NAM and the Liberty League had advocated intransigence, many corporate CEOs looked toward more moderate and conciliatory voices like that of the CED and the Business Advisory Council (later renamed the Business Council) for leadership. But all that changed in the 1970s.

The CEOs of large banks and corporations helped to create during that decade a powerful network of national organizations, think tanks, trade associations, policy groups, and lobbies, headquartered in Washington. Blue-chip corporations like General Motors and banks like Chase Manhattan began contributing to conservative political groups. Bankers like Citicorp's Walter Wriston, who had backed President Johnson earlier, gravitated to the Republican right. Of course, there were still sharp conflicts among industries and business organizations, and between large and small business, over specific provisions and bills. But businesses, believing that they faced common organized adversaries, created overlapping and interlocking organizations, which, when directed toward a single end, such as the revision of the tax code or the reduction of labor's influence on Capitol Hill, were irrepressible.

The first efforts at reviving business's influences took place at the NAM and the Chamber. Both organizations had become irrelevant during the 1960s, but in 1973 the NAM's new chairman, Bert Raynes, decided to move the NAM's headquarters from New York to Washington. Explained Raynes, "The thing that affects business most today is government. The interrelationship of business with business is no longer so important as the interrelationship of business with government."[24] Raynes converted the NAM's twenty-eight-person policy staff in Washington to lobbyists on Capitol Hill, and established a full-time liaison with other corporate lobbyists in Washington. The NAM and the Chamber also discussed merging. It didn't happen, but they did establish a joint political action committee and began to work together for the first time on specific issues. By the late seventies both groups were being credited with helping to turn Congress around. The Chamber itself enjoyed a revival in the last half of the seventies. Its membership grew 30 percent a year; it went from a $20 million budget and 50,000 members to $65 million and 215,000 members by 1983, with a staff of 1,000.[25]

But the main thrust of business lobbying came from an entirely new organization. Two of the industries that first experienced the slump of the late 1960s were construction and steel. Construction companies found their profits eroded by the high wages they had to pay for hard-to-find skilled workers. Steel companies worried not only about a slowdown in construction but also about foreign competition. Foreign imports controlled less than 2 percent in 1958; by 1968, they accounted for almost 18 percent of American steel consumption. Steel company profits plummeted from 1968 to 1970.[26] At the instigation of former U.S. Steel president Roger Blough, one hundred steel and construction companies formed the Construction Users Anti-Inflation Roundtable in 1969 to pressure unions to hold down their wage demands.

Then, in 1972, Fred Borch, the chairman of GE, and John Harper, the chairman of Alcoa and a member of Blough's group, went to Washington to meet with Secretary of the Treasury John Connally, Deputy Treasury Secretary Charls Walker, and Federal Reserve Board Chairman Arthur Burns about the growing hostility toward business. Connally, Walker, and Burns urged the executives to found a new organization that would be confined to CEOs and that would lobby Congress and the White House directly. With Bryce Harlow also advising them, Borch and Harper organized the March Group, which they intended to be a small, select body. But growing interest among CEOs persuaded them to merge with Blough's group to form the Business Roundtable in 1973. Within five years, the Business Roundtable boasted 192 member companies, including 113 of the top *Fortune* 200. Together, the Roundtable's companies accounted for nearly half of the country's GNP.[27]

The Roundtable was different from past business organizations in several important respects. Unlike the Chamber of Commerce and the NAM, it was strictly limited to major corporations and to their CEOs. John Harper was the first president, followed by Thomas Murphy of General Motors, Irving Shapiro of Dupont, and Borch's successor at GE, Reginald Jones. These CEOs actually did much of the lobbying. Writing in *Harvard Business Review* in 1981, Albro Martin commented:

> The Business Roundtable almost seems a belated recognition of the frequently demonstrated historical principle that royalty always commands more attention, respect and awe than the lesser nobility. Neither the National Association of Manufacturers nor the U.S. Chamber of Commerce can do what a uniquely conceived and specially powered lobby of the largest and most responsible economic interests in the country can achieve.[28]

The Business Roundtable differed from the Committee on Economic Development (CED), an organization that had also attracted *Fortune* 500 CEOs. The CED was not a lobby, but a research organization that publicized its results in order to promote policies and directions. The Roundtable lobbied for and against specific initiatives. In its initial decades, the CED's businessmen and social scientists did not see themselves as members of an interest group. Business leaders like Paul Hoffman and

Beardsley Ruml and economists like Herbert Stein attempted to be above both party and class. They framed their proposals in terms of the national interest and argued for their worth on the objective grounds of social science. The CED occupied a gray area between an interest group and an elite policy organization. The Business Roundtable was purely an interest group led by CEOs looking out for their own companies' balance sheets. It didn't employ intellectuals like Stein, but publicists and press flacks. Unlike the CED, it also didn't respect the parameters of countervailing power. It had been founded by men who wanted to quash government regulation of corporations. That remained its thrust, even while, on purely social matters that didn't threaten the power or profitability of their institutions, a few of the Roundtable's leaders might embrace the cause of the downtrodden.

The New Think Tanks

Kristol, Powell, and Simon convinced many corporate leaders that it was important to wage a battle for public opinion. Businessmen and corporate foundations began steering their money to opponents of corporate regulation. They endowed university chairs for free enterprise studies, financed special business institutions, and gave money to new kinds of think tanks. These think tanks bore roughly the same relationship to Brookings that the Business Roundtable bore to the CED. They were not, in Robert Brookings's words, "free from any political or pecuniary interest," but were expressions of political and economic interests. Yet their experts and spokesmen sought and often enjoyed the same exalted status as the social scientist from Brookings.

The two most important new think tanks were the American Enterprise Institute (AEI) and the Heritage Foundation. The AEI had begun as an ideological trade association, founded as the American Enterprise Association in 1943 by Lewis H. Brown, the president of Johns-Manville, and a group of like-minded businessmen. Brown had been a tentative supporter of the New Deal, but had become uneasy about Keynesian economics and public works spending, which he believed would undermine the work ethic. Other early association backers were much more stridently anti–New Deal. With a budget of only $80,000, the association hired academics to write reports that were indistinguishable from those of the NAM. In 1954, General Electric executive A. D. Marshall, who had become the association's president after Brown's death in 1951, was ready to shut the association down. But as a last resort he appointed a Chamber of Commerce economist, William Baroody, to be its executive vice president.*

Baroody, like Nader, was the son of Lebanese Christian immigrants. Born in Manchester, New Hampshire, in 1916, he worked in New Hampshire's Unemployment Compensation Agency in the 1930s and in the Veterans Administration after World War II before joining the Chamber of Commerce, where he met and impressed Marshall. Baroody was not himself an intellectual, but he had a deep appreciation for the role of ideas. He wanted to convert Brown's association into a Roosevelt-style "brain trust" for a future conservative administration. He recruited two little-known economists, Milton Friedman from the University of Chicago and Paul McCracken from the University of Michigan, as academic advisors. He also persuaded the trustees to change the name to the American Enterprise Institute to distinguish it clearly from a trade association. (Baroody himself wanted the even more neutral name, the Institute for Public Policy Research.)

In 1964, Baroody organized a "brain trust" for Goldwater's presidential campaign. But this proved to be a thankless task in more ways than one. After the election, Representative Wright Patman's House Subcommittee on Small Business subpoenaed AEI's tax records, and the IRS began a two-year investigation of whether Baroody, by his participation in the Goldwater campaign, had violated AEI's tax-exempt status. Baroody became very guarded in how he characterized AEI, and he recruited token liberals and Democrats to justify his claim that the institute was nonpartisan.[29] Baroody also got his staff to produce torturously even-handed and often out-of-date legislative analyses of Congressional bills.

*Marshall also recruited another Chamber of Commerce economist, Glenn Campbell, to become the association's research director. Campbell soon left to join the Hoover Institution, where he eventually became the director. Campbell and Baroody would remain close friends and serve on each other's boards.

But Baroody retained his older vision of a conservative brain trust. He argued that policy research was monopolized by liberals and liberal institutions, among which he included Brookings, even though Brookings for most of its history had been seen as probusiness. He claimed that by funding AEI, businesses and foundations would be preventing a monopoly of ideas. His favorite line, borrowed from McCracken, was that "a free society can tolerate some degree of concentration in the manufacture of widgets, but it will have trouble surviving a monopoly or near-monopoly of ideas as they affect public policy."[30]

Under Baroody, the AEI's funding rose steadily—from $230,000 in 1960 to $600,000 in 1965 to $900,000 in 1970—but it was still considerably less than the $5.5 million Brookings spent annually. Then, in 1971, Harlow and Laird, who was an old friend of Baroody and for whom Baroody's son, William, Jr., served as press secretary, kicked off a $25 million fund-raising dinner for the AEI at Laird's private Pentagon dining room. Over the next decade, AEI's annual budget climbed to $4.1 million in 1975 and to $9.7 million in 1980, $500,000 more than Brookings. AEI became the favorite cause of corporations that were worried about government regulation and the power of Nader and the AFL-CIO. By 1981, more than 600 corporations were contributing 40 percent of their annual budget. Baroody was now able to recruit the top CEOs to fund-raising posts, including Walter Wriston of Citibank, Willard Butcher of Chase Manhattan, David Packard of Hewlett-Packard, Thomas Murphy of General Motors, and Reginald Jones of General Electric. The AEI also enjoyed the support of corporate foundations, which, heeding the advice of Kristol and Simon, began to concentrate their donations on organizations like AEI. These included Olin, the Sarah Mellon Scaife Foundation, the Smith Richardson Foundation, and the J. Howard Pew Freedom Trust. The Pew Foundation alone (based on Sun Oil stock) gave $6 million to AEI between 1976 and 1981.

Baroody continued to insist publicly that AEI was above politics, but beginning in November 1976, it became the government-in-exile for Ford and Nixon administration officials. Gerald Ford himself joined AEI, as did Robert Bork, Arthur Burns, and Simon. Its fellows and scholars produced hundreds of studies decrying government regulation of business and attacking legislation offered by the consumer, environmental, and labor movements. Many of its studies on regulation were written by James C. Miller III, who would become head of the Federal Trade Commission in the Reagan administration, and Murray Weidenbaum, who also edited the AEI journal *Regulation*. Simon chaired its program on tax policy; former CEA chairman Herbert Stein put out the *AEI Economist*; Jude Wanniski wrote his primer of supply-side economics, *The Way the World Works,* as an AEI fellow; former Secretary of the Treasury George Shultz served on the board of advisors for regulatory policy; and Kristol and Michael Novak developed the political outlook that would be labeled neoconservative. The *Economist* magazine characterized AEI as "always unapologetically conservative."[31] When Reagan won the election in 1980, he would call on more than thirty AEI fellows to join his administration.

The Heritage Foundation, which opened its doors in 1973, sought to influence Congress and the White House not simply over the long term, but on a daily basis. Except in the strictest legal sense, it was a lobby. It did not produce scholarship, but quick takes on policy and op-ed pieces. And it was the coordinated expression of a political faction within the Republican Party. Yet, like Brookings, it sought to present itself as a think tank. Instead of presenting its experts as being above politics, it marketed them as a counterbalance to the views of Brookings and to prevailing "liberal" opinion in Washington.

Heritage was the invention of two Capitol Hill political aides, Paul Weyrich and Edward Feulner. In the spring of 1971, two days *after* the Senate had defeated the Nixon administration's plan to fund a supersonic transport plane (SST), Weyrich, who was working for Colorado Republican Senator Gordon Allott, received an analysis of the SST plan from the AEI. When Weyrich called AEI to find out why the report had arrived late, he was told that Baroody, still fearful of the IRS, didn't want to be seen as influencing the actual vote. At breakfast the next day, Weyrich expressed his frustration to Feulner, and the two men decided the Republicans needed a research organization that would have what Feulner later called "quick response capability."[32]

That fall, Weyrich heard from Allott that beer magnate Joseph Coors wanted to help stem the tide of antibusiness sentiment in the country. Coors had been "stirred," he explained later, by Lewis Powell's call to arms against the critics of free enterprise and had become convinced that business was "ignoring" a crisis.[33] Weyrich persuaded Coors to give $250,000 to begin an Analysis and Research Association on Capitol Hill. After a year of squabbling at the new association, Coors told Weyrich to find a new venue, and Weyrich and Feulner turned to the Schuchman Foundation, named after a young conservative who had died at age twenty-seven. Heritage was started as part of this foundation and then, when it received tax-exempt status, broke off on its own. In the process, Weyrich and Feulner also recruited a new financial angel: Richard Mellon Scaife.

Scaife, an heir to the Mellon fortune, had been a financial backer of Barry Goldwater and of AEI during the 1960s. After his mother, Sarah Mellon Scaife, died in 1965, he and his sister inherited control over the Sarah Mellon Scaife Foundation, the Carthage Foundation, and the Allegheny Foundation. From 1965 to 1973, he fought with his sister, who wanted to spend the foundations' money on art and population control, but in 1973, Scaife became chairman of the Sarah Mellon Scaife Foundation and won control over the family funds, which he then used to back new right, conservative, and business organizations and publications. Scaife initially put up $900,000 for Heritage—more than triple Coors's contribution—and over the next eight years contributed at least $3.8 million.[34]

In 1973, Heritage was incorporated with Weyrich as its director and Forrest Rettgers of the NAM as its chairman. Weyrich only lasted a year. In 1977, Feulner was persuaded to leave the House Republican Study Group, of which he was the director, to become the president of Heritage. Edward Feulner was like William Baroody: an extraordinary promoter and fund-raiser who appreciated the power of ideas. In his first eighteen months at Heritage, he raised its annual budget from less than one million dollars to $2.8 million. Feulner was not only able to lure foundations like Smith Richardson and Olin, but also *Fortune* 500 corporations and banks, including General Motors, Chase Manhattan, Pfizer, Mobil, and Sears. One of Feulner's biggest catches was oilman Edward Noble and his Samuel Robert Noble Foundation. (When Noble later became the head of the Synthetic Fuels Corporation in the Reagan administration, Heritage suddenly fell silent about the waste generated by this ill-begotten agency.)[35]

Feulner also established Heritage's political style. Unlike the AEI, it defined itself openly as a "conservative" organization. With few exceptions, Heritage did not hire recognized scholars, but Ph.D. candidates and aspiring journalists and publicists to produce "backgrounders" on current legislative battles and foreign policy issues, which were then mailed (and later faxed) to politicians, public officials, and journalists. The backgrounders were article-length. Heritage vice president Herb Berkowitz later explained that Feulner "wanted products to meet a briefcase test, so a busy executive can throw it into his briefcase and read it in an hour or less."[36] Unlike the AEI legislative analyses, Heritage's backgrounders took sides and recommended action. Journalist Burton Pines, whom Feulner made director of research and later vice president, said, "We're not here to be some kind of Ph.D. committee giving equal time. Our role is to provide conservative public-policy makers with arguments to bolster our side."[37]

In Feulner's first years, Heritage was probably more successful at marketing itself than marketing its recommendations. It was less important than AEI in altering the debate over business and the economy in Washington. Other organizations, such as Paul Nitze's Committee on the Present Danger, played a more decisive role in attacking the Carter administration's foreign policy toward the Soviet Union. But when the Reagan administration and Senate Republicans took power in 1980, Heritage, with its backlog of backgrounders, which it synthesized into a large volume, *Mandate for Leadership 1980,* was best positioned of all the new institutions to play a decisive role in Congress and the White House. By 1985, its annual budget would equal that of AEI and Brookings.

Budgets of Think Tanks and Policy Groups
(selected years, in millions of dollars)[38]

	1965	1970	1975	1980	1983
CED	1.7	2.1	1.9	2.6	3.1
AEI	.6	.9	4.1	9.7	10.6
Heritage			2.8('78)	5.3	10.6
CFR	1.7	2.1	2.3	3.9	6.5('84)
Brookings	3	5.5	7.8	9.2	11.9

Besides Heritage and AEI, business funded scores of other think tanks and policy groups inside and outside of Washington—from the Capital Legal Foundation (an anti-Nader outfit) and the Center for Strategic and International Studies to the Institute for Contemporary Studies in San Francisco and Murray Weidenbaum's Center for the Study of American Business at Washington University in St. Louis. It also subsidized sympathetic economists, including Milton Friedman, Karl Brunner, and James Buchanan. Together, these think tanks, policy groups, and academics inundated the pages of magazines and newspapers and filled up the mailboxes of journalists and Congressional staff with their own version of economic and social reality.

The New Ideology

This version of reality pivoted on a simple formula: government rather than business was responsible for America's ills—from inflation and high energy prices to the slowdown in growth and the rise in unemployment. It was a reassertion of Jacksonian economics and an attempt to undermine the basis of democratic reform in the twentieth century. AEI economist Warren Nutter put it this way: "The serious economic pains now being experienced are symptoms of political ills, not of flaws in the economic system. The basic problem is too much government, not too little."[39]

Inflation was caused by government deficits rather than by corporate greed or OPEC. Slow growth was caused not by overcapacity and a lack of demand, but by government regulations, which increased business costs, government spending, and taxes, which deprived the private sector of funds, and by rising wages. Faster growth could be achieved by eliminating costly environmental, workplace, and product regulations, reducing government welfare spending, cutting taxes, and easing wage growth. These measures would increase growth by increasing the "supply" of capital for investment. Wrote General Electric CEO Reginald Jones in *Harvard Business Review* in 1975, "Business must convince an indifferent public and skeptical Congress that this country is facing a severe capital gap."[40]

This analysis was presented in articles in the AEI's *Regulation* and Kristol's *The Public Interest* and in books and studies published by AEI, the Institute for Contemporary Studies, and other think tanks and policy groups. It reached America's business and professional classes through the editorial page of the *Wall Street Journal, Fortune, Forbes,* and other business publications. It reached the general public through the *Reader's Digest* and the business and editorial pages of many newspapers, including the *Washington Post.* Said Weidenbaum of his critique of regulation and big business, "We helped business get interested in the thing. We knew we scored when we got into comic strips. You change public understanding that way. Broom Hilda did five comic strips in a row showing OSHA penalizing her for her broom."[41]

Business won the public to its view of reality. Americans' distrust of government regulation and intervention began about 1973—at the same time when simultaneous unemployment and inflation, or "stagflation," was taking hold and when the think tanks, policy experts, and CEOs were beginning to make their opinions known. Distrust of government economic intervention then rose steadily through the decade. By the early 1980s, it had begun to surpass the distrust of big business or corporate power. (See polls 1, 2, and 3.) That change in attitude was rooted in a change in economic reality, but it was reality as interpreted by Herb Stein, Murray Weidenbaum, and the AEI.

Changing Attitudes Toward Business and Government: National Opinion Polling Results, 1966–81

1. Gallup: "Would you say that you, yourself, have been better off or worse off as a result of government control and regulation of the business practices of large corporations?"[42]

DATE	BETTER OFF	WORSE OFF	NO DIFFERENCE	DON'T KNOW
1966	37%	21%	18%	24%
1970	43	15	22	20
1977	28	26	26	20
1981	24	40	17	19

2. Opinion Research Corporation: "Government regulation is a good way of making business more responsive to people's needs."[43]

DATE	AGREE	DISAGREE	DON'T KNOW
1973	60%	27%	13%
1975	53	34	13
1977	50	38	12
1979	49	41	10

3. Gallup: "In your opinion, which is most responsible for inflation—government, business, or labor?"[44]

DATE	GOVERNMENT	BUSINESS	LABOR	DON'T KNOW
1972	38%	19%	29%	14%
1973	46	18	24	13
1974	47	17	18	18
1975	48	16	19	16
1978	51	14	20	16

By challenging the public perception of stagflation, these policy experts made it easier to defeat proposals aimed at strengthening regulation and prepared the public for the effort in the early 1980s to weaken regulations and regulatory agencies.

The Rise of K Street

To counter environmental and consumer movements and to influence Congress and the new regulatory agencies, the CEOs also hired thousands of lawyers and public relations specialists to lobby on their behalf. Together, these hires created a new political culture in Washington dominated by the Gucci-shod lobbyist. They gave business an enormous advantage in the policy and political arena over its adversaries.

In 1971, only 175 businesses had registered lobbyists in Washington. By 1982, 2,445 had.[45] The number of corporate offices increased from 50 in 1961 to 500 in 1978 and to 1,300 by 1986.[46] By 1978, 1,800 trade associations were headquartered in Washington, with 40,000 employees; by 1986, there were 3,500 associations employing 80,000.[47] From 1973 to 1983, the number of lawyers grew more than threefold from 11,000 to 37,000.[48] By 1988, 1,634 out of every 100,000 Washingtonians was a lawyer, the highest proportion of any American city.[49] A few of these were public interest lawyers and lobbyists for women's, consumer, and environmental groups, but the great majority worked for businesses. By 1978, businesses were spending about $1 billion on lobbying in Washington and $1 billion on politics and public relations.[50]

Many of the new lawyers and lobbyists specialized in regulatory issues. From 1887 to 1963, fourteen new federal agencies and commissions had been established. From 1964 to 1975 alone, fifteen new federal agencies and commissions were added (see table). As a result of the 1946 Administrative Procedure Act, these agencies were highly susceptible to pressure and review from lobbyists. Regulators from these agencies had to involve affected parties at every phase in the determination of rules; and almost every step in rule-making could be subject to court challenge. Decisions were finally made not by an authoritative bureaucracy—the entirely misleading stereotype promulgated by the enemies of regulation—but through what political scientist Hugh Heclo called "issue networks" that linked government officials, regulatory agencies, and cabinet departments with lawyers, lobbyists, policy groups, journalists, and judges and the courts.*

Regulatory Agencies and Commissions

Interstate Commerce Commission	1887
Federal Reserve System	1913
Federal Trade Commission	1914
Packers and Stockyards Commission	1916
Federal Power Commission	1930
Food and Drug Administration	1931
Federal Deposit Insurance Corporation	1933
Federal Communications Commission	1934
Securities and Exchange Commission	1934
Federal Maritime Commission	1936
Agricultural Marketing Service	1937
Civil Aeronautics Board	1938
Federal Aviation Administration	1948
Animal and Plant Health Inspection Service	1953
Equal Employment Opportunity Commission	1964
Federal Highway Administration	1966
Federal Railroad Administration	1966
Postal Rate Commission	1970
National Highway Traffic Safety Commission	1970
Environmental Protection Agency	1970
Securities Investor Protection Commission	1970
Farm Credit Administration	1971
Consumer Product Safety Commission	1972
Mining Safety and Enforcement Administration	1973
Drug Enforcement Administration	1973

*As the agencies themselves grew in number arithmetically, the number of lobbyists grew geometrically, dwarfing the growth of government workers. From 1955 to 1980, federal regulations (as indicated by pages in the *Federal Register*) sextupled. Yet federal employment grew by less than 20 percent. In 1960, federal workers accounted for 40 percent of the Washington area workforce; by 1976, only 23 percent. The real story of the postwar era was not the rise of big government, but of K Street.

Occupational Safety and Health Administration	1973
Energy Regulatory Administration	1974
Commodities Future Trading Commission	1975
Nuclear Regulatory Commission	1975

These new lobbyists not only had to possess some technical expertise, they also had to master the complexities of the post-Watergate Congress. In the Eisenhower years, for instance, lobbyists had primarily relied on their connections to House speaker Sam Rayburn, Senate majority leader Lyndon Johnson, and a handful of committee heads to make political deals. The speaker and majority leader would also tell a lobbyist whose campaigns to fund. But the political reforms of the 1970s made things more difficult. Partly in response to Watergate but largely as a result of the civil rights struggles of the 1960s, Democrats did away with the seniority system, which had vested power automatically in aged Southern House members and senators who inherited control over key committees. After 1974, committee chairs had to be elected by the Democratic Caucus, and could no longer command the automatic loyalty of junior members. The House and Senate leadership could still control the appointment to committees, but the committees began to spawn scores of subcommittees, so that almost every politician who was reelected could command a position of authority. In 1945, there were 135 committees and subcommittees in Congress; by 1975, there were 313.[51] Each House member and senator had to develop his or her own position, which might often be at odds with leadership. The lobbyist could no longer simply rely on a connection to the majority leader or the speaker; he or she had to establish connections with hundreds of legislators and be prepared to help, cajole, and if necessary pressure them from within their districts or states.

In 1974, Congress, in response to Watergate, passed campaign finance reform. It limited the amount of money that a candidate could receive from any contributor while authorizing corporations and unions to form political action committees to donate money to candidates. The legislation made it less likely that a candidate would become the ward of a single large contributor. But after the Supreme Court in 1976 threw out the limits on candidate expenditures, while retaining the limits on campaign contributions, candidates had a much harder time raising enough money. Fund-raising became a major part of their job. And they looked for lobbyists for help—not so much for their own contributions, but for organizing fund-raising events and bundling donations. Thomas Boggs, one of Washington's most successful lobbyists, became known for hosting events for as many as 125 politicians during each election season.[52]

Few lobbyists could contact several hundred House members and a score of senators, draft complicated amendments, organize grassroots pressure in multiple districts, and raise money. So companies now hired teams of lobbyists, policy experts, public relations flacks, and pollsters. And the law firms themselves diversified. Arnold & Porter, one of the city's largest law firms, started its own lobbying firm, APCO Associates, which included nonlawyers in its management. Washington law firms also routinely hired economists, and in 1990 the District of Columbia Bar ruled that nonlawyers could become partners in law firms.[53] Several law firms, including Robert Strauss's Akin, Gump, Strauss, Hauer & Feld, started their own political action committee.

There was an intimate relationship between the lawyers, lobbyists, policy specialists, and PR men of K Street and the new business think tanks and policy groups. They worked together to counter the consumer, environmental, and labor movements and to thwart or subvert the new regulatory agencies. No lobbyist better symbolized the breadth of this relationship than Charls Walker, a voluble Texan who would later be credited with alchemizing Carter's efforts at tax reform into a business tax cut and with securing the bountiful business provisions of Reagan's 1981 tax cut. In 1973, frustrated that he would never become Secretary of the Treasury, he left the government to form a lobbying firm of his own, Charls Walker Associates. He immediately attracted high-profile corporate clients, including Harlow's Proctor and Gamble, AT&T, General Electric, and the Business Roundtable itself, which he had helped to found.[54]

Walker understood that lobbying could not be confined to buttonholing legislators. In 1975 he took over a faltering organization called the American Council for Estate and Gift Taxation and converted it into a coalition aimed at winning new tax breaks for business. Renamed the

American Council for Capital Formation and housed initially on 1425 K Street, it stood for the view that American business's problems were due to a lack of capital to invest and could be solved by granting a range of very generous tax breaks, from a reduction in capital gains tax rates to accelerated depreciation on investment. Walker was the chairman; Robert Keith Gray, a Nixon White House official turned public relations expert, was the president. Walker quickly recruited a raft of *Fortune* 500 members who contributed $200,000 the first year to its operation. Walker also recruited powerful Democrats like Clark Clifford, former Secretary of the Treasury Henry Fowler, and super-lawyer Edward Bennett Williams to serve on the board of directors.

The American Council adopted a coalition strategy. Instead of trying to win individual concessions for companies, Walker got a group of them to back a common position. (The NAM and the Chamber of Commerce were also coalitions, but they were so large that they could usually only reach agreement on what to oppose.) The council engaged in influence-peddling (Walker numbered among his friends Senate Finance Committee chairman Russell Long), along with grassroots lobbying in the districts of members who resisted his entreaties. Walker pioneered the tactic of getting local company officials, armed with local job loss and gain figures, to meet directly with their House or Senate member.

Most important of all, Walker used the fiction of the "council"—a name suggesting an ordinary policy group or administrative body—to present self-interested lobbying in the guise of social science. He appointed a board of scholars that included three future chairs of the Council of Economic Advisors—Murray Weidenbaum, Harvard's Martin Feldstein, and Stanford's Michael Boskin. The council's scholars issued studies—many of them subsidized by the council—that purported to show that business tax breaks would benefit all Americans. Walker himself wrote op-eds in which he was identified not as a lobbyist, but as the chairman of the council or simply a former Treasury official. The ploy allowed the public to believe that the council's positions were based entirely on disinterested social science and on the knowledge and expertise gained from public service.

Walker's council summed up the multidimensional strategy of the business counteroffensive of the 1970s that Lewis Powell and Irving

Kristol had helped to inspire. He understood that it wouldn't be enough just to grab legislators in the Capitol cloakrooms. Lobbyists had to organize political campaigns, raise money for candidates, and hire academics and other policy professionals to lend legitimacy to their positions. This strategy would eventually corrode the public's faith in elite opinion and encourage a perception of K Street as a vipers' nest of corruption. But in the late 1970s it worked brilliantly.

[6]

The Triumph of Conservatism

In 1969, Kevin Phillips, an aide to Nixon's Attorney General John Mitchell, published a book, *The Emerging Republican Majority,* declaring that the election of 1968 had ushered in a "new era" in American politics that would be dominated by Republican conservatives rather than Democratic liberals.[1] Nixon's landslide in 1972 appeared to prove Phillips right, but then Watergate came. In the 1974 elections, Democrats captured a two-to-one majority in the House of Representatives and a thirteen-seat majority in the Senate, which they maintained in 1976, when Democrat Jimmy Carter was elected president.

These Democratic victories set the stage for a final conflict that would help define American politics and democracy for the next decade, and in some respects for the rest of the century. On one side was what remained of the old liberal movement, led now by an increasingly desperate AFL-CIO. On the other side were the lobbies, think tanks, and policy groups created by business and their conservative allies in the early 1970s. The battleground was the U.S. Congress.

The Liberal Rout

As Carter took office, liberal politicians, the AFL-CIO, Nader's Congress Watch, and civil rights groups drew up a far-reaching legislative agenda, some of which Carter enthusiastically supported, but none of which he opposed. The leading group in the liberal coalition was the AFL-CIO. During the sixties, it had been overshadowed by the antiwar and civil rights movements, but as these movements lost their fervor, the labor federation reemerged as the key player in the liberal coalition.

The AFL-CIO saw Carter's election as an opportunity to reverse through legislation the setbacks it was suffering in the workplace. Organized labor's share of the workforce had steadily fallen—from 34.5 percent in 1956 to 30.7 percent in 1964 and to 25.1 percent in 1978.[2] The decline in union membership was partly President George Meany's fault. When the two federations merged in 1955, union leaders expected that the merger would facilitate organizing and bring in new recruits by eliminating jurisdictional disputes between rival AFL and CIO unions. But Meany, a former plumber who had never walked a picket line, quickly lost interest in funding recruiting drives. Before the merger, the rival federations had spent almost half of their dues income on recruiting new members. Afterward, the new federation spent 11.2 percent its first year, 4.9 percent in 1957, 2.4 percent in 1959, and less than 1 percent by 1974.[3] Meany made the federation's Washington office into a kind of labor Vatican that devoted more resources to foreign policy ventures than to domestic organizing.

But Meany's indifference to organizing explained at most the slow erosion of support during the federation's first fifteen years. The precipitous decline that took place in the 1970s—from 27 percent of private sector workers in 1973 to 22 percent in 1979—was the result of American businesses adopting more aggressive tactics to keep out or get rid of unions. Management began hiring antilabor consultants to contest organizing campaigns, and, in violation of the Wagner Act, began firing union organizers to intimidate workers. According to NLRB statistics, the number of employer unfair labor practice charges tripled between 1960 and 1980, and the number of workers ordered to be reinstated because of being fired illegally rose fivefold in the same period.[4] To block these tactics, Meany wanted a labor law reform bill that would increase the penalties on companies that violated the law and eliminate arduous appeal processes that companies used to evade holding or accepting the results of union elections.

Meany and the civil rights movement also backed a full employment bill sponsored by Senator Hubert Humphrey and Representative Augustus Hawkins to commit the government to reducing unemployment to 3 percent—if necessary, through government job creation. The backers of these bills maintained that they would restore the balance between business and labor that had been undermined by business's new offensive and the decline of union membership. Humphrey-Hawkins's economics was suspect—it is doubtful that the country could have achieved 3 percent unemployment in the 1970s without provoking further inflation—but labor law reform was a justifiable defense of democratic pluralism.

While the AFL-CIO's chief priority was labor law reform and Humphrey-Hawkins, Nader and the consumer movement were pressing for a new federal office of consumer representation that would consolidate all the different government consumer departments, represent consumers before federal agencies and courts, and conduct research on their behalf. Nader and the unions also backed tax reform that would remove the loopholes for oil profits, capital gains, and overseas profits. And they supported a national health insurance bill that Senator Edward Kennedy was sponsoring.

Carter championed the new consumer agency and tax reform. He was more hesitant about the labor measures and Humphrey-Hawkins, but he promised to sign whatever bill the Democrats passed. He also introduced a comprehensive energy plan that would regulate prices and production; he opposed national health insurance as too far-reaching, but proposed a bill to hold down the rapid rise of hospital prices; and he enthusiastically backed campaign and lobbying reform. Carter and the Democrats believed they would get their bills. The Senate had already passed a bill establishing a consumer protection agency in 1970 and 1975; and the House had passed a similar proposal in 1971, 1974, and 1975, only to see final approval blocked by a Republican White House.

The Business Roundtable led the opposition to Nader's idea for an office of consumer representation. It established a Consumer Issues Working Group of 400 businesses and organizations including the Chamber of Commerce and the NAM. It got plant managers and CEOs in the districts of vulnerable House members to pay them personal visits. It hired former Watergate counsel Leon Jaworski to produce a public statement opposing the bill that it then ran in advertisements. The Roundtable also paid the North American Precis Syndicate to send around editorials and cartoons to 3,800 newspapers and weeklies that they could run for free.[5] All in all, the business organizations spent several million dollars fighting the bill. By contrast, the Consumers Federation of America, Nader's Congress Watch, and the National Consumers League, the three main supporters of the bill, spent $352,000.[6]

The business groups claimed that the tiny $15 million agency would contribute to "big government"—a ludicrous charge that nonetheless proved effective. The bill did not even make it through the House of Representatives. In explaining the defeat of the consumer agency, Mark Green, who headed Nader's Congress Watch, told *Congressional Quarterly* that House members repeatedly informed him, "I'm with you on the merits, but I can't convince my constituents that this bill is not a move toward big government."[7]

Labor law reform looked more promising. The House quickly passed it in 1977. But then it got held up in the Senate in the winter and spring of 1978 as the debate over the Panama Canal treaty dragged on. That delay allowed business to mobilize against it. The Chamber of Commerce, the NAM, and the construction industry trade associations set up a National Action Committee that ran ads and distributed editorials. Together, the organizations got their members to inundate Congress and the White House with eight million letters. In the last week of the debate, 97 percent of letters to the White House opposed the bill.

The committee's editorials charged that the bill was inflationary and would tip the balance of power of the country toward labor. "The last thing we need now is to amend the NLRB to tilt it more on the side of the labor monopoly," declared one of the editorials circulated by the coalition.[8] The coalition made the issue the survival of small business, even though the measure exempted small businesses from its provisions. Two political scientists commented on the lobbying strategy:

> Business succeeded in capturing the political center by portraying the issue as a union power grab and the union movement as greedy. In particular, the elevation of the small businessman to the exalted position of potential victim of big labor—even though the bill's im-

pact on small business would have been minimal—was a skillful exploitation of a key American value.[9]

The Business Roundtable, many of whose firms were unionized and wanted to retain an amicable relationship with labor, was initially neutral, but in August 1977, its policy committee, prodded by Sears Roebuck, voted to oppose the measure. In the last week of the debate, Roundtable CEOs flew into Washington on corporate jets to lobby against the bill. The AFL-CIO tried to get unionized businesses to endorse the measure, but the business community, which had been mildly sympathetic to union issues in the 1950s and 1960s, was now united against labor. Recalled AFL-CIO secretary-treasurer Tom Donahue, "It was a matter of absolute solidarity. The auto companies sent out letters to their suppliers saying they should not break ranks. It was an unbroken chain of employers."[10] Altogether, business outspent the AFL-CIO by $7 million to $2.5 million.[11] In the final tally, the measure could not get the sixty votes it needed in the Senate to stop a filibuster by the bill's opponents.

Carter's proposals for hospital cost containment, public financing of campaigns, and stricter disclosure by lobbyists were also defeated. Humphrey-Hawkins finally passed, but only after business lobbyists had forced its sponsors to remove the provisions requiring government to meet the 3 percent target. Richard Lesher, the president of the U.S. Chamber of Commerce, accurately described the final bill as a "toothless alligator."[12] Carter's energy program ended up deregulating rather than regulating prices. The president's tax reform package made out worst of all. Its fate summed up the liberal rout.

Carter's initial proposal raised the rate on capital gains taxes, which he aptly described as "tax windfalls for millionaires," and limited business deductions for entertainment and meals. This time, the lobbyists didn't just block the administration's bill, they rewrote it. The key player was Charls Walker. In March 1978, Walker, Ed Zschau, the president of the American Electronics Association, and Mark Bloomfield, the deputy research director of Walker's Council for Capital Formation, met with Republican Representative William Steiger, a member of the House Ways and Means Committee. At the meeting the three men persuaded Steiger to sponsor an amendment that Walker and Bloomfield wrote up cutting the capital gains tax in half. When Steiger's amendment ran into trouble in Russell Long's Senate Finance Committee, Walker got Democrat Henry Fowler, a member of the council's board, to negotiate a suitable rewording with Long. The final bill *lowered* the effective tax rate on capital gains from 49 to 28 percent, preserved business tax exemptions, and lowered corporate tax rates.

Together, these defeats dealt a death blow to the democratic reform movement that had begun early in the century, foundered in the 1920s, revived in the 1930s, survived in the 1950s, and then flourished in the 1960s. Reform had required using the power of unions and, later, of the consumer, environmental, and civil rights movements to win government measures regulating and limiting the behavior of private corporations. By convincing the public that "big government" was to blame for all the nation's ills, the business lobbyists undermined the argument for reform. Emboldened by their victories in the first two years of Carter's term, they now began to target the reforms adopted in the 1960s. Toward that, they made common cause with a group of politicians and political activists whom, in the past, they had kept at arm's length.

The Conservative Movement

In the early twentieth century, there was no such thing in American politics as a conservative movement. The right was an unwieldy collection of anti-Semites, libertarians, fascists, racists, anti–New Dealers, isolationists, and Southern agrarians who were incapable of agreeing on anything. It was only in the mid-1950s that a coherent movement began to emerge. Its intellectual voice was William F. Buckley, Jr.'s, *National Review* and its political champion was Arizona Senator Barry Goldwater. These conservatives were united by opposition to the New Deal, including Social Security, and to any accommodation with the Soviet Union, which they viewed as an immediate threat to America's survival.

Their basic outlook combined nineteenth-century corporate individualism, set forth by Milton Friedman and other economists, and militant Cold War anti-Communism, expounded by former Communist Whittaker Chambers and former Trotskyist James Burnham. The conservatives opposed progressive taxation, including the income tax, and most federal government spending except on the FBI and the military. They blamed unions for unemployment and higher prices and blamed welfare recipients for the persistence of their own poverty. They wanted not merely to contain but to roll back Communism—by the threat, if not the use, of nuclear weapons.

There was an integral connection between the conservatives' opposition to Communism and their opposition to domestic liberalism. Communism was, to the conservative view, what would occur if liberalism were allowed to grow unchallenged. Chambers summed up this connection in *Witness*:

> When I took up my little sling and aimed at Communism, I also hit something else. What I hit was the force of that great Socialist revolution which in the name of *liberalism,* spasmodically, incompletely, somewhat formlessly, but always in the same direction, has been inching its icecap over the nation for two decades.[13]

The early conservative movement was limited in its popular appeal. As Goldwater discovered in 1964, most Americans didn't want to get rid of Social Security or go to the brink of war with the Soviet Union. Over the next sixteen years, however, America changed in ways that made the conservative message more palatable. School integration drove white Southerners into the Republican Party—the Deep South was the only region Goldwater won in 1964. Busing, affirmative action, and rising welfare costs, coming in the wake of the ghetto riots, split the the New Deal coalition in the North and made many white ethnic Democrats receptive to conservative appeals. Conservatives, who had opposed the civil rights acts out of either racism or support for state's rights, suddenly found their political base immeasurably widened. Northern whites also became more receptive to conservatives' harsh message on welfare and crime.

The U.S. defeat in Vietnam, coupled with advances in Soviet influence in Africa and Central America, made the conservatives' militant message on Communism far more credible, while the economic downturn that began in the late 1960s lent credence to conservative arguments for free-market capitalism. And the court rulings on abortion and school prayer, along with the continued spread of the counterculture and the women's movement, produced an entirely new constituency for conservatism.

Conservative politicians and intellectuals also adapted their own message to take advantage of these opportunities. In his 1966 California gubernatorial campaign, Ronald Reagan exploited the historic distrust of government and of elites to rally voters to his side. He reminded voters that he had once been a union leader, while directing his fire at students, whom he described as "elitists" disrupting the universities that middle-class taxpayers were financing. He didn't attack welfare capitalism itself, but attacked welfare cheaters (invariably black or Mexican-American in voters' minds). He didn't openly favor segregation, but he opposed a fair housing measure on the ballot. Because Reagan was running for governor rather than senator, he didn't have to take positions on the old conservative bugaboos of Social Security or nuclear war.

In the early 1970s, a group of young conservatives, who became identified as "the new right," tried to take advantage of the backlash against the civil rights movement and the counterculture. Instead of railing against budget deficits, they focused on the "social" issues that had emerged during the sixties, including abortion, busing and racial integration, drugs, school prayer, and gun control. Their motives were tactical: they recognized the political limitations of the older conservative movement and wanted to create a politics that could unite business conservatives with working-class Democrats disillusioned by the civil rights movement, antiwar protests, and the counterculture of the sixties.

Richard Viguerie, the son of a Texas petrochemical executive, came to New York from Texas in 1963 to become executive secretary of the Young Americans for Freedom (YAF). He became expert in using direct mail to finance campaigns. In 1968 he worked as a fund-raiser for George Wallace and from 1973 to 1976 raised money for Wallace's American Independent Party through the mailing lists he created. Unlike other conservatives who disdained Wallace's racism and anti-elitism, Viguerie was drawn to his campaign. "My working with Wallace was the beginning of my thinking in terms of coalition politics," Viguerie recalled.[14] In 1975, Viguerie began using his rapidly growing mailing lists to raise money for a conservative movement that would attract Wallace supporters.

Viguerie helped raise funds for Howard Phillips, a Harvard graduate and founder of YAF who began the Conservative Caucus; for John "Terry" Dolan, who founded the National Conservative Political Action Committee (NCPAC); and for Paul Weyrich, who, after leaving the Heritage Foundation, established the Committee for the Survival of a Free Congress, and was also meeting with Wallace. Between 1976 and 1980, hundreds of conservative groups sprouted up in Washington, many of them funded from Viguerie's lists. Most of these organizations were different from the older membership groups like the AFL-CIO and Chamber of Commerce. They were directed by their staffs and financed by whatever they could raise in the mail. The membership consisted primarily of direct mail donors, who in return received newsletters. (See table.)

Budgets, Staffs, and Membership Activity of Conservative Organizations, 1978

ORGANIZATION	BUDGET	STAFF	ARE MEMBERS ACTIVE?
American Conservative Union	$2,800,000	19	yes
ACU Education and Research Institute	350,000	5	no
American Enterprise Institute	7,000,000	150	no
American Legislative Exchange Council	600,000	4	yes
American Security Council	1,961,285	19	no
American Tax Reduction Movement	5,830,000	15	no
Americans for Constitutional Action	100,000	4	no
Christian Voice	1,000,000	7	no
Citizens Committee for the Right to Keep and Bear Arms	1,021,703	15	no
Citizens for the Republic	2,000,000	20	no
Committee for the Survival of a Free Congress	1,175,000	12	no
Conservative Caucus	2,000,000	12	no
Conservative Victory Fund	392,000	3	no
Council for Inter-American Security	750,000	5	no
Eagle Forum	250,000	5	no

ORGANIZATION	BUDGET	STAFF	ARE MEMBERS ACTIVE?
Heritage Foundation	2,800,000	50	no
Institute for American Relations	800,000	6	no
Intercollegiate Studies Institute	750,000	12	yes
National Conservative Political Action Committee	1,500,000	7	no
National Legal Center for the Public Interest	1,600,000	12	no
National Right to Work Committee	7,000,000	90	no
National Right to Work Foundation	3,500,000	45	no
National Taxpayers Union	1,192,000	18	no
Pacific Legal Foundation	3,000,000	55	no
Washington Legal Foundation	800,000	7	no
Young Americans for Freedom	800,000	12	yes

Sources: James C. Roberts, *The Conservative Decade,* Westport, Conn., 1980; Alan Crawford, *Thunder on the Right,* New York, 1980; Matthew C. Moen, *The Transformation of the Christian Right,* Tuscaloosa, Ala., 1992. Interviews with author.

The new right scorned the older politics of precinct workers and party organizations. It understood the importance of gaining the attention—favorable or unfavorable—of the media. Viguerie, Weyrich, and other activists poked at the open wounds created by court decisions on abortion and busing and by a decade of fierce battles on Capitol Hill. Perhaps their greatest success was achieved when, because of their focus on social issues, they were able to recruit white Fundamentalists and Pentecostals into conservative Republican politics.

In the early twentieth century, Protestantism had split into two camps. On one side were the liberalizers and modernizers who believed that biblical doctrine had to be adapted to modern conditions and scientific discoveries, including the theory of evolution. On the other side were the Pentecostals, who stressed faith-healing and speaking in tongues, and the Fundamentalists, who believed in biblical inerrancy. A political division was superimposed on this theological division. While many of the modernizers and liberals, working through the Federal Council of

Churches (later the National Council of Churches), espoused the progressive social gospel, many Fundamentalists and Pentecostals rejected politics altogether. They were premillennialists who believed that Christ would spirit away the true believers before Armageddon and the millennium took place, and they aimed to be among those who ascended to Heaven with Christ while the earth was consumed in flames.

Those Fundamentalists who did participate in politics identified with the extreme right wing of the Republican and Democratic parties. In 1941, Carl McIntire established the American Council of Christian Churches, from which he attacked the National Council for its support of the New Deal. In the 1950s, McIntire and Billy James Hargis were at the front of anti-Communist crusades that charged that Communists with infiltrating the U.S. government. But most of the Fundamentalists and Pentecostals had no interest in politics. The Rev. Jerry Falwell declared in 1965, "I would find it impossible to stop preaching the pure saving gospel of Jesus Christ, and begin doing anything else—including fighting Communism or participating in civil rights reforms."[15]

Falwell and other religious conservatives began to reconsider their abstention from politics when the Carter administration ruled that segregated Southern private schools would lose their nonprofit tax exemption. The Fundamentalists and Pentecostals had established religious schools in the South, which, after *Brown* v. *Board of Education* in 1954, became outposts for white parents not wanting to send their children to integrated schools. A group of ministers, including Falwell and Robert Billings, wanted to organize in protest, and they began discussions with Weyrich and Phillips, who suggested to them that they found a new political organization.

The new organizations that emerged—Falwell's Moral Majority, Christian Voice (which pioneered the tactic of sending out report cards rating politicians' morality based on their voting record), the Religious Roundtable, and Billings's National Christian Action Coalition—would enjoy a genuine mass following, organized through the ministers and their churches. Falwell, using the mailing list from his television series, "Old Time Gospel Hour," had recruited 300,000 dues-paying members, including 70,000 ministers, by mid-1980.[16] The organizations focused on abortion and school prayer, but they also aligned themselves with the economic individualism and militant anti-Communism of Republican conservatives and the new right.

While the new right and their newfound allies in the Moral Majority attacked the Supreme Court's decisions on abortion and school prayer, another group of conservative activists took aim at rising federal and state taxes. Federal taxes had increased primarily because of "bracket creep," as inflation forced taxpayers into higher brackets without increasing their real incomes. State taxes had grown because of the growing budget for social services. The National Taxpayers Union, which was founded in 1969, had 200 chapters by the end of 1979. In California, Howard Jarvis, a classic free-market conservative, led a successful referendum campaign in June 1978 for Proposition 13, leading to a drastic cut in property taxes. "We are telling the government, 'Screw you,' " Jarvis declared that year.[17]

The intellectual rationale for the conservative tax cutters came from economist Arthur Laffer and *Wall Street Journal* editorial writer Jude Wanniski. In Irving Kristol's journal *The Public Interest,* Wanniski argued that by cutting taxes and tightening the money supply, the government could raise revenue, increase investment, create jobs, *and* curb inflation.[18] Most economists regarded this theory, called "supply-side economics," as crackpot, but it gained a wide following among conservatives because it allowed conservatives to advocate tax cuts without abandoning their opposition to budget deficits. In March 1976, Congressman Jack Kemp, who was influenced by Wanniski, and Senator William Roth introduced a bill in Congress cutting tax rates by 30 percent. After the victory of Proposition 13, the Republican Party officially adopted the Kemp-Roth bill as its main campaign issue and organized a three-day, seven-city tour to publicize its virtues.

The final ingredient in this new conservatism was ex-liberals and -leftists like Kristol, who turned right sometime between 1968 and 1972 as the Democratic Party became more identified with opposition to the Vietnam War, support for affirmative action, and toleration of urban violence. The neoconservatives, Kristol quipped, had been "mugged by reality." But while the neoconservatives became staunch opponents of Johnson's Great Society and the regulatory reforms of the first Nixon administration, they never repudiated New Deal programs like Social Security, which, they argued, provided a "safety net" for the poor and aged. Their conservatism was directed at the liberalism of the late sixties rather than the New Deal or even the early sixties. In this way, they provided an important bridge to voters who were alienated by the explosion of the welfare state, but continued to back Social Security and Medicare.

The first indication that the new conservative movement was nationally viable came in 1978. That fall, Republicans picked up 319 state legislative seats, 6 governorships, 12 House seats, and 3 Senate seats. The most impressive gains were by Republican conservatives. In Colorado, Iowa, and New Hampshire, Republicans identified with the party's far right and defeated liberal Democratic incumbents. In Mississippi, a Republican—the first since Reconstruction—succeeded Democrat James Eastland. In Georgia Newt Gingrich was elected to Congress that year.

Reagan and Business

Before the 1978 election, business lobbies and corporate political action committees had tended to divide their contributions equally between Democrats, the incumbent party, and Republicans, the more probusiness party. But in that election, PAC contributions began to shift toward Republicans. From January 1 to October 1, 1978, corporate PACs split their contributions between Democratic and Republican Congressional candidates; but during the last six weeks of the elections, as the potential for Republican upsets loomed, corporate PACs gave 72 percent of their money to Republicans, particularly to those challenging Democratic incumbents.[19] This infusion of cash was an important factor in the Republican successes.

As the 1980 elections approached, business leaders and PACs decided to cast their lot with the Republicans, but for the presidential nomination they were still leery of supporting a full-blown conservative like Ronald Reagan. Most business leaders had backed Gerald Ford against Reagan in the 1976 primaries. In 1980 they backed either John Connally or George Bush against Reagan. They doubted the seventy-year-old Reagan's competence as a chief executive. They were uncomfortable with his blustering statements about the Soviet menace. And they were worried that under the influence of Kemp and Wanniski, he would prove as fiscally irresponsible as the Democrats. But once it became clear in the spring of 1980 that Reagan had sewn up the nomination, the Californian and business leaders began to move closer to each other.

Reagan formed a policy council chaired by George Shultz and including Alan Greenspan, Ford's chair of the Council of Economic Advisors, Burns, Simon, McCracken, and Walker.[20] He asked Greenspan to draft his speeches and to accompany him during the campaign. The economists and former economic officials provided legitimacy for Reagan's promise that he could raise defense spending, cut taxes, and still balance the budget. In September they would conceal their own doubts as they stood behind him as he introduced a highly implausible plan for balancing the budget by 1983. (Arthur Burns told Herbert Stein that he endorsed the plan because "if you dissented from it, your whole usefulness in the organization was lost.")[21] Reagan also created a forty-member business advisory group that included CEOs and chairmen from many of the top banks and *Fortune* 500 corporations. Sensing that they would get much of what they wanted from his administration, the business leaders lent their support. Businesses also threw their support to Republican Congressional candidates, helping Republicans win the Senate in November 1980. During 1979–80, corporate PACs gave $12.29 million to Republicans and $6.87 million to Democrats.[22] By the last month of the election, the Republican Senatorial Campaign Committee had outraised its Democratic counterpart by twenty-five to one.[23]

Once in office, President Reagan fulfilled business's fondest wishes. Reagan's tax program included the supply-side cuts, but it also featured a set of generous business tax cuts devised and lobbied for by Walker, whom Reagan had put in charge of his transition team on tax policy. Administration members who imagined they could defy their business allies got a rude awakening. Reagan's budget director David Stockman thought he could modify Walker's proposed cuts for business in order to make room for other cuts. But he discovered business's power on K Street: "Within days . . . Walker, the Chamber of Commerce, and most of K Street would come at us like a battalion of tanks. The firing lasted four days, then abruptly stopped. Walker got everything he wanted."[24] Some of Walker's cuts were so egregious that they had to be repealed the next year when Robert McIntyre of Citizens for Tax Justice revealed that they were allowing some large and profitable corporations to pay no taxes at all.

The individual tax cuts enacted under the new administration were just as egregious. Earlier in the century, progressives had fought to create an income tax because, in contrast to a sales tax or tariff, it could be used to reduce economic inequality. Reagan's tax cuts increased economic inequality. From 1980 to 1985, the share of after-tax income of the top 5 percent increased, while the share of the bottom four-fifths fell.[25] The effective federal tax rates on the top 1 percent of earners fell from 31.8 percent in 1980 to 24.9 percent in 1985, while the tax rate on the bottom four-fifths *rose* from 16.5 to 16.7 percent.[26]

Reagan attempted to gut the regulatory agencies established during Nixon's first term. He cut the budgets of the Consumer Product Safety Commission by 38 percent, the National Highway Traffic Safety Administration by 22 percent, and the EPA by 10 percent. He used the time-worn strategy of putting foxes in charge of the chicken coop. He appointed Thorne Auchter, the owner of a Florida construction company that OSHA had repeatedly cited for violations, to head the agency; and two outspoken opponents of the environmental movement, James Watt and Anne Gorsuch, were put in charge, respectively, of the Interior Department and the Environmental Protection Agency. The three appointees drastically reduced the budgets for enforcement. Watt reversed federal land policies. While he could not sell federal lands directly back to ranchers or miners, he transferred over 20 million acres back to state control, where they could be given or sold to private interests.[27]

The new administration went after regulatory policies that dated from the Progressive Era. The budget of the Federal Trade Commission was cut by 28 percent and it was discouraged from pursuing antitrust cases. Reagan sent a clear message to business and the labor movement by firing and then refusing to rehire striking air controllers. He appointed probusiness conservatives to the NLRB who consistently ruled against unions in cases that came before the board. Under the Ford administration in 1975–76, the board had favored business 35 percent of the time. In 1983 and 1984, it favored business in 72 percent of the cases.[28]

These policies represented a repudiation of the reform tradition that began in the Progressive Era and a return to the principles of corporate individualism that governed America in the late nineteenth century. While Reagan had given a nod to pluralism in his campaign—boasting of his own union past—his administration made a mockery of democratic pluralism by throwing its weight behind business and attempting to crush business's adversaries. Reagan would sometimes compare his administration with that of Eisenhower, but it did not show a trace of the "balanced" government that Eisenhower and Arthur Larson had advocated. It was a throwback not to Eisenhower, but to Coolidge and to the corrupt post–Civil War administrations.

Reagan also revived a nineteenth-century view of the federal government that was consistent with business's antiregulatory stance. He portrayed government as the enemy of popular democracy. In his first inaugural address, he declared:

> In the present crisis, government is not the solution to our problems; government is the problem. From time to time, we've been tempted to believe that society has become too complex to be managed by self-rule, that government by an elite group is superior to government for, by, and of the people. Well, if no one among us is capable of governing himself, then who among us has the capacity to govern someone else?[29]

He also fiercely attacked what he referred to as the "bureaucracy"—the permanent civil servants that since 1883 had replaced patronage appointees. Accusing them of "bureaucratic sabotage" of his programs, he lamented "the permanent structure, that they've been here before you got here and they'll be here after you're gone and they're not going to change the way they're doing things."[30] Like Reagan's denigration of government, his attack against the bureaucracy implied that the alternative was individual self-rule, but Reagan's promise of "self-rule" was a cruel hoax. What it really meant in practice was dominance over government decisions by business and K Street lobbyists—by the "issue networks" that had grown up around Washington in the 1970s.

The Conservative Mood

From 1978 to 1986, Republican conservatives and their business allies thoroughly dominated American politics. One reason they prevailed was that business itself was united. Faced with fierce competition from abroad and from the labor, environmental, and consumer movements at home, all the different sectors of business—small, large, Northern, Southern, service, industrial, and agricultural—united against what they perceived was a common enemy. That had occurred in the early 1920s and occurred again in the late 1970s.

The liberal movement was also divided and in disarray. George Meany and Lane Kirkland, who succeeded Meany as head of the AFL-CIO in 1979, disdained the movements of the sixties. In the wake of the legislative defeats in 1978, the new United Auto Workers president Douglas Fraser attempted to create a new coalition called the Progressive Alliance that would unite labor with the movements of the sixties. But the AFL-CIO undermined Fraser's effort by discouraging its unions from joining. In 1980, Fraser and other leaders of industrial unions, along with many of the consumer, civil rights, and community organizing groups that had come out of the sixties, backed Senator Edward Kennedy's primary challenge to President Carter, while Kirkland and many of the Democratic politicians stood by Carter. The split weakened the liberal movement and made Reagan's victory in 1980 more likely.

There was no doubt that in his first term Reagan and his policies also had popular support. Reagan and the Republicans were able to do to Carter and the liberal Democrats what Roosevelt had done to Hoover and the Republicans: associate them with whatever unpleasantness had happened in the prior decade. Voters blamed Carter and the Democrats for everything from stagflation to America's loss of face internationally, and they saw in Reagan's policies hope for change. Identifying activist government with what they took to be Carter's failures, the public also backed Reagan's Jacksonian view of government. From September 1973 to February 1981, the percentage of Americans agreeing that "the best government is the government that governs least" rose from 32 percent to 59 percent.[31]

Reagan and the conservative movement also benefited from a dramatic change in Americans' priorities. During the sixties, the transition from the older industrial culture of self-denial had manifested itself in new political and social movements and in a quest for new forms of communal salvation, similar to the early Christians or the Americans of the 1740s and 1830s. The quest for earthly happiness that replaced the quest for otherworldly salvation was itself conducted through political movements rather than singly or by family. But with the disappearance or fragmentation of the main political movements, and with the downturn in the economy, Americans, and particularly younger Americans, turned inward—not back to otherworldly religions, but to psychological and quasi-religious methods of seeking happiness.

The Americans of the seventies read pop psychologists like Thomas A. Harris, the author of *I'm OK—You're OK,* Shere Hite's *Hite Report* on female sexuality, and Nancy Friday on becoming a "fully sexual woman." San Francisco's Haight Ashbury gave way to the sexual and gastronomic fads of Marin County, brilliantly satirized in Cyra McFadden's novel *The Serial.* "For starters," McFadden describes one dinner party,

> she and Ginger Gallagher had had this great conversation about choosing a gynecologist who could really relate to women even if he wasn't one. Ginger had said the critical thing was whether or not he had *Our Bodies Ourselves* in the waiting room instead of *Penthouse* and *Field and Stream.* Frank Gallagher and Sam Stein had talked for *hours* about the energy crisis and how they were going to build solar heating units for their swimming pools. Fran said that if everybody else did the same thing, we wouldn't have to worry about the Arab oil cartel anymore. And over the bisque, Marsha Wilson, who sold real estate, had filled them all in on the housing market, which made Kat feel a lot more *secure* about her own socioeconomic status.[32]

The change in mood showed up dramatically in the surveys of college freshmen conducted by the UCLA Higher Education Research Institute. The UCLA researchers found a continuing shift in young people's priorities from 1968 to 1987. In 1968, 40.8 percent of the freshmen thought being "very well off financially" was an "essential" or "very important objective." By 1980 it had risen to 63.3 percent, and by 1987 to 75.6 percent. In 1968, 82.5 percent of the freshmen thought that it was essential to "develop a meaningful philosophy of life." By 1980 the percentage had dropped to 50.4 percent, and by 1987 to 39.4 percent.[33] This change in attitude may not have been entirely congenial to Reagan conservatism, but it was altogether alien to the politics of the new left or of New Deal liberalism. It led either to withdrawal from politics or to sympathy toward the kind of economic policies promoted by conservative tax-cutters.

There was, however, one other factor that accounted for the triumph of business and Republican conservatives. In the past, elites and elite organizations had remained steadfast in their support for a politics that sought to reconcile democratic ideals of equality with the fact of corporate capitalism. Even in the hostile environment of the 1920s, the elite organizations had persevered. But that did not happen in the late seventies and the eighties. Far from providing a counterweight to corporate individualism and to the attack against pluralism and government, they came to reinforce it.

[7]

The Apostasy of the Elites

In the 1980s there were clearly individuals, like Greenspan, Burns, Simon, former Secretary of Defense Clark Clifford, and former Secretary of State Henry Kissinger, who could, and did, claim to be part of the nation's establishment. They were appointed to presidential commissions, asked to testify before Congress as disinterested "wise men," and invited to vent their expert opinions on op-ed pages and on Sunday television news shows. But many of them—like those who had eagerly endorsed Reagan's balanced budget plan in September 1980—no longer behaved, or functioned, as elites. They were interested, rather than disinterested, participants; what they said often meshed subtly or crassly with the interests of business clients or political patrons.

There were also organizations that claimed to be part of the establishment. "We are delighted to be members in good standing of the Washington Establishment," the president of the American Enterprise Institute declared.[1] Washington and New York abounded in "foundations," "institutes," "institutions," "centers," "committees," and "councils"—the labels that once distinguished elite groups from trade associations and PR firms. But many of these organizations were really the intellectual arm of business lobbies or political factions. They had little in common with the National Civic Federation, the Brookings Institution, or other original elite institutions. A similar gulf separated the newer foundations like Olin and Smith-Richardson from the older Ford and Rockefeller foundations. Irving Kristol had said it best when he declared that the new "corporate philanthropy should not be, and cannot be, disinterested."[2]

The older elite organizations had helped make democratic pluralism possible. They stood for defining the national interest in terms that took account of business, labor, and the other competing groups in society. But the new organizations, foundations, and think tanks were designed to undermine democratic pluralism—to further the rule of business and of its K Street lobbyists over the political process. By the end of the seventies the new organizations had carried the day—through their own self-promotion and through intimidating the other elite organizations.

The Intimidated Elites

In the early 1970s, conservative intellectuals, with the support of business leaders, began attacking the older elite think tanks, policy groups, publications, and foundations. They argued that Brookings, the Ford Foundation, and the *Washington Post* and *New York Times* were not independent, objective, and impartial in their political judgments and reports, but liberal and left-wing. Wrote former Nixon speechwriter and new right leader Pat Buchanan in 1975, "The Brookings Institution, policy institute of the left, works hand-in-glove with bureaucrats and Democrats. . . . The national press is the silent partner of the political and social movements of liberalism."[3] These charges put those institutions on the defensive. They tried to demonstrate their impartiality by embracing the views of their critics.

In the past, elite organizations had not merely survived attacks from business and labor, but flourished. In the Progressive Era, the National Civic Federation was denounced by both the NAM and the Socialist Party. In the sixties, the radical right and the radical left had both attacked the Ford Foundation. With powerful critics on both sides of them, the elite organizations could perform a mediating role between business and its adversaries. But beginning in the 1970s, Brookings, the CED, the Ford Foundation, and the *New York Times* editorial board could no longer play a mediating role. Their critics were almost entirely to their right.

In addition, the elite groups remained predominately upper-class in their membership and dependent upon bankers and businessmen for much of their financial support and political legitimacy. During the Progressive Era, the 1930s, and the post–World War II decades, there had been a sizable group of business leaders like George Perkins and Paul Hoffman who insisted that businessmen had to focus on the long-term national interest. But by the 1970s they had become an anachronism. There were some holdovers like banker Felix Rohatyn, but most of the investment bankers who meddled in government policy were like William Simon or Walter Wriston, the CEO of Citicorp and prime mover behind AEI. They were primarily interested in protecting their own.

One could draw a sharp contrast, for instance, between Robert Brookings, the initial funder of the Brookings Institution, and Richard Mellon Scaife, who supplied much of the funding for Heritage and other policy groups. Brookings, who migrated to St. Louis at age seventeen, was a self-made millionaire who sold bowls, clothespins, and other wooden products in the West. His real passion remained, however, history and music, and at thirty-five he quit his dry-goods firm to go to Berlin to study the violin. When informed by his teacher after a year's study that he would never be better than a talented amateur, he returned to St. Louis and business. Having reamassed a fortune, he retired ten years later in 1896 and devoted the rest of his life to philanthropy. He became the president of Washington College, which he made into Washington University. Much of St. Louis's intellectual and cultural life still bears Brookings's mark. He was a founding member of the Carnegie Corporation, a trustee of the Smithsonian Institution, and was active in the National Civic Federation. He served on commissions in the Taft administration and on the War Industries Board in World War I.[4]

Scaife, by contrast, was a reclusive millionaire. Born in 1933, he inherited his wealth from the Mellon fortune. He flunked out of Yale and did not seem to have any occupation until 1969, when he purchased a small-town newspaper. His principal work seems to have been funding conservative policy organizations, think tanks, and publications. Over four decades, he would give $620 million (in 1999 dollars) to conservative organizations. In 1994 he set up a fund to investigate whether former Clinton aide Vincent Foster was murdered by someone associated with the Clinton administration, even though police reports had ruled that Foster's death was a suicide. He appears to have been a man of fevered imagination and narrow, visceral hatreds.[5]

There was also a sharp difference between the religious and moral outlook of the older elite and that of the new funders of foundations and think tanks. The older elite had been deeply influenced by the Protestant social gospel and carried on a tradition of noblesse oblige. But many of the men who funded the AEI, Heritage, and the new policy groups were closer to the conservative wing of Protestantism that had risen in opposition to the social gospel. J. Howard Pew of Sun Oil, for instance, who was a prime contributor to Billy Graham and *Christianity Today*, pressured evangelicals to embrace a radical right stance on economics and foreign policy.[6] Pew's foundation would later be one of the largest contributors to the AEI. Other wealthy conservative Christians included Richard M. DeVos, the president of Amway Corporation; Nelson Bunker Hunt of Hunt Oil; and Art DeMoss, the chairman of the National Liberty Insurance Corporation.[7]

Few of the investment bankers and corporate CEOs who served as trustees of the foundations and think tanks and as outside directors of the great newspapers, and who helped fund policy research in the 1970s, shared Robert Brookings's view of the world. They may not have been virulently partisan like Scaife or as religiously conservative as Pew, but they focused on the threat to their company's profitability from government intervention and hostile political movements. They were largely oblivious to the ethic of noblesse oblige or to older strains of the Protestant social gospel. They were the upper-class counterparts to the Marin suburbanites that McFadden satirized. Instead of making sure that the elite organizations played their mediating role, they threw their money and weight behind the new conservative-business alliance.

In the face of withering attacks, some of the older elite organizations made modifications, but they maintained their identity. Brookings, for instance, hired a conservative publicist and recruited a monetarist and an anti-Soviet hawk to buttress its claim to being nonpartisan and nonideological. When its president Kermit Gordon, a former economic advisor in the Kennedy administration, died in 1977, it appointed Bruce MacLaury, who had been in the Nixon Treasury Department before becoming president of the Minneapolis Federal Reserve Bank, as his successor. But several organizations underwent more significant upheaval in the 1970s. These included the Ford Foundation, the *New York Times*, and the *Washington Post.*

Under McGeorge Bundy the Ford Foundation had come under heavy criticism from Congress in 1969 for its role in Ocean Hill–Brownsville, its funding of voter registration in Cleveland's mayoral race, and Bundy's award of resettlement grants to wealthy former aides of the late Robert Kennedy. In response, Congress had inserted new requirements in the 1969 tax reform bill that prohibited foundations from seeking to influence legislation or elections with their grants. Bundy and the foundation weathered that crisis, but in the next decade they faced a new challenge from business critics outside and inside the foundation.

What brought the wrath of business leaders down on Bundy's head was the foundation's role in backing the environmental and consumer movements. Ford underwrote the growth of public interest law firms. It was the main source of funds for the Center for Law in the Public Interest, the Environmental Defense Fund, the Sierra Club Legal Defense, the Natural Resources Defense Council, the Institute for Public Interest Representation, the Center for Law and Public Policy, the Citizens Communication Center, the Public Advocates, the Education Law Center, and the Center for Law and Public Policy. These firms often sued the U.S. government to force it to make companies comply with the new environmental and consumer legislation.

Bundy and the foundation also incurred the wrath of business through its work on energy conservation. In 1971, Bundy launched what would become a three-year, $4 million study of U.S. energy use. The final report, *A Time to Choose,* was released in October 1974, but the research was finished by the time the energy crisis hit in late 1973. The project staff was called upon to testify on Capitol Hill, and its recommendations became the basis of a House bill. The report laid out three options: continued use of oil and gas at the present rate, a "technical fix" that would cut the rate of increase in half, and a "zero-growth" option that would hold energy use increase after 1985 at 2 percent a year. The report recommended either the technical fix or the zero option and argued that either could be achieved without causing a recession by adopting improved automobile gas mileage, better building construction, and greater industrial efficiency. To oversee either the technical fix or the zero option, the report called for the creation of a federal "energy policy council."[8]

In retrospect, the report's recommendations were wise, prudent, and moderate—just the kind of thing one would expect from a dispassionate, but also cautious, application of social science. Over the next decade, the nation would go considerably farther than the report called for. The report's technical fix and zero option called for U.S. energy consumption to go from 73 quadrillion BTUs in 1974 to about 90 quadrillion BTUs in 1985. In fact, consumption would go from 73 to 74! A recession would occur in 1982, but it would not be caused by energy conservation. And Congress and the Carter administration would establish not just a new policy council, but an entire new cabinet department. All in all, the report succeeded, as one energy expert concluded in 1984, in shifting "the orientation of public policy somewhat closer to a conservationist ethic."[9]

Some energy and environmental experts applauded the report. Michael McCloskey of the Sierra Club said, "It is a pity that the report of the Energy Policy Project was not available a couple of years ago to help guide us through the turmoil of the energy crisis."[10] But from the moment the Ford panel began releasing its findings, it was hounded by industry representatives. Against the wishes of the project's director, S. David Freeman, the foundation created an advisory board that included prominent industry representatives, including William P. Tavoulareas, the crusading president of Mobil Oil; John D. Harper of ALCOA, the first president of the Business Roundtable; Donald C. Burnham, the president of Westinghouse; J. Harris Ward, the director of Commonwealth Edison; and Minor S. James, the vice president of the Independent Petroleum Institute of America. When the report was issued, the industry representatives hit the roof. Tavoulareas denounced it at the National Press Club. James declared, "In my considered judgment, this report is seriously lacking in objectivity and is not an appropriate guidance tool for evaluating or determining public policies as to energy." Ward objected to the report's wariness about the safety of nuclear reactors. "A proposal to defer nuclear development in this country is dangerous to the national security and the national welfare," he wrote.[11]

Several think tanks issued reports and studies attacking the report. The Institute for Contemporary Studies, a conservative think tank funded by Olin and Scaife money, put out a book of essays, *No Time to Confuse*. Its critics, drawn from business and engineering schools, rejected the report's contention that energy conservation was economically feasible. The report's scenarios were "worthless," *No Time to Confuse* declared.[12] And they warned that government intervention could work "only in the context of a police state."[13]

The Ford Foundation panicked at the torrent of vitriol. Bundy agreed to publish a critique of the report by Tavoulareas, titled *A Debate on a Time to Choose*. The foundation also appointed a team to review the process, headed by John Deutch, an MIT professor and energy expert who would become Undersecretary of Energy in the Carter administration and later serve as CIA director in the Clinton administration. Instead of soberly evaluating the report, Deutch's team seconded the conclusions of the critics from industry. It called the report "extremely naïve regarding the feasibility of effectively implementing many of the policy proposals" and accused it of a "pervasive anti-market, pro-government bias."[14] It concluded ominously:

> What is of legitimate concern is the general atmosphere of an adversary nature that seems to have existed between the project and the representatives of industry on the Advisory Board. As a result, an attitude of hostility to the project has spread in the business community. This hostility has limited the useful impact of the project. If the Energy Policy Project was to be influential in the long term public debate on energy policy, it was essential that the project have credibility with leaders of energy industries.[15]

Deutch didn't understand the irony of this point: to have had credibility with leaders of the energy industry, the report would have had to abandon its support for government-sponsored energy conservation, exactly the alternative that the country would turn to, and that Deutch himself would oversee. The business leaders and their lobbyists had succeeded in intimidating not only the foundation but also prominent social scientists like Deutch.

The year after Deutch's report, the final blow fell on the foundation. Henry Ford II resigned in protest from the board of trustees. In his letter of resignation, Ford took direct aim at what he believed was the foundation's hostility to business:

> The Foundation exists and thrives on the fruits of our economic system. The dividends of competitive enterprise make it all possible. . . . In effect, the Foundation is a creature of capitalism—a statement that, I'm sure, would be shocking to many professional staff people in the field of philanthropy. It is hard to discern recognition of this fact in anything the Foundation does. . . . Perhaps it is time for the Trustees and staff to examine the question of our obligations to our economic system and to consider how the Foundation as one of the system's most prominent offspring might act most wisely to strengthen and improve its progenitor.[16]

Ford's resignation clearly reflected business's dissatisfaction with the foundation. It became the basis for Irving Kristol's attack on "disinterested" corporate philanthropy. Bundy had resisted this kind of criticism before, but now he took steps to accommodate it. To mollify the critics of his funding environmental public interest firms, he began funding new firms that claimed to mediate between the public interest firms and the government. He also appointed a new pro-industry panel to do a new energy report. It appeared in 1979 and was ignored. Its principal argument was that conservation and the development of alternative sources of energy could best be achieved through "decontrolling" energy prices.[17]

In 1979, Bundy reached mandatory retirement age. The foundation's trustees appointed Franklin Thomas to succeed him. Thomas's appointment appeared to confirm the foundation's independence. He was the first black to become the head of a major foundation. An Ivy Leaguer, he had shunned corporate law to make his name as the head of a large Ford-funded poverty project in the Bedford-Stuyvesant area of New York. But Thomas, it turned out, represented an innocuous social liberalism that calmed the fears of the foundation's business critics. He was interested in funding poverty programs and promoting affirmative action inside and outside of the foundation. He upped Ford's commitment to ghetto redevelopment and women's rights. While other foundation officials balked at the Reagan administration's request that private foundations make up for the loss in government social programs for the poor, Thomas, in effect, complied.* At the same time, Thomas abruptly abandoned the foundation's commitment to consumer, environmental, and energy programs that might have ruffled the business community.

One of Thomas's first acts was to end funding for public interest law firms. A Ford official claimed that the foundation wanted the organizations to become "self-sustaining institutions," but this was laughable.[18] In Washington, public interest firms were already being outspent about twenty-five to one by their corporate counterparts.[19] Ford's withdrawal of funds meant that the balance between consumers and large corporations would be tipped even farther in business's direction. With Thomas's appointment, business had won its decade-long struggle to emasculate the Ford Foundation.

At the same time, business leaders began to attack the press for being "antibusiness." Corporations began monitoring newspapers and television shows to demonstrate bias. Chevron sponsored a project on "The Influence of Reporter Bias on TV Viewer Opinion." Other surveys were

*J. Roderick MacArthur, who won control of the fabulously wealthy John D. and Catherine T. MacArthur Foundation of Chicago from rival William Simon in 1981, seemed to have a clear idea of what was wrong with Ford and what a cutting edge foundation should do. MacArthur said:

> I personally think that both we and other foundations should refuse to pick up where government is pulling back. The government was doing little enough as it was, and the whole idea that this society should move back to the nineteenth century just because the government wants to save money is absurd. . . . In effect, private foundations should not encourage the government to go backwards. We should be out there in the forefront, ahead of where government thinks it's safe to be. Only in that way can we use the unique ability that a private foundation has. If we don't use that unique ability, why should we have the privileges we enjoy? Waldemar A. Nielsen, *The Golden Donors,* New York, 1985, pp. 110–11.

But MacArthur failed to put his words into practice. His main innovation before he died in 1984 was the "genius grants"—grants that won their donor and the recipients enormous publicity, but that did little to put the foundation itself at the forefront of social progress.

funded through the AEI and the Institute for Contemporary Studies. In 1976, Mobil Oil, Proctor and Gamble, and other corporations set up the Media Institute in Washington to monitor media coverage of business. Its advisory board included Bryce Harlow, Murray Weidenbaum, and Herbert Schmertz, the vice president of Mobil Oil who pioneered corporate advocacy ads. One business editor, recalling the early 1970s, described "the visceral hatred and contempt that most businessmen had for the media."[20] Much of this hatred became known to the publishers of major newspapers when they solicited advertising or when they met with their boards of directors.

The *New York Times* always prided itself on being immune to outside pressures, but it was among the first publications to succumb. Arthur "Punch" Sulzberger became publisher of the newspaper in 1963. The editor of the editorial page was John Oakes, Sulzberger's second cousin. Oakes had been in charge since 1961 and had been on the editorial board since 1949. One of the nation's most distinguished editors, he was responsible for the introduction of the op-ed page in 1970 (the first of its kind) and for the *Times*'s prescient warnings about U.S. intervention in Vietnam. But his evenhanded editorials on business and labor—many of them written by A. H. Raskin (a distinguished labor reporter) or Leonard Silk (later an outstanding business columnist)—and his support for consumer and environmental legislation began to provoke protests from businessmen close to Sulzberger. Whenever Sulzberger made his annual pilgrimage to Detroit to help the advertising department sell ads to the Big Three, he would return filled with complaints about the editorials questioning car safety or bemoaning auto pollution.

Sulzberger hired a Harvard management expert, Chris Argyris, to analyze the relationships among the paper's different departments. Argyris's report was subsequently published with the names of the paper and its editors changed (the *New York Times* was called the *Daily Planet*). The exchanges between Sulzberger ("P" in the book) and Oakes ("T") reveal the growing tension over business coverage:

> [Oakes] then said that one of the problems of being a paper with a conscience was that such a paper served the community best by being critical: "We're helping our city by being critical of all the things

> that are wrong with it. I think that the best way to help the city is to be critical. Of course, this is different from the typical booster view." [Sulzberger] interrupted to ask [Oakes], "Are you anti-big business?" [Oakes] answered, "No, I'm not." "The editorial page," [Sulzberger] retorted, "could give some people the idea that we're anti-big business." "That's because businessmen don't like some of the criticisms that we made," [Oakes] replied. "I would say that we're as critical of big labor as we are of big business."[21]

At a second session, Sulzberger, turning against Oakes for his anti-business views,

> described his feelings when, on a few occasions, several of his corporation board members, men whom he respects greatly, read the paper to find their company's actions condemned. [Oakes] said that he had never thought of that embarrassment. However, he still believed that the correct action for the paper was to condemn the companies even if their chief executive officers were on the corporate board. [Oakes] continued, "These businessmen are great human beings, but they have no feelings for the tradition of a great newspaper." [Sulzberger] replied, "Let us be clear that news and editorial matters are not discussed by these businessmen. But it is still not easy to divorce myself when I know [that we have attacked] someone who sits on our board of directors. . . . None of these men would even think of trying to influence our positions. But they might say, "You are certainly entitled to print anything you wish, but how on earth did you arrive at such-and-such a position?"[22]

By the mid-1970s, Sulzberger had resolved to change the newspaper's image among businessmen. Sulzberger told biographer Joseph Goulden that he had wearied of defending the newspaper to his business friends.[23] In October 1976, to symbolize his determination to change, he fired Oakes two years before he was to retire and replaced him with Max Frankel. Within a year both Silk and Raskin were also gone.

An almost identical course of events took place at the *Washington Post*. In 1967, Philip Geyelin had become editor of the editorial page.

Katharine Graham, who had become publisher in 1963, hired Geyelin, a former *Wall Street Journal* diplomatic correspondent, partly because she wanted to move the paper away from its identification with Johnson's policy in Vietnam. Geyelin, like Oakes, was by no means a radical, but he backed a negotiated peace in Vietnam and was amenable to the new Washington-based environmental and consumer groups. In its earlier versions, the *Post* had backed Nader's plan for a federal consumer protection agency, even though its defeat had become a paramount goal of the Business Roundtable and its allies.

At the end of 1977, Graham called in Geyelin and asked for his resignation. Graham wrote later that it was because he was in a "prolonged slump" after Watergate.[24] But other *Post* editors believe that she, like Sulzberger at the *New York Times*, had come under pressure from friends in business and *Post* directors who thought that the newspaper's editorial policy was antibusiness. Geyelin pleaded for another chance, and Graham agreed. The next February, when the consumer protection agency bill came up for a vote, Geyelin informed Colman McCarthy, who had written the earlier editorials, that the newspaper was going to change its position and oppose the bill. He gave the job of writing the editorial to a woman who was becoming close to Graham and would later become her speechwriter.

In its editorial, the *Post* explained that it was changing its position because "both the legislation and conditions have changed." But the changes, it acknowledged, had been to "cut back" rather than enlarge the agency's authority. What, then, was its beef? The $15 million cost! Argued the newspaper: "The bill's sponsors maintain that the $15-million budget of the new agency would be more than offset by transfer or elimination of existing consumer programs in over 20 agencies. We find the net-savings claim a bit hard to swallow."[25] The newspaper rested its case on the most implausible grounds. In fact, the pricetag on the agency hadn't gone up since the *Post* had first endorsed the agency—if anything, it had gone down. And no one had ever suggested that a $15 million expenditure amid $505 billion in outlays—approximately 0.003 percent of the federal budget—could threaten insolvency. The weakness of the argument revealed the newspaper's true motive: not to prevent an unwise and unwarranted expenditure that could expand the deficit, but to give a signal to business that it was on its side on an issue that had great symbolic importance to it.

Graham at this point had turned extremely hostile to the consumer movement and the Federal Trade Commission. When FTC chairman Michael Pertschuk met with Graham to try to reduce her animosity, Graham surprised him by denouncing the *Washington Post*'s consumer reporter, Morton Mintz, a journalist who had broken the Thalidomide story in 1962 and had been one of the first reporters to write about Nader and auto safety. "She delivered a diatribe against Morton Mintz saying that he doesn't realize that for the *Post* to survive it has to make a profit. I had the sense that the *Post* had to thrive and consumer reporting was inimical to that," Pertschuk recalled.[26]

After that, the newspaper regularly opposed consumer legislation. It denounced a bill to regulate advertising on young children's television shows—a proposal violently opposed by cereal companies. "It is a preposterous intervention that would turn the agency into a great national nanny," the newspaper declared.[27] Geyelin himself only lasted through the year. When Graham's son Donald took over as editor the next year, one of his first acts was to fire Geyelin and replace him with his deputy Meg Greenfield. Geyelin later explained his firing: "I've been told that he felt we were too liberal."[28]

Neither the *New York Times* nor the *Washington Post*—nor, for that matter, the Ford Foundation—became mouthpieces for the Business Roundtable or the Heritage Foundation, but they showed that they were subject to intimidation from the powerful bloc of conservatives and business lobbies that dominated American politics in the late 1970s.

The Counterestablishment

The goal of conservatives like Irving Kristol, John Simon, and Pat Buchanan was to create what they later called a "counterestablishment." Richard Viguerie argued that the Heritage Foundation should "become to the Eighties what the Ford Foundation and Brookings Institution were to the last couple of decades."[29] Heritage, the AEI, the American Council for Capital Formation, the Olin Foundation, and the other new institutions of the counterestablishment appeared outwardly to be elite organizations. They attracted prominent former officials as their sponsors and directors and often persuaded big-name social scientists to put their names on reports. Many conservatives, who knew little of American history, believed that the organizations they had created *were* the rightful heirs of the older elite groups. They were, however, fundamentally different.

Instead of creating a new elite, they undermined what it meant for the country to have one. The new groups, in contrast to the old, did not seek to be above class, party, and ideology. On the contrary, they were openly probusiness and conservative. Some were factions in the Republican Party. They did not seek to mediate conflicts, but to take one side. They had no ties to labor unions or to the environmental, consumer, or civil rights movements that had emerged in the sixties, but only to the business counteroffensive against them. They were not committed to reconciling democracy with corporate capitalism, but merely to defending corporate capitalism. They did not seek to produce objective results by means of social science. On the contrary, they were willing to use social science to achieve partisan results. As Eric Wanner, the president of the old-line Russell Sage Foundation, put it: "The AEIs and the Heritages of the world represent the inversion of the progressive faith that social science should shape social policy."[30]

Conservatives would later attack the "relativism" of the new left, but neoconservatives like Irving Kristol and new right intellectuals like Buchanan unwittingly mirrored the worst anti-intellectual tendencies of the new left. Just as the new right activists mimicked the guerrilla mentality, the moralism, and the apocalyptic thinking of the new left, the conservative counterestablishment perpetuated the radical new left's rejection of social science as "ideology." While the new left rejected social science as being implicitly "probusiness" or "promilitary," the new right and its think tanks rejected it for being "antibusiness" and "left-wing." The conservatives rejected the very idea of a dispassionate and disinterested elite that could focus on the national interest. Their real case against Brookings or the *Washington Post* wasn't that they were liberal rather than disinterested, but that they were liberal rather than conservative.

* * *

The career of Murray Weidenbaum and of the American Center for the Study of Business is a case in point. On the surface, Weidenbaum and his Center had all the earmarks of the older establishment. Weidenbaum was a full professor at Washington University, a prestigious private university in St. Louis whose superior reputation in social science dated from Robert Brookings's tenure as its president and chief benefactor. (In the 1920s, Washington University and the Brookings Institution had even run a Ph.D. program together.) In 1975, Weidenbaum established the American Center for the Study of Business within the university. Its reports, mostly written by Weidenbaum himself, were widely cited in the press as authoritative accounts of what was wrong with government regulation. In 1981, Reagan appointed Weidenbaum to chair the Council of Economic Advisors, a post previously held by distinguished economists like Arthur Burns, Walter Heller, Herbert Stein, and Charles Schultze.

In fact, Weidenbaum and the Center had little in common with the social scientists and the institutions of the older establishment. Weidenbaum himself was far from being a leader in his profession. After earning a Ph.D. in 1949, he became a corporate researcher—with General Dynamics and Boeing in Washington. He was the economist as lobbyist. He went to Washington University in 1964 to head up a project on aerospace and got an appointment to its economics department, while beginning to work on projects with the AEI. In 1969 he was appointed Assistant Secretary of the Treasury in the Nixon administration. In 1975 he returned to Washington University as Mallinckrodt Professor, a chair endowed by a firm for which Weidenbaum did consulting work.

Soon after Weidenbaum returned, he had a conversation over lunch with the university chancellor and vice-chancellor. According to Weidenbaum, the three of them were worried about the left-wing reputation the university was acquiring and wanted a business think tank to counter it. "At that point all the community heard were loud radical voices," Weidenbaum said. "We decided they shouldn't be the only voices that you hear. It would be nice to have a serious research body that had a more sympathetic view of the private enterprise."[31] Weidenbaum claimed later that they tried not to set up "one of these institutes to promote free enterprise," but it was hard to distinguish the American Center from similar efforts that business groups and their foundations initiated in the 1970s and 1980s.

Weidenbaum received an initial grant from the Olin Foundation, which continued to back the Center. During the rest of the decade he was its only prominent fellow, and the Center's purpose was largely to promote and publish his ideas and those of his research associates on the prohibitive costs of government regulations. Unlike the National Bureau of Economic Research, the Center did not fund a diversity of viewpoints. Unlike the NBER, its steering committee contained no labor leaders. It consisted, outside of the university chancellor and Weidenbaum, of prominent conservative businessmen.

Its purpose was clearly to advance business's war on regulation, but this aim was clothed in politics and ideology rather than being stated straightforwardly. The Center claimed to be defending the new being of the sixties—the "consumer"—against the ravages of regulation. Stated the Center's brochure: "The single most effective national issue the Center has developed thus far is the position that over-regulation of business is not in the public interest because it increases the prices that consumers pay for the products they buy."[32]

Weidenbaum's reports were extremely influential. In 1978 he and a research assistant produced a study of business regulation that made the highly provocative claim that government regulations would cost business $96 billion in 1978. The study was then published by the American Enterprise Institute, whose magazine *Regulation* Weidenbaum co-edited with future Supreme Court justice Antonin Scalia. Republicans then arranged for Weidenbaum to testify on the results of his study before the Joint Economic Committee of Congress. And the *Reader's Digest*, whose foundation funded the AEI, printed a short, popular version of the study titled "Time to Control Runaway Inflation."[33] Weidenbaum's numbers were cited repeatedly in arguments for regulatory reform.

The study itself was open to obvious objections. Its purpose appeared to be overtly political. It cited gross costs without attempting to estimate benefits. While singling out OSHA and EPA for criticism, it failed to note that the agencies accounted for a small percentage of Weidenbaum's gross costs—OSHA 5 percent and EPA 13 percent in 1976.[34] When the Congressional Research Service (CRS), which is run by the Library of Congress and used by both parties, studied Weidenbaum's numbers, it found they were based on unjustifiable assumptions. His gross costs included general social costs in addition to the direct costs that a business incurred from installing a seat belt or pollution control device. His figures included the costs of import quotas and wage regulations; and they were based on an exaggerated estimate of paperwork costs, which failed to distinguish between the costs of complying with the regulations and the costs of filling out IRS or government loan forms. The cautious CRS, which had rarely taken a critical stance, concluded that the study had "enough questionable components to make the totals arrived at suspect and of doubtful validity."[35] Yet Weidenbaum prevailed. His views became the vogue. He became chairman of the Council of Economic Advisors.

The new think tanks and policy groups created by conservatives and their business allies began to overshadow their rivals. The press, on the defensive itself, began treating the products of the AEI, Heritage, and the American Center with the same respect as those of Brookings, NBER, or a university economics department. They accepted the canard that different views simply reflected different ideologies and that to be fair, both left and right, liberal and conservative, had to be represented. Once this concession was made, the conservatives triumphed, because in the late 1970s and 1980s they had far more money than their rivals with which to broadcast, publish, and promote their opinions.

In this way the conservative strategy worked. It achieved credibility for their ideas and reduced the influence of those of their rivals. Weidenbaum's numbers and Arthur Laffer's supply-side curve both got taken far more seriously than they ever deserved. In the long run, however, the creation of a "counterestablishment" undermined the credibility of the very concept of elites. It was like a monarch debasing the coin of the realm by adding nickel to the silver. Once the public figured out that many of the silver coins contained nickel, all the coins became worthless.

"Doing good to do well"

Just as some older elite organizations abdicated their responsibility during the 1980s, so, too, did many of the individuals who had earned a reputation as disinterested public servants. By the mid-1980s there were over a thousand former officials in Washington working as lobbyists, including over 200 former members of Congress. They weren't working simply as lawyers who were knowledgeable in FDA or FCC policies. They were selling their reputations and even their convictions. Many of the former officials would trade on their reputation as members of the elite in the crassest manner: they would defend their clients' positions in speeches, interviews, and op-ed pieces without identifying themselves as lobbyists. Elliot Richardson was not known as a lobbyist for Japanese companies but as "Mr. Ambassador" and the man who had defied Nixon during Watergate. Henry Kissinger was not known as a highly paid consultant for companies and governments but as the distinguished former Secretary of State.

Some of the lobbyists clearly believed in what they were doing. Wisconsin Senator Gaylord Nelson, a champion of environmental causes, became the head of the Wilderness Society after he was defeated for reelection in 1980. But many others were simply working for the highest bidder. Former Congressman James Corman, a leading liberal Democrat who was defeated in 1980, went to work for a Washington law firm where he lobbied for Nissan and Texas Air, but not for the causes or institutions he supported as a Congressman. Corman explained, "People don't hire lawyers to work on the things I worked on when I was in Congress. When you're in public office you have the privilege of representing the public interest. When you work for a law firm, you represent your client."[36] In fact, companies preferred to hire officials who had regulated or negotiated against them or former politicians like Corman who had opposed them. Former opponents not only had a better chance of convincing their former colleagues, but their opinion, appearing to represent a conversion, carried more weight and attracted more attention.

These officials did not become lobbyists because of the conservative counteroffensive but because of the sheer growth of K Street and of the demand for effective lobbyists and consultants. Former officials could easily earn over a million dollars a year on K Street—more than ten times what they had made as public officials. This kind of temptation had not existed in the 1930s when Harvard Law graduates flocked to Washington to take jobs in government.

The law firms themselves changed in character. Firms that had formerly prided themselves on their detachment from pecuniary concerns became "profit centers" that measured the success of their partners and associates by their "billable hours." "By the 1980s," Harvard Law professor Mary Ann Glendon writes, "the billable hour had evolved from a sensible tool of office management to a frenetic way of life."[37] And the men and women who joined these firms also changed. Once the heirs of the American tradition of public service, they became businessmen and -women. The new business culture of the law firm, Stanford Law professor Robert Gordon writes, worked

> to discourage the development of any values beside making money for the collective. The pressures to seek and take on new clients and to pile up billable hours wipe out most of the time and energy that lawyers might otherwise have for outside activities. Firms treat the partner engaged in politics and the associates who want to do pro bono work as parasites, free riders on the income-producing efforts of others.[38]

The move from the White House and Capitol Hill to K Street had begun in the last years of the New Deal. One of the first officials to become a lobbyist was Thomas "the Cork" Corcoran, who was a student of Frankfurter at Harvard and had helped write the Securities and Exchange Act and the Public Utility Company Holding Act. From 1936 to 1939 he served as Roosevelt's closest advisor until he was supplanted by Harry Hopkins. When Roosevelt did not appoint him solicitor general in 1940, Corcoran quit and set up a law practice. He turned his back on the New Deal and on the ideal of disinterested law. He became known as a "fixer" for his ability to solve problems for his corporate clients. He did little actual law; most of his work was done through phone calls to contacts in the White House, the cabinet, and Capitol Hill.

Other important officials followed a similar parth, including former Undersecretary of the Interior Abe Fortas, former Truman aide Clark Clifford, and Eisenhower aide Bryce Harlow.* But the trickle of recruits in the 1950s and 1960s became a raging torrent in the 1970s. During the Carter administration, the practice of parlaying government service into a lucrative lobbying career became known as "doing good to do well." Former chairmen of the Federal Communications Commission went to work for television networks.[39] Former Securities and Exchange officials represented Wall Street companies under investigation by the SEC. A host of former U.S. trade officials became lobbyists for Japanese companies.†

*If there were an original sin in this story—equivalent to Eve's eating the apple—it would be Abe Fortas's choice of his first client after leaving the Department of the Interior. While he was Undersecretary, Fortas had worked closely with Rexford Tugwell, who was governor of Puerto Rico. When Tugwell had requested permission in 1945 to hire a private counsel for the island to help with its legal problems, Fortas had killed the idea. "I believe that continuing representation of a Government or a governmental agency by private attorneys is unsound and unwise," Fortas wrote. Fortas's first act after leaving the Interior Department was to go to Puerto Rico and to arrange that his new firm handle its affairs. It became one of the firm's most lucrative accounts—not only for its own sake, but because of other clients like Phillips Petroleum that had, or sought to build, facilities on the island. See Bruce Allen Murphy, *Fortas,* New York, 1988, pp. 74–75.

†Here are some examples, drawn from *Washington Representatives*.

Regulators lobbying for the regulated: Former Ford administration chairmen of the Federal Communications Commission Richard Wiley hired out to CBS. Charles Ferris, who succeeded Wiley and served until 1981, signed up with Japanese television firms accused of copyright violations and later for Turner Broadcasting. William Ruckelshaus, head of the Environmental Protection Agency in the Nixon administration, represented the plastics industry before the EPA. Lynn Coleman, the former general counsel for the Department of Energy in the Ford administration, became a lobbyist for Occidental Petroleum and other oil and gas producers.

Tax and securities experts: Donald C. Alexander, former Internal Revenue Service commissioner in the Ford administration, lobbied for REITs (Real Estate Investment Trusts) and for a host of financial corporations. Bruce S. Mendelsohn, the former head of the Office of Regulatory Policy at the Securities and Exchange Commission in the early Reagan administration, left to lobby for Drexel Burnham and Lambert when the SEC began to investigate it.

The Japan lobby: Former U.S. trade representative William Eberle and former deputy trade representatives Harald Malmgren and William Walker began lobbying for Japanese companies in the 1970s. Former U.S. trade representative Robert Strauss advised Japanese companies on trade and foreign investment issues. Former senator Frank Church and former CIA director William Colby lobbied for Japanese companies.

Some of these former public officials refused to be described as lobbyists. Former State Department official Stanton Anderson, a lobbyist for numerous Japanese companies, insisted that he was a "trade-policy specialist," not a lobbyist.[40] Former Nixon administration counsel Leonard Garment, who represented Toshiba, said, "I am not really a lobbyist, I am a trial lawyer."[41] Former U.S. trade representative Robert Strauss, who advised Japanese companies, explained, "I don't lobby. I want to be helpful, but I don't know a fucking thing about it."* Of these, only Strauss had a point, but not a very good one. According to the legal definition of lobbying, which lobbyists themselves helped to write, a lawyer did not lobby unless he or she actually buttonholed a Congressmember on behalf of a client. Strauss, Clark Clifford, and the other "superlawyers" usually didn't do this work themselves. They attracted the client to their firm, gave the company advice, spoke and wrote on the relevant issues, but then let junior members of the firm do the actual lobbying. Meanwhile, the Congressmembers or White House officials knew that the message was ultimately coming from them.

These lawyer lobbyists bore the same relationship to the older elite of Theodore Roosevelt, Stimson, Brandeis, and Frankfurter that policy groups like Heritage and the American Council for Capital Formation bore to Brookings and the CED. Just as the American Council for Capital Formation aspired to be seen as a CED, Strauss wanted to be seen as a Stimson. In the short run, this strategy of deception worked, but in the long run, it proved to be self-defeating and corrosive.

By becoming business lobbyists, the former officials deprived the country of responsible mediating voices. By making it appear that even the most distinguished Americans could be bought, they contributed to

*Strauss is even touchier about being named as a lobbyist for the Japanese. When Strauss feared that former Commerce Department official Clyde Prestowitz was going to name him in his book, he got Richard Rivers, Strauss's former deputy at USTR and a partner at Akin, Gump, to call Prestowitz. Prestowitz recalled, "His firm was retained by Toyota. He was on the board of directors for Toyota USA. When I was writing my book, his firm got wind I might name him. Dick Rivers called me. . . . He explained that Toyota came, but we said we'd only do legal work. You get into this gray area. But the reason his law firm was singled out was because of who he was" (interview with author).

public cynicism about all political opinion, including that of elites. Like the social scientists who lent their name to supply-side economics or to outlandish estimates of regulatory harm, they undermined the tradition of dispassionate expertise on which twentieth-century American democracy had relied.

The Kissinger Precedent

The single act that contributed most to public cynicism about elite opinion was former Secretary of State Henry Kissinger's establishment of Kissinger Associates, his own global consulting firm, in 1982. Before joining the Nixon administration in 1969, Kissinger had been a professor of government at Harvard and was also on retainer to Nelson Rockefeller. But by the time he left office in 1976, he was one of the most famous and respected men in the world. His opinion on any subject from Somalia to soccer carried great weight with government officials around the world and with the general public.

Kissinger could have followed the course of two other famous public officials, George Kennan and Paul Nitze. After serving in the State Department in the Truman administration, Kennan accepted an appointment at Princeton's Institute for Advanced Study, where for the next four decades he had enormous impact on American foreign policy through his books, articles, and public statements. Nitze, after resigning from the Nixon administration in 1973, established the Committee on the Present Danger, through which he almost single-handedly transformed U.S.-Soviet relations during the 1970s. But Kissinger chose instead to cash in on his own fame and reputation by setting up the world's most prestigious consulting service.

He himself tried to keep the entire operation secret. The Park Avenue office wasn't even listed in the building's directory. But on the basis of financial forms filed by his clients and disclosure statements from former employees who joined the government, journalists were able to construct a rough picture of what went on. Kissinger initially charged American and foreign banks and businesses $200,000 a year to provide advice and consultation. He charged them up to $150,000 a month for helping with concrete problems. These were huge sums in the early 1980s.

Kissinger denied that he used the reputation and contacts he had acquired as Secretary of State to open doors for his clients, but it appears that he did so frequently. In Asia, and particularly China, any businessman who wanted to see a government official needed an intermediary or door-opener like Kissinger. Explained Roger Sullivan, the former president of the National Council for U.S.-China Trade, "The Chinese have all the traditional views toward business. It's crass, lower-class. Higher-level officials don't like businessmen that much. You have to have someone else with you if you want to see them."[42] Kissinger opened doors for American Express, American International Group, GTE, H. J. Heinz, ITT, and other companies that employed him. He was equally influential in Singapore, Malaysia, and Indonesia. And he could command audiences in Mexico, where many of his clients had interests, and in the Persian Gulf.

The architect of Nixon's China opening also maintained political ties to the Chinese government. In 1987, China's ambassador asked Kissinger to set up what he called a "lobby" to create U.S. support for China. Kissinger created the American-China Society, which he ran out of Kissinger Associates and which held luncheons and dinners at which visiting Chinese officials met with American businessmen and opinion makers. Kissinger denied that it was a lobby, and legally it was not. But it was a perfect example of what political scientists call "grassroots lobbying." It didn't affect legislation or governmental action directly, but it tried to change the political environment in which decisions about U.S.-Chinese relations were made.

While he was running Kissinger Associates, setting up the American-China Society, and serving as a partner in an investment scheme in China called China Ventures, Kissinger continued to comment on world affairs. He was on retainer from ABC and also had a column that was syndicated by the *Los Angeles Times*. Much of what he wrote pertained directly to his business and his clients. He promoted U.S. government help for countries that couldn't pay their debts to American banks, some of which were his clients. He defended authoritarian rulers in Asia from whom he was receiving favors. Yet even though he had a very direct and immediate financial stake in what he wrote, Kissinger was merely identified as a former Secretary of State. Neither ABC nor the *Los Angeles Times* cited his interests as the head of Kissinger Associates. Instead, he spoke and wrote as a high-ranking member of the foreign policy establishment. That gave his opinions added cachet and credibility, and in turn enhanced his ability to attract clients and open doors.*

Like Corcoran, Kissinger set an example that other members of the foreign policy elite followed. He himself hired former Undersecretary of State Lawrence Eagleburger and former national security advisor Brent Scowcroft. He inspired Alexander Haig, after he was forced to resign as Reagan's Secretary of State in July 1982, to set up his own version of Kissinger Associates, called Worldwide Associates.[43] By the 1990s, one prominent former official after another was setting up a "Group" or an "Associates" in his or her own name. On K Street, such practices were seen as an effective way to make money. But they thoroughly compromised the ideal of the disinterested public servant. They confirmed the public's perception that everyone was for sale.

*In 1989, Kissinger spoke on ABC television and wrote in his *Los Angeles Times* column urging that the United States not overreact to the Tiananmen massacre in China. When *Wall Street Journal* reporter John Fialka (Sept. 12, 1989) revealed that Kissinger had financial ties to China and to clients with interests in China, some newspapers belatedly began acknowledging his business interests, but still did not say whether they had any relationship to what he was writing about. In 1992, the *Washington Post* began accompanying his columns with the words, "The writer, former secretary of state, is president of Kissinger Associates, an international consulting firm which has clients with business interests in many countries abroad."

[8]

The Conservative Crack-up

Many conservatives believed Ronald Reagan's victory in 1980 had ushered in a political realignment even more dramatic than the liberal realignment that Roosevelt's victory in 1932 had brought about. They spoke of "the Reagan revolution." Wrote conservative columnists Rowland Evans and Robert Novak, "Not since the political threshold year of 1932 had a change of political power resonated with the promise of real change in government policy. But even the coming of the New Deal forty-eight years earlier could not compare with the arrival of Reagan in Washington in its revolutionary portents."[1] Reagan's victory and his first term did decisively tilt American politics away from the liberal spirit of the sixties and from the model of democratic pluralism that the New Deal had established. It also witnessed the consolidation on K Street of a new power base in American politics. But Reagan's governing coalition of business and the very diverse conservative movement barely survived his two terms in office. By the end of the 1980s, it was in disarray.

The Reagan majority collapsed partly because of its own success. By thoroughly defeating the movements of the sixties and the labor movement, it removed the outside threat that had united business and conservatives. By helping to speed the Cold War's end, the Reagan administration also deprived conservatives of the single issue on which they could all unite. But the Reagan coalition, like the business coalition of the

1920s or the New Deal coalition, also had to contend with an economic downturn—one that its own policies had helped to bring about. This downturn undermined the alliance between business and the conservative movement and eventually contributed to defections from the conservative ranks.

Business Defectors

Beginning in the early 1970s, business leaders, bankers, and lobbyists in Washington had united against what they believed to be a revolutionary threat from the labor, consumer, and environmental movements. With the dissipation of that threat—which was wildly overstated to begin with—the potential for internal discord *within* business ranks recurred. In 1986, high-tech and service industries fought with rust belt companies over the bipartisan tax simplification bill—hotels and software developers were happy to get rid of loopholes in exchange for lower corporate tax rates, while Charls Walker's auto and steel companies wanted to hang onto their credits and subsidies. Businesses and banks also argued about whether the corporate raiders and junk bond specialists should be disciplined. And they quarreled about the deficit, with *Fortune* 500 CEOs and top-tier investment bankers urging a tax increase to cut the deficit, while small business and Wall Street speculators held out against any tax increases.

But what really turned business leaders against each other and against the Republican conservatives was the continuing difficulty of adjusting to a post–Bretton Woods world. In the 1980s the country faced yawning trade deficits, concentrated in manufacturing, and growing budget deficits. The trade deficit rose from $27 billion in 1979 to $159 billion in 1987. In 1979 the trade deficit had largely been brought about by oil imports. By 1987, more than half the deficit was in manufactured goods from Japan ($57 billion) and Western Europe ($27.5 billion), while the deficit with OPEC countries was only $13.7 billion.

The trade deficit stemmed from Japanese trade barriers, which kept out American steel, semiconductors, and automobiles, and from the failure of American companies to keep up with their competitors in new technology and work organization. During the 1980s, Japan's leading automobile companies became capable of producing better cars for lower costs, irrespective of wages.[2] From 1980 to 1988, the United States lost 46 percent of the world market in automobiles, 36 percent in computers, 26 percent in microelectronics, and 17 percent in machine tools.[3] In the early 1950s the nation had produced almost 100 percent of its consumer electronics, but by the late 1980s its share of this rapidly growing market was 5 percent.[4]

Reagan's supply-side plan promised to eliminate the budget deficit by 1983, but the deficit soared from $40.2 billion in 1980 to $149 billion in 1988.[5] The nation accumulated more federal debt in the Reagan years than it had accumulated during the previous two hundred years. From 1980 to 1990, federal debt went from 34 to 59 percent of GNP, and interest payments on the debt rose from 9 to 15 percent of the budget, contributing further to the annual deficits and posing the threat of interest rate rises that could have brought about economic collapse.[6] In the past, budget deficits had played a useful role in mitigating economic downturns, but the deficits of the 1980s depressed the economy as much as they stimulated it. These deficits ensured that the real interest rates (the nominal rate minus inflation) that banks charged business borrowers would remain unusually high. From 1966 to 1980, real interest rates hovered around 1.25 percent; from 1981 to 1990, they were generally above 5.5 percent and as high as 8.1 percent. By the mid-1980s, business leaders were beginning to pressure the administration to hold down the deficit.*

*Some Reagan administration officials argued that our trade deficit was the result of our budget deficit, a novel doctrine that became extremely popular in Tokyo. There was a connection between the two deficits, but it was not what the administration economists claimed. In the early 1980s, the Reagan administration could have stemmed the rising trade deficit with Japan by pressuring the Japanese to eliminate their extensive barriers to American imports and by reducing the American budget deficit, which would have reduced consumer demand for imports. But it chose not to do this. It was unwilling to risk antagonizing Japan, which was an important Cold War ally, and to reduce the budget deficits, which were primarily caused by tax cuts and increases in military spending. Instead, as Taggart Murphy, a former banker turned economic historian, showed in his book *The Weight of the Yen* (New York, 1996), the Reagan administration struck a devil's bargain with Japan. While the administration largely ignored Japanese trade barriers to American goods, the Japanese used the enor-

In 1988, as the Federal Reserve began raising interest rates in response to rising deficits and falling unemployment, economic growth began to slow; it stopped altogether in the summer of 1990. The economy would not fully recover until 1996.[7]

Beginning in the mid-1980s, business leaders began to disagree vehemently over how, and whether, the government should respond to the decline of American manufacturing and to the threat posed by Japanese and Western European manufacturers. In the early 1980s, liberal intellectuals and maverick investment banker Felix Rohatyn had called for a government "industrial policy" to make American firms more competitive. By Reagan's second term, some of his supporters in the business community were beginning to reconsider their opposition to big government and to industrial policy. The most important defector was John Young, the CEO of Hewlett-Packard—not only because he was so widely admired among businessmen, but also because of the way he came to his conclusion that the conservative approach was wrong.

In 1983 the Reagan administration tried to head off Rohatyn and the liberal Democrats' support for industrial policy by co-opting the issue. Carefully avoiding the term "industrial policy," the White House set up a President's Commission on Industrial Competitiveness, and they asked Young to head it.[8] A lifelong Republican, Young had already become worried about "losing to Japan."[9] He wanted a serious, nonpartisan commission rather than the typical letterhead group that would rubber-stamp the administration's opposition to market intervention. "We need to realize that Republicans and Democrats, management and labor, smokestack and high-technology have more interests in common than we might have presumed," Young told a House committee.[10]

Young objected when White House counsel Edwin Meese presented him with a list of members that included no one from labor. Meese proposed to find labor members, but admitted to Young two weeks later that

---

mous surplus in dollars that they were accumulating from the U.S. trade deficit to buy up American factories, office buildings, movie studios, farms, golf courses, and Treasury bills. By shipping dollars back to the United States, the Japanese saved the U.S. administration from having to finance the deficit through double-digit interest rates that would have choked off the recovery.

the administration didn't know any labor officials. Young found them himself. The White House had wanted a report finished before the 1984 election, but Young—not eager to become caught up in the election—waited until the next year to preview "Global Competition: the New Reality" at a cabinet meeting. Young's report violated a number of conservative taboos. He wanted government to spend more money on worker training and education, and he wanted to fund civilian research and development into applied technology. He was concerned about the diversion of scientists and engineers into military work, and rejected the outdated view that military technology would create net benefits for the civilian economy through spin-offs. He also proposed new cabinet-level departments of trade and of science and technology. The White House, displeased with the report, decided not to issue it under its own name, but under that of the Commerce Department—which meant that it would not be taken seriously by the press. Young's commission was disbanded and he returned to Palo Alto.

Later in 1985, Alexander Trowbridge, the president of the NAM, visited Young. Trowbridge, who had been Secretary of Commerce in the Johnson administration, had become worried about the rising deficits under Reagan and about the administration's indifference to the decline of manufacturing industry. Trowbridge offered Young $75,000 to start up a council on competitiveness as a private organization. In August 1986, Young opened the council on Seventeenth Street just north of the White House. Young's executive committee was composed of business and labor leaders, university presidents, prominent scientists, and newspaper and magazine publishers. In its composition and its insistence on being above the factional fray, Young's group was very much in the tradition of the elite policy organization.

Over the next six years, the Council on Competitiveness issued a series of major reports calling for more spending on education and on infrastructure, on civilian research and development, and on applied technology rather than simply pure science. Young and his two directors, Alan Magazine and Kent Hughes (who had worked for Senator Vance Hartke when he was championing Burke-Hartke), became adept at capturing the attention of the business press and of Democrats and moderate Republicans. The council gained currency for the idea that there were "critical technologies" that were important not for military purposes, but for the nation to retain its place in the world economy.

Young and the council failed, however, to make any headway with the Reagan or Bush administrations. The Bush administration set up its own Council on Competitiveness under Vice President J. Danforth Quayle, but Quayle's council became merely a White House back-channel for businesses that wanted to fight environmental or worker safety regulations. When council members met with Quayle, he was less than interested. Recalled Alan Magazine:

> We brought in a Who's Who of top corporate and academic leaders, who . . . kept regaling Quayle with the recommendations we had. Every now and then he would look up from his food and he'd ask a question, just to get it going. He didn't make one declarative sentence the entire time we were there. It was as though he didn't understand these issues and couldn't care less.[11]

When Young, John Sculley of Apple Computer, John Akers of IBM, and other council members visited White House chief of staff John Sununu, they met a similar fate. That meeting at the White House marked a turning point for Young and for Sculley, who, like Young, had been a lifelong Republican. In 1992, when the council attempted to interest the presidential candidates in its work, the Clinton campaign was the most receptive. Young and Sculley met with Clinton just before the Democratic convention. When the two men complained that Clinton didn't have a technology policy, he asked them to draft one. Their report, "Technology: the Engine of Economic Growth," became the campaign's position paper, and in September 1992, Young, Sculley, and twenty-nine other Silicon Valley CEOs—most of whom had been either Republicans or Independents—endorsed the Democratic nominee. The endorsement helped Clinton and the Democrats. Many business leaders, including Young's predecessor at Hewlett-Packard, David Packard, continued to endorse Bush and the Republicans, but what had been an unbreakable link to conservative Republicans was broken.

Another key Republican defector was Clyde Prestowitz. At the same time that Young was founding his private policy group, Prestowitz, counselor to Secretary of Commerce Malcolm Baldrige, was negotiating a semiconductor agreement with Japan. Prestowitz, a former foreign service officer and businessman in Tokyo, spoke fluent Japanese and had an extensive knowledge of Japan's trade strategy. In December 1982, after Prestowitz and other Commerce Department officials had visited Japan, they had presented a report to Reagan and the cabinet in which they warned that the United States was "losing ground and was likely to continue to do so unless new policies were developed."[12] Reagan's budget director David Stockman and other administration economists had rebuked them, and Reagan himself showed little interest in the subject. By the time Prestowitz was negotiating the semiconductor agreement, eleven of the thirteen American companies had been driven out of business by their Japanese competition, which was "dumping" their goods on the U.S. market well below the prices they were being sold for in Japan. Prestowitz worried that the agreement was too little, too late to save the American semiconductor industry.

Prestowitz had been raised on the economics of free trade internationalism, but as Japanese firms, protected by their own formal and informal trade barriers, began to drive American firms out of business, he began to rethink his position. He continued to support free trade when it was reciprocal, but he rejected free trade as a unilateral strategy for the United States to follow. Prestowitz also became enraged at former American officials who were lobbying for the Japanese and taking their side during the semiconductor negotiations. "When Americans represent those people in the political dealing in Washington, they unwittingly or wittingly become instruments of foreign national policy, which is sometimes aimed at undermining American interests or overtaking American interests," he explained.[13]

After the agreement was signed, Prestowitz left the Commerce Department for the Carnegie Endowment in Washington to write a book about U.S.-Japanese relations. Published in 1988, *Trading Places: How We Allowed Japan to Take the Lead* attracted considerable attention in Congress and among corporate and business officials who were becoming worried about Japan's challenge. One businessman who was particularly impressed with Prestowitz was South Carolina billionaire Roger Milliken, the CEO of Milliken & Co., the country's largest family-owned textile company. Milliken had been one of principal funders of the conservative movement. He had given money to *The National Review* since 1955; he had underwritten the Goldwater campaigns of 1960 and 1964; and he had been a major contributor to the Heritage Foundation in the 1970s. As a textile manufacturer, Milliken had always been concerned about the threat from low-wage foreign imports. By the 1980s he had become an out-and-out opponent of the free trade orthodoxy that prevailed in Washington. John Nash, Milliken's Washington lobbyist, explained the textile magnate's enthusiasm for Prestowitz's book. "It was written by a Republican who was on our side," he said.[14] That summer, Milliken bought a copy of *Trading Places* for every delegate at the Democratic and Republican conventions. He also encouraged Prestowitz to set up a think tank or policy group that would promote a tougher line on trade.

Two years later, Prestowitz founded the Economic Strategy Institute. Milliken provided a million dollars and sublet an office on the same floor of the institute's Connecticut Avenue headquarters. But Prestowitz, like Young, was determined that his organization not be identified with a political faction, or with business to the exclusion of labor. He got Chrysler, Ford, Motorola, Corning Glass, TRW, the AFL-CIO, the Steelworkers, the United Auto Workers, and Intel to pledge large annual grants, and he appointed Howard Samuel, who was retiring as the president of the Industrial Union Department, as a vice president. Unlike John Young's Council on Competitiveness, Prestowitz wanted a think tank that would publish research under authors' names rather than a policy group that would issue statements on behalf of its members.[15]

Prestowitz's institute became known for "powernomics"—a strategic approach to foreign trade and investment based on competing national interests rather than on a simple market model of world commerce.[16] The institute's studies accused the Bush administration of letting Japan off the hook in trade negotiations and of overestimating the benefits of a new GATT treaty. It published detailed studies of how trade agreements affected specific industries. Like Young, however, Prestowitz got blank stares from the Republican White House. In February 1992, Milliken and Chrysler gave Prestowitz money to go to New Hampshire to air the institute's views during the presidential primary. The only candidates who expressed interest were Clinton, Pat Buchanan, who was running against Bush in the primary, and Nebraska Senator Bob Kerrey, who soon dropped out. The institute itself took no position in the election, but that October, writing under his own name, Prestowitz, the former Republican, endorsed Clinton in a *Los Angeles Times* op-ed piece.

Besides trade and the deficit, the other issue that brought business into conflict with the conservatives was health care. In the late 1980s many business leaders began to worry about rising health care costs—and to demand government action to hold them down. From 1970 to 1989, employer spending on wages, counting for inflation, rose just 1 percent, while spending on health benefits rose 163 percent.[17] But the Reagan and Bush administrations, as well as the conservative think tanks, ignored business's concerns. As a result, CEOs began to consider more seriously plans for national health insurance and to make common cause with unions, social scientists, and liberal Democrats who favored these plans.

In 1986, Henry Simmons, a doctor who had served in the Department of Health, Education, and Welfare under Carter, and who had become a vice president of the advertising firm J. Walter Thompson, set up a commission of experts in health care that included academics and representatives from business and labor. Four years later, building on the interest shown in the commission's reports, Simmons organized a National Leadership Coalition for Health Care Reform that included major companies and unions as well as health care organizations. Bethlehem Steel, Burlington Coat Factory, Chrysler, Ford, General Motors, H. J. Heinz, LTV Steel, Maytag, Safeway, Scott Paper, Westinghouse, and Xerox were among the corporations.

In 1991 the coalition came out with its recommendation for a national insurance system. All employers would be required either to buy insurance for their employees or to pay into a government fund that would provide insurance. The cost would be kept down through national regulation of insurance charges. The proposal was called "pay or play" and became the basis for a bipartisan bill in Congress that was introduced the next year. Dupont and a few other companies in the original coalition found the plan too radical and dropped out, but most endorsed it. The bill never passed Congress—the Bush administration countered with a vague plan of its own—but what was significant was not the plan's details, but the fact that major corporations had endorsed a measure that was anathema to conservative Republicans.

The rift was clear, and so was the opening for a different political coalition—one that could build on the defections of Young's Council, Prestowitz's Economic Strategy Institute, and Simmons's Leadership Coalition for Health Care Reform. These organizations not only expressed business's dissatisfaction with Reagan conservatism, but they also occupied the gray area between interest groups and elite organizations. They represented the revival of the Progressive Era model and appeared to foreshadow the emergence of a new post-Reagan political system.

Conservative Schisms

While business groups were sundering their ties with conservatives, the conservative movement itself was falling apart. The new right's attempt to tie working-class Democrats and Protestant evangelicals to secular, business conservatives began to unravel. By the end of the decade, few of the organizations that had sparked the upsurge of conservative politics in the late 1970s were still standing.

The new right political strategy depended upon working-class Democrats subordinating their broader economic populism to concerns about gun control, abortion, racial integration, affirmative action, high taxes (for the wealthy as well as the working class), and the threat of Communism. These voters began returning to the Democratic column during the 1982 recession and then came back in droves during the downturn of the early 1990s. In West Virginia, for instance, Republican conservative Cleveland Benedict, a Proctor & Gamble heir and a favorite of the National Conservative Political Action Committee (NCPAC), won an open House seat in 1980, claiming that God had summoned him and Reagan to run. When he ran for reelection on similar grounds during the 1982 recession, he was soundly beaten by Democrat Robert Wise. (Benedict, presumably on God's instructions, went on to become a lobbyist in Washington for the Chamber of Commerce.) In 1986, NCPAC and Viguerie targeted nine Democrats for defeat, but lost every race. NCPAC dissolved soon afterward. By 1987, Viguerie was more than $1.5 million in debt from bad business investments, an unsuccessful race for lieutenant governor in Virginia, and mailings that failed to achieve adequate returns.[18]

The Protestant evangelicals who worked with Jerry Falwell's Moral Majority or Pat Robertson's Freedom Council in the 1980s continued to identify themselves as conservatives, but they began to change their attitude toward the conservative movement. The new right organizers and conservative political consultants had envisaged the evangelical ministers and their flocks as loyal foot soldiers, but as their numbers grew, and as Reagan and the Republican conservatives in Congress failed to deliver on abortion or school prayer, the evangelicals began to see themselves as an independent, and even leading, force in the conservative movement. They began to battle secular conservatives for control of state Republican parties and for primary nominations. In 1986, two evangelical candidates in Indiana won Congressional primary victories over conservative candidates chosen by local party officials.[19] In Iowa, Nebraska, Michigan, Minnesota, Texas, and Washington, evangelicals were on their way to taking over the state parties. In the 1988 presidential primary, Robertson challenged Congressman Jack Kemp for the conservative Republican presidential vote.

If the conservative movement sputtered during Reagan's second term, it began to break down during Bush's presidency. Most of the disparate conservatives and conservative organizations, who had backed Reagan, had been united by their fear and hatred of Soviet Communism, which they saw as an imminent threat to America's survival. The end of the Cold War, which coincided with the crumbling of the Berlin Wall in 1989, represented a personal triumph for Reagan and George Shultz, but it also spelled doom for the postwar conservative movement. Without an underlying basis for unity, the different factions and groups that had tolerated each other's existence fell to quarreling. There was no longer an overriding reason to close ranks behind candidates and parties.

Many conservatives of the 1970s and 1980s were also bound together by common assumptions about the way the economy worked. Along with the business lobbies, they believed that the principal threat to American prosperity came from government intervention in the free market at home. They blamed the stagflation of the Carter years on high taxes and growing regulatory costs. But these assumptions were severely tested by the trade and budget deficits of the 1980s and by the subsequent slowdown. The slowdown revived differences over deficits, trade, foreign investment, and immigration that had been common in American politics sixty years before, but that had been suppressed by the Cold War and by American economic superiority.

The one event that most clearly signaled the breakup of the Reagan coalition was the battle over the budget and taxes in 1990. Bush, who had pledged not to raise taxes in his 1988 campaign, announced a five-year budget agreement in October that included $140 billion in tax increases. Both the Business Roundtable and the National Association of Manufacturers had urged Bush to reach an agreement that would reduce the deficit, even if that meant raising taxes, but the Chamber of Commerce, the National Federation of Independent Business, and the supply-siders at the *Wall Street Journal* editorial page denounced it. Meanwhile, conservatives in Congress were bitterly divided over the bill. In the Senate, 23 Republicans voted for the agreement and 22 opposed it.

In the wake of the budget battle, thirty prominent conservatives met in Easton, Maryland, to discuss a primary challenge to the president in 1992. Both former Delaware governor Pierre "Pete" du Pont and Pat Buchanan were mentioned as candidates. In the Heritage Foundation's *Policy Review*, foundation vice president Burton Pines compared Bush to Theodore Roosevelt's successor William Howard Taft, warning that he would suffer the same fate as Taft, who was defeated when Roosevelt led the Progressive Republicans out of the party in 1912. The next month, of course, Bush proved his mettle in the war against Iraq, and the Easton meeting was forgotten, but it proved a portent of things to come.

The other issue that split both the business community and conservatives was trade. Before World War II, Republicans had favored high tariffs to protect American manufacturers against low-wage imports from abroad. They proudly called themselves "protectionist," but the enormous superiority of American industry after World War II undercut the arguments of protectionists. American industry didn't need protection against imports. It needed countries to revive and prosper so they could buy its exports. Postwar conservatives eventually became enthusiastic free traders, envisioning free trade on the world market as the extension of the free market at home. But beginning in the late 1960s, American industries that were threatened by foreign competition, including textiles, steel, and shoes, abandoned their unequivocal support for free trade. Some of the managers and owners of these firms had been leading conservatives, and in the 1980s they helped revive the older protectionist tradition.

In 1984, Roger Milliken withdrew his support from the Heritage Foundation when they opposed protection for U.S. textile manufacturers. Two years later, a steel company executive tore up his check in front of Heritage vice president John Von Cannon to protest the think tank's opposition to steel import quotas.[20] In the mid-1980s, Milliken threw his considerable financial support to a smaller policy group, the U.S. Business and Industrial Council. It had been founded in 1933 to fight the New Deal and had lobbied against labor unions and the minimum wage. Most of its 1,500 members were mid-sized manufacturers who did not have overseas branches and were worried about foreign imports. By the early 1980s, Business Council president Anthony Harrigan had begun to turn against free trade. By the late eighties he was describing his position as "economic nationalism" and "economic containment."[21] But the council remained an isolated dissenter within Washington conservative circles. That began to change when Pat Buchanan became an opponent of the free trade orthodoxy.

For almost fifteen years, since he had bested the Watergate Committee, Buchanan had been one of the premier conservative intellectuals. After leaving the Nixon administration, he became a successful syndicated columnist and a regular on television talk shows. In 1985 he joined the Reagan administration as its director of communications, where he became an outspoken defender of Oliver North. In 1987 he resigned to return to his column and television appearances and to write his autobiography. Buchanan had always been a free trader. When Roger Milliken came to him in 1986 for help with a textile bill, Buchanan demurred.[22] But in the first year after he left the Reagan administration, Buchanan watched with alarm how Congress and the White House dealt with Toshiba's selling submarine technology to the Soviet Union. "When Congress tried to impose sanctions," he recounted later, "U.S. lobbyists were all over Capitol Hill, pleading for amnesty—even though Toshiba had put at risk U.S. national security and the lives of American sailors. Did trade trump patriotism?"[23] That experience set in motion four years of rethinking that climaxed in his becoming one of the country's most outspoken critics of foreign trade barriers and American multinationals.

Buchanan was also instrumental in the reconsideration of another key tenet of postwar conservatism. Before World War II, many Republicans had described themselves as isolationists. Citing George Washington's and Thomas Jefferson's warning against "entangling alliances," they rejected American participation in the League of Nations and in any treaty arrangements that might have forced the nation unwittingly into war when its national interest was not directly threatened. They opposed American entry into the war against Nazi Germany until December 1941, when, after the Japanese attacked Pearl Harbor, Germany joined Japan in declaring war on the United States. After World War II, the old debates between the isolationists and internationalists temporarily revived, but the onset of the Cold War and of the global threat of Soviet Communism removed the basis for disagreement. The conservatives of the 1950s were still skittish about international institutions such as the UN and International Monetary Fund, but they did not reject American participation in a system of alliances against the Soviet Union.

With the end of the Cold War, some conservatives—calling themselves "paleoconservatives" as opposed to "neoconservatives"—began to revive the idea of America First. Many of them wrote for *Chronicles*, a small-circulation magazine published by the Rockford Institute in Rockford, Illinois. *Chronicles* opposed foreign aid and intervention, except when the nation was directly threatened, and favored restrictions on immigration (particularly of dark-skinned peasants) and on low-wage imports. By the late 1980s, *Chronicles* and the paleoconservatives were in a nasty fight with their neoconservative enemies. While the neoconservatives accused *Chronicles* and its authors of being bigots, *Chronicles* accused the neoconservatives, many of whom favored an active U.S. presence abroad, particularly in the Mideast, of wanting to subordinate the U.S. national interest to that of Israel.

By 1989, Buchanan was taking *Chronicles*' side in the debates with the neoconservatives. He denounced AEI fellow and neoconservative Ben Wattenberg's proposal for focusing U.S. foreign policy on the expansion of democracy as "messianic globaloney." "We are not the world's policeman, nor its political tutor," Buchanan wrote.[24] Buchanan acknowledged later he was deeply influenced by *Chronicles*: "They made me aware of a really totally different tradition. I used to keep [back issues of] *Chronicles* in my basement. It was one of the magazines I would hold onto because in many cases on immigration and other issues, you'd read them and they had a different perspective."[25]

In the fall of 1990, Buchanan and *Chronicles* opposed U.S. participation in the war to liberate Kuwait after the Iraqi invasion. In a highly controversial column that invited charges of anti-Semitism, Buchanan accused American Jewish neoconservatives of serving Israel by trying to get the United States to go to war against Iraq's Saddam Hussein. Buchanan's and *Chronicles*' opposition to the Gulf War did not attract extensive support among conservatives, and the furor over it obscured the popularity of his neoisolationism among many grassroots conservatives.

In September 1991, as he was beginning to consider running against Bush, Buchanan restated his position more generally in a *Washington Post* op-ed piece:

> At the American Enterprise Institute, Brookings and Heritage Foundation seminars, phrases like America First may yet get a big howl—as the boys decide the fate of the Punjab—but in a nation that hasn't seen real growth since Old Dutch rode off to Rancho Cielo, questions are being asked: What are we getting for $15 billion in foreign aid? Why, 46 years after WWII, are we defending Germany and Japan while they steal our markets? Why must we pacify the Persian Gulf when women walking dogs in Central Park are slashed to death by bums?[26]

That position—rejecting the millenarian premise of twentieth-century American foreign policy—won considerable support in 1992 and would gain further adherents over the decade. With the revival of protectionism and isolationism, there was no longer a single position on any major foreign policy issue—from the enlargement of NATO to human rights in China to GATT and the World Trade Organization—on which conservatives could claim unity. The end of the Cold War had not laid the basis for a new consensus, but rather for chaos and dissension.

* * *

While the economic downturn of the late 1980s befuddled business conservatives in Washington and New York, it gave new impetus to Christian conservatives by providing seeming proof of their premillennial thesis that the nation was in inexorable decline. Just as the ranks of conservative evangelicals swelled during the pessimistic early 1970s—evidenced in the popularity of Hal Lindsey's *The Late Great Planet Earth*—they expanded again in the gloom of the late 1980s. This time many of the new evangelicals joined political organizations.

Both Falwell's Moral Majority and Robertson's Freedom Council had perished in the first phase of movement decline, but in September 1989, Robertson founded the Christian Coalition and hired Ralph Reed, a protégé of ruthless Republican operative Lee Atwater, to run it. Robertson intended the coalition as the vehicle for another presidential run—he had promised his followers at a secret gathering at the Republican national convention that he would be back in 1996—but Reed turned the Coalition into an effective national political organization. By 1992 it claimed almost a million dues-paying members, an extensive network of loyal ministers and their parishioners, and was helping to field candidates all over the country.

Conservative politicians heralded the rise of the Coalition and other Christian right groups, which seemed to provide the movement with a mass base comparable to the Democrats' labor movement. But the Christian right's trajectory was different from that of other conservatives. It was deeply concerned with abortion, homosexuality, and what it claimed to be the "destruction of the family," but its members did not necessarily agree with the positions of other conservatives on economic and foreign policy. Robertson, a millionaire businessman and the son of a Virginia senator, was an upper-class Republican whose views on trade, taxes, and multinational corporations echoed those of other CEOs; but many of the Christian rank and file were economic populists who would be much closer to Buchanan and Ross Perot in 1992 than to Robertson's choice of George Bush. The only issues on which they were invariably willing to join forces with other conservatives were precisely those social issues on which many business Republicans took opposing stands.

The Christian right's political strategy was at odds with that of other conservatives. Its aim by then was not to buttress Republican candidates, but to take power itself. At the Christian Coalition's national convention in September 1992, Guy Rodgers, the national field director, explained, "I believe God is taking us to the point in the nineties where we have to learn how to govern."[27] Just as conservative evangelicals regarded mainstream Christian denominations as not being truly "Christian," the political true believers of the Christian right came to regard other conservatives as not being genuinely conservative. There was a similarity, in fact, between the Christian right and the sectarian antiwar left of the late 1960s. Randall Terry of Operation Rescue was Mark Rudd of Weatherman reborn. The Christian home schoolers were the Communards of the 1990s. As the Christian right grew in members, the battles between it and other conservatives became uglier, and in the absence of the Cold War, there was little except the prospect of transient political victory that could unite the feuding factions. In 1992 that proved insufficient, as many Christian conservatives refused to join conventional, secular conservatives in backing George Bush.

By a pollster's enumeration, there were probably many more self-identified conservatives in 1992 than there were in 1980. But in 1980, the whole was greater than the sum of its parts, while in 1992, it was far less, because each of the parts claimed to be the whole. Buchanan and the economic nationalists wanted to re-create the high-tariff isolationist party of Coolidge, while the Christian right wanted to recruit a Cromwellian army of God. Meanwhile, business leaders, worried about budget deficits, health care costs, and foreign competition, increasingly shunned their former conservative brethren; and two of the main three factions of conservatives—the Christian right and Buchanan's economic nationalists—expressed either indifference or hostility toward these same business leaders.

Popular Disaffection

When Ronald Reagan left office in January 1989, he was as popular as ever, but not the party or the movement he had helped bring to power. While Reagan's backers insisted that the 1980s were the best of times—

Wall Street Journal editorial page editor Robert Bartley would write a book, *The Seven Fat Years,* to praise Reagan's years in office—the public shared business's perception that the economy was in decline. By the late 1980s, as the Japanese began buying up prime real estate, including Rockefeller Center, and major movie studios, panic was setting in. It was evidenced in best-selling books like Paul Kennedy's *The Rise and Fall of the Great Powers* and Kevin Phillips's *The Politics of Rich and Poor*, both of which portrayed America as being in inexorable decline.[28]

In 1989 pollsters Stanley Greenberg and Celinda Lake found that 55 percent of Americans believed the country was going on the "wrong track" and only 36 percent on the "right track." Eighty-eight percent thought "foreign investors buying up American companies and land" was a serious problem; 90 percent worried about "America's trade imbalance with foreign countries"; and 87 percent were concerned about "the loss of America's lead in technology."[29] Most Americans blamed the Republicans for this decline. In 1986 the Republicans lost the Senate. In 1988 they would have lost the presidency if the Democrats had not nominated Massachusetts Governor Michael Dukakis, a remarkably inept candidate. And in 1990 the Democrats increased their margin of control in Congress.

The public also became skeptical about Reagan's message of economic individualism and his claim to be restoring political self-rule. Wall Street was wracked with a series of scandals that raised questions about whether business, left to its own devices, would act in the public interest. Dennis Levine, Ivan Boesky, and Michael Milken were the lead actors in a drama that began in May 1986 when the Securities and Exchange Commission accused Levine—a trader at Drexel Burnham Lambert—of making $12.6 million on insider profits and ended four years later with junk bond king Milken being sentenced to jail for ten years.[30] The savings-and-loan debacle, which cost taxpayers and depositors hundreds of billions of dollars, showed the fruits of Reagan era deregulation.

A spate of scandals on K Street demonstrated that the alternative to government administration was not self-rule, but the empowerment of Washington's lobbying community. During Reagan's second term, Michael Deaver, Lyn Nofziger, and other former top Reagan aides and cabinet officials were indicted for using their connections in government illegally to reap millions as lobbyists and consultants. In Deaver's first year as a lobbyist in 1985, he gleaned $4.5 million in contracts, primarily from foreign governments and companies.[31] And the slap on the wrist that the Toshiba Co. and a Norwegian firm received from Congress for selling critical submarine technology to the Soviet Union—due largely to Toshiba's massive lobbying effort on Capitol Hill—showed the power of K Street and the indifference of its lobbyists to America's national interests.

During the late 1980s the public became increasingly convinced that lobbyists representing "special interests" or "big interests" were running the government in Washington for their own benefit. The University of Michigan election studies showed a steady climb of voters who believed that "government is pretty much run by a few big interests looking out for themselves" from 55 percent in 1984 to 64 percent in 1988 to 75 percent in 1992. (By contrast, it was 29 percent in 1964.)[32] In the spring of 1992, one poll found that 83 percent of Americans believed that "special-interest groups have more influence than voters," 74 percent believed that "Congress is largely owned by special-interest groups," and 69 percent believed that "the current incumbents will *never* reform the political system."[33] In 1992, third-party candidate Ross Perot would crystallize this public disgust with lobbyists and special interests into a viable presidential candidacy. At the same time, there was a growing conviction that government had to do something about the nation's economic and social problems. In an ABC/*Washington Post* poll, the proportion believing that "government should do more to solve our country's problems" rose from 38 percent in January 1985 to 45 percent in September 1990 to 49 percent in June 1992.[34] These sentiments represented a repudiation of the Reagan revolution and seemed to provide an opening to a new democratic pluralism.

There was also a visceral disgust with the individualism that Reagan encouraged. Prosperity in the age of Reagan was also inordinately concentrated among the wealthiest Americans, while many poor and working- and middle-class Americans did worse than before. (From 1979 to 1989, the earnings of men in the highest fifth of the income brackets increased by 9 percent while men in the lowest three-fifths saw their earnings decline by 6 to 11 percent.[35] From 1983 to 1989, the top 0.5

percent of the population reaped 55 percent of the increase in household wealth.[36]) The contrast between boarded-up factory towns and Wall Street opulence fed a growing revulsion with the ethic of greed and individualism that flourished during the age of Reagan. As Kevin Phillips put it in *The Politics of Rich and Poor*:

> The 1980s were a second Gilded Age, in which many Americans made and spent money abundantly. Yet as the decade ended, too many stretch limousines, too many enormous incomes and too much high fashion foreshadowed a significant shift of mood. A new plutocracy . . . had created a new target for populist reaction.[37]

The counterreaction took the form of a growing idealism and altruism. In 1981 the percentage of students describing themselves as "conservative" outnumbered those calling themselves "liberal"—by 19.6 to 18.1 percent—for the first time since 1966 when the survey reported in *The American Freshman* began. These numbers stayed relatively even until 1989, when the percentage calling themselves "liberal" began to climb. By 1992, 5.4 percent more students described themselves as "liberal" than "conservative." The proportion of students who wanted to "become involved in programs to clean up the environment" climbed from 26.1 percent in 1989 to 33.6 percent in 1992. During the same period, the proportion of those who wanted to "help promote racial understanding" grew from 35.3 percent to 42 percent.[38]

There was also an organized backlash to the Reagan years. Both the environmental and consumer movements picked up new members in response to Reagan's attempt to sell off federal lands, privatize the parks, and gut the Environmental Protection Agency and the Federal Trade Commission. The ten leading environmental groups, including the Sierra Club, the World Wildlife Fund, the Natural Resources Defense Council, and Greenpeace, took in $218 million in 1985; by 1990, they were bringing in $514 million. Membership in these groups went from 3.3 million in 1985 to 7.2 million in 1990.[39] Local organizations also sprouted up. In 1986, the Citizens Clearinghouse for Hazardous Wastes, which grew out of the Love Canal incident, oversaw activities of 1,700 local organizations trying to combat chemical contamination; by 1990, it boasted about 7,000 groups.[40]

The environmental groups adopted a range of political approaches—from the more sedate Environmental Defense Fund to the radical Greenpeace and Earth First! to the Green parties. Greenpeace alone went from 240,000 members in 1980 to 1.5 million members a decade later.[41] The growth of the movement reflected a growth in public support for environmental protection. One 1990 Gallup Poll revealed that 76 percent of Americans considered themselves "environmentalists." A poll the same year by the *New York Times*/CBS found that 74 percent of Americans believed that "protecting the environment is so important that requirements and standards cannot be too high, and continuing environmental improvements must be made regardless of cost"—up from only 45 percent who agreed with this statement in 1981.[42]

In November 1988, Nader and the consumer movement, which had failed two years earlier to defeat a referendum in California restricting the right to sue corporations, successfully passed an initiative in California that rolled back automobile and property insurance rates. It was the movement's first initiative victory and led to efforts in other states to curb insurance costs. Feminist and civil rights organizations also prospered. In 1988 these organizations successfully lobbied Congress to override Reagan's veto of a bill that strengthened the hand of government in punishing institutions that practiced racial and sexual discrimination.

There were even signs of life in the labor movement. Unions that organized public workers and workers in the service sector actually began to increase their membership. From 1980 to 1993, the Service Employees International Union (SEIU) increased its membership by 400,000. The United Food and Commercial Workers increased the number of unionized workers in retail grocery stores from 67 percent in 1988 to 72 percent in 1993 and in meat packing from 50 to 65 percent. The American Federation of County, State, and Municipal Employees (AFCSME) grew so rapidly that it was on the verge of displacing the Teamsters as the largest union. Several major unions, including the Teamsters and the United Mine Workers, ousted corrupt leaders and installed reform administrations.[43]

* * *

For all these harbingers of a new progressivism and democratic pluralism, however, there were equal indications that the country might not be ready for a new era of reform. The growth of the environmental, consumer, and civil rights organizations during the late 1980s was largely in the size of their budgets and in their paper memberships. Outside of public and some other service employees, union membership continued to decline—down to only 16 percent of the nonagricultural workforce by 1992. Liberals in the late 1980s did not have a mobilized citizenry behind them. On the other side, while conservatives and their business allies had lost their governing majority, they remained a considerable force on K Street and in the government.

During the Bush years, liberal groups blocked legislation that deeply offended their constituencies, but, outside of a civil rights bill and a small and belated increase in the minimum wage, they failed to pass any legislation of their own. A renewal of the Clean Air Act passed, but only after its key provisions were shaped by business lobbyists who wanted to delay the implementation of tougher standards. The bill that most clearly epitomized the new balance of forces was Bush's heralded 1990 budget, which split the conservative movement. It contained no reform initiatives. It cut some social programs while modestly increasing others. It raised taxes across the board, but unlike the Reagan budgets did not egregiously favor the wealthy or business. Fiscally speaking, it was an important corrective to the bloated budgets of the 1980s, but it failed to alter the balance of political or social forces in the country.

The Reagan years and the business counteroffensive also left their mark on popular sentiment toward reform. In 1964, on the eve of the Great Society, 76 percent of Americans said they could "trust the government in Washington to do what is right" either "most of the time" or "just about always." By 1992, this percentage had fallen to 29 percent.[44] This was an indication of dissatisfaction with the Bush administration, but it also reflected a residual distrust of government itself that a new administration would find it difficult to overcome.

[9]

The Frustration of Reform

During his 1992 presidential campaign, Bill Clinton promised that his new administration would be similar to Franklin Roosevelt's New Deal. "I would want to have another one of those hundred day periods like Roosevelt did. I think the American people are looking for real action," Clinton declared in August just after the Democratic convention.[1] The next February, Clinton journeyed to Roosevelt's birthplace of Hyde Park and reiterated his admiration of the father of the New Deal. "We are in a rut," he said in Hyde Park. What we need is Roosevelt's style of "bold, persistent experimentation."[2] Two years later it was Clinton himself who was in a rut, and it was Newt Gingrich's time to crow. After the Republicans had won the House of Representatives for the first time since 1952, Gingrich, who was expected to become the new speaker of the House, told ABC News, "I represent a revolution."[3] Gingrich then compared himself to Mark Hanna and Theodore Roosevelt.

These bold comparisons typified a decade of politics in which the historical pretensions of political leaders far outweighed their actual achievements. In Clinton's first two years, he advanced a serious agenda for reform that had been forged by liberal elites during their time in the political wilderness. While Clinton compared it to the New Deal, it was, in fact, an attempt to resume the spirit of the early 1960s. Clinton's efforts initially enjoyed popular support, but were blocked by the revival of the alliance between conservative Republicans and business lobbies on

K Street. Gingrich then attempted to marshal those same forces in order to carry forward the "Reagan revolution," but found that while sufficient to stymie a liberal agenda, they were not strong enough to pass their own agenda. Both Clinton and Gingrich scaled the rhetoric of Mount Rushmore, but what they actually accomplished was a continuation of the stalemate that had marked Bush's presidency.

The New Liberal Elites

Two groups of policy elites played a critical role in defining Clinton's initial agenda. One was the Democratic Leadership Council (DLC), which was founded in 1985 to move the party away from what it called "liberal fundamentalism." The other was a loosely defined collection of intellectuals who had been reformers rather than revolutionaries during the late sixties and who had spent fifteen years trying to recast the liberal agenda. Clinton had close ties to both groups. He had been a founding member of the DLC and was its president in 1990 and 1991. He and his wife, Hillary Rodham Clinton, were charter members of the post–new left intelligentsia, many of whom he had met when he was a Rhodes Scholar, a Yale Law School student, or a worker on McGovern's presidential campaign in 1972.

The DLC was started by Al From, a young political operative who had been director of the House Democratic Caucus during Reagan's first term. From was a protégé of Senator Edmund Muskie, whom he backed for president in 1972, and of Bob Strauss, with whom he worked in the Carter White House. After Walter Mondale's landslide defeat in 1984, From became convinced that the Democratic Party had to move to the center by distancing itself from the AFL-CIO, the National Organization for Women, Jesse Jackson's Rainbow Coalition, and other liberal groups that had dominated the Democratic National Committee and set the tone for national campaigns.[4] With help from Strauss (who raised much of the initial money), Senator Sam Nunn, and Virginia Governor Chuck Robb, From established the DLC with himself as executive director and Will Marshall, who had worked with From on Capitol Hill, as the policy director. In the first year, 110 politicians signed up, including

Congressmen Dick Gephardt and Al Gore, Arizona Governor Bruce Babbitt, Delaware Senator Joe Biden, and Clinton, all of whom would later run for president.

The DLC began as a factional group within the Democratic Party. At the outset, many of its proposals, such as the creation of "Super-Tuesday" presidential primaries in the South, were designed to enable someone like Robb to capture the Democratic presidential election, but after Bush defeated Dukakis in 1988, From and Marshall established a research organization, the Progressive Policy Institute, to develop a platform for a Democratic candidate to run on. The DLC and PPI produced a hybrid of positions. Some—intended to "inoculate" Democrats against Republican attacks by moving the party to the center on capital punishment, affirmative action, and other hot-button issues—were purely tactical; some positions on trade and statements on labor unions mimicked Reagan conservatism; but other PPI stances broke new ground for liberalism.

From and Marshall promoted a national service program—originally developed by Northwestern University sociologist Charles Moskos—that would require young people who wanted student loans to serve in either the armed forces or a new citizens corps that would assist the poor and help in state conservation efforts. The DLC evoked John Kennedy's nationalism—"Ask not what your country can do for you, but what you can do for your country"—in presenting this proposal.[5] From and Marshall also unveiled a welfare reform plan based on the concept of "mutual obligation." After two years, welfare recipients would be given a choice between taking a private sector job or enrolling in the national service corps. It also championed a new strategy of "reinventing government" developed by policy intellectual David Osborne that was intended to defend government's historic role by improving its efficiency. Its central idea was summed up in the slogan that government should "steer, not row."[6] With these efforts, the DLC was trying to counter the individualism of the Reagan era with a communitarian and nationalist politics that recalled, but also went beyond, the politics of the early 1960s.

The other key group consisted of liberal intellectuals who had worked together in different commissions and campaigns and had written for the same publications, and who were attempting to develop a new politics that took account of the post–Bretton Woods world economy. They included academics (Robert Reich, Derek Shearer, and Laura Tyson), lawyers (Mickey Kantor, Harold Ickes, and Susan Thomases), businessmen and business consultants (Ira Magaziner and Eli Segal), and journalists (Strobe Talbott, Robert Kuttner, and Sidney Blumenthal). Many of them had attended the annual Conference on Alternative State and Local Politics in the 1970s or had served on the two Cuomo Commissions during the late 1980s. They had read and written for *Working Papers*, *The Washington Monthly*, *The New Republic*, and *The American Prospect*. And they had worked on the Hart, Mondale, Dukakis, and Jackson campaigns.

They had been part of the sixties new left, but sought reform rather than "revolution now." They were much closer to the sunny utopianism of early SDS, the Kennedy administration, and Martin Luther King's "I have a dream" speech than to the dark apocalyptic spirit of Weatherman and the Black Panther Party. They had opposed the Vietnam War because they thought it violated America's democratic mission in the world. Some of them initially thought of themselves as socialists, but they eventually became progressive elites in the tradition of Croly, Lippmann, Frankfurter, Tugwell, Arthur Schlesinger, Jr., and Nader. They believed that through the application of social science they could devise programs that would solve the country's deepest problems. They believed in government and what Reich called the "power of public ideas." They differed from the progressives and New Dealers primarily in their social and political priorities. They had come of age during the sixties, when the "labor question" ceased to preoccupy the nation's intellectual and political leaders. Instead, their framework was shaped primarily by the civil rights, antiwar, feminist, consumer, and environmental movements.

Like Nader, they wanted to create democratic structures that checked the power of corporations. Indeed, many of them, like Derek Shearer, got their start working for Nader. They shared the utopian impulse of the early new left, typified by "The Triple Revolution." They believed that through government planning, people could solve the major problems of society—from access to health care to the competitiveness of American businesses. Shearer advocated European-style planning, while

Reich and Magaziner embraced an "industrial policy" and later a "national economic strategy" that was borrowed from Japan's MITI. They were internationalists who believed that the United States benefited from the elimination of trade barriers, but they fretted that under the mantle of free trade, multinational corporations were forcing down wages and environmental standards.

The leading figure was Robert Reich. Reich had been on the respectable fringe of the antiwar movement, working in 1968 in Eugene McCarthy's presidential campaign. When he came back from Oxford as a Rhodes Scholar in 1971, he told a reporter that European-style democratic socialism was "inevitable" for the United States.[7] But his thinking evolved into a much more typically American, and progressive, mixture of public regulation and private initiative. What became most important to Reich was using the power of government to subject the private market to overall public direction.[8]

In *Minding America's Business*, written with Ira Magaziner in 1981, Reich proposed putting federal research and development funding, antitrust policy, and trade relief under a new agency that would coordinate federal policy to improve industries' competitiveness. This agency would use the promise of subsidies and trade and antitrust relief to exact changes in behavior from industry. Ten years later, Reich was still worried about competitiveness, but he now had a different take on how the United States could adjust to post–Bretton Woods international capitalism. In *The Work of Nations*, Reich argued that because of the ability of corporations to transfer operations wherever they pleased, there would soon be no such thing as a "national corporation."[9] Government policy, Reich maintained, should be oriented toward making American workers more competitive and therefore able to attract the most profitable enterprises of the future, whatever their national origin:

> The real economic challenge facing the United States in the years ahead . . . is to increase the potential value of what its citizens can add to the global economy, by enhancing their skills and capacities and by improving their means of linking those skills and capacities to the world market.[10]

Within this new economy, Reich also worried about the tendency of the new information technology to divide the workers into a "fortunate fifth" that enjoyed its benefits and a mass of lower-paid service workers who lacked health insurance and pensions and access to the kind of worker training that could lift them onto a higher tier. Reich favored

> public spending within each nation in any manner that enhanced the capacities of its citizens to lead full and productive lives—including pre- and postnatal care, childcare and preschool preparation, excellent primary and secondary education, access to college regardless of financial conditions, training and retraining, and good infrastructure.[11]

He rejected the calls for trade protection and subsidies to specifically American companies, but, echoing Burke-Hartke, he warned against trade agreements that were really designed to speed the flight of capital rather than the sale of goods. "Instead of pushing other nations to open their markets to [investments by] American firms," Reich wrote in *The New Republic* in 1991, "the U.S. trade representative should insist that foreign nations allow in the work-products of Americans."[12]

By the early 1990s a new liberal politics had emerged from these sources: Reich's ideas of a new "positive nationalism" focused on increasing the skills and decreasing the economic insecurity of American workers, the DLC's innovative social policies, Clyde Prestowitz's and John Young's emphasis on increasing American competitiveness, and the programs for national health insurance being pressed by Henry Simmons's Leadership Coalition for Health Care Reform. It was not altogether consistent, but it was a program that addressed both the weaknesses of the older liberalism, with its single-minded emphasis on welfare spending, and the failings of Reagan conservatism, with its blithe acceptance of economic inequality and insecurity.

Clinton's Promise of Reform

Clinton was as much a product of the new left as Reich or Magaziner were. Before he went to Oxford he championed civil rights in Arkansas and worked at Georgetown and in Senator William Fulbright's Washington office to end the war in Vietnam. In the 1970s and 1980s, Clinton was a participant in, and not simply an observer of, the debate over industrial policy and national economic strategy. But he was also a Southern politician who had to win reelection in a political environment dominated by Reagan conservatism and a small-state governor who had to cultivate the good will of multinational corporations and Wall Street banks. Throughout his career the two mentalities of progressive reformer and realistic Southern politician vied for supremacy, but during his 1992 campaign and his first year in office the progressive reformer was firmly in command.

Clinton adopted most of the political agenda that the DLC, the post–new left intellectuals, and other dissenters from Reagan conservatism had developed. His campaign pledge to "end welfare as we know it" and his commitment to a communitarian "new covenant" bore the mark of the DLC. His campaign manifesto, *Putting People First,* was drafted by Magaziner, Reich, and Shearer. Clinton backed both the DLC's citizens corps and welfare reform plan, Simmons's call for national health insurance, and the post–new left intellectuals' approach to worker retraining, trade, and multinational corporations. He supported large increases in public investments on education and infrastructure and called for tax reform that would discourage corporations from awarding CEOs multimillion-dollar salaries. In the months after Clinton's election, it looked as if he was going to lead the country into a major reform era. But Clinton got almost none of the things that he asked for.

Clinton backed off his plan to limit the deductions corporations could take on CEO salaries. He couldn't get Congress to increase public investment. The budget it finally passed provided less for education, bridges, water systems, and other infrastructure than the last Bush budget had projected. Republicans reduced Clinton's plan for a citizens corps to a pilot program—a contradiction in terms for a program intended to unify the national community, not to reward a few ambitious teenagers. The administration fared no better in attempting to amend the North American Free Trade Agreement (NAFTA), and in getting Congress to vote on, let alone adopt, its health care plan. In each case, the reason for defeat was the same. Business lobbyists and conservative Republicans were able to draw off enough moderate Democrats to undermine Clinton's agenda. With some programs, like Reich's plan to finance worker retraining from corporate payroll taxes, business opposition was so adamant that the administration backed off even before Clinton was inaugurated. But the most telling defeats were on NAFTA and the health insurance program.

George Bush had negotiated and signed NAFTA in 1992, but had never sent it to Congress for ratification. Like other recent trade pacts, it had as much, if not more, to do with regulating the flow of foreign investment as with reducing tariff barriers between countries. About one-fourth of the thousand-page treaty was devoted to eliminating barriers and restrictions that Mexico placed on American foreign investment and protecting American firms from the threat of expropriation. It was exactly the kind of "free trade" treaty that Reich had criticized in *The Work of Nations*.

During the campaign, Clinton couldn't decide what position to take on the treaty. His advisors were split on whether to back it. Polls showed that a majority of Americans opposed the treaty. But Shearer and Richard Rothstein, a former SDS leader who had spent a decade organizing for the textile workers, sent Clinton a series of memos urging him to back NAFTA on the condition that the treaty include the establishment of commissions that would ensure that Mexico would abide by its own strict, but laxly enforced, labor and environmental standards. Shearer and Rothstein believed that regardless of whether NAFTA passed, companies would continue to move across the border in search of lower wages and unenforced environmental regulations. What NAFTA could do was gradually bring Mexican labor and environmental standards up to those of the United States, benefiting workers on both sides of the border. Clinton endorsed their approach in a speech during the last month of the campaign, and when he took office, he instructed Mickey Kantor, the U.S. trade representative, to get the labor and environmental commissions added to the treaty.

But when Kantor made the proposal for the commissions, he ran into stiff opposition from corporate lobbyists, who had organized an umbrella lobbying group, USA*NAFTA, which was run by former Carter administration aide Anne Wexler. USA*NAFTA included over two thousand businesses. These businesses worked through other national organizations like the NAM and the Business Roundtable and set up local and state groups such as the Illinois NAFTA Coalition to pressure senators and House members.[13] The American Enterprise Institute and other business-funded think tanks also got into the act. Two AEI economists published a study estimating that the United States would be running a $7–9 billion trade surplus with Mexico and would gain 171,000 jobs by the end of 1995. (The economists later admitted that they had not included in their book a finding that over the long term, the United States would suffer a net loss of jobs.)[14] And Republican senators announced that they would not support the treaty if the commissions were included. By July of 1993, Clinton and Kantor gave in. The commissions were included in the treaty, but they lacked any enforcement or independent investigate powers.* Clinton claimed the passage of NAFTA as a victory, but the battle bitterly divided his supporters and the final result failed to include what had been most novel and positive in his own approach.

Clinton's health care program epitomized the progressive impulse of the new administration. Hillary Rodham Clinton, who was put in charge of the plan, called it "the Social Security Act of this generation, the reform that would establish the identity of the Democratic Party and be the defining legislation for generations to come."[15] The plan, modeled on a proposal from Paul Starr, a Princeton sociologist and co-editor of *The American Prospect*, and Walter Zelman, an aide to California insurance

*The labor and environmental commissions lacked the power to subpoena witnesses or to enforce their mandate, and their mandate (especially in the case of the labor commission) was extremely narrow. The environmental panel had slightly stronger powers partly because some environmental groups sought to influence rather than simply block the treaty, while the labor commission was toothless. In 1996, the labor commission asked Cornell University industrial relations researcher Kate Bronfenbrenner to submit a report on the effect that NAFTA had on union negotiations. Bronfenbrenner's report showed that by providing employers with the threat of moving, NAFTA had had a significant chilling effect on wages and union recognition efforts. But the three-nation labor commission confined the report's results to a page and a half of a 110-page report on NAFTA that it issued in June 1997 and did not issue the report itself. See the *Ithaca Journal*, May 8, 1997.

commissioner John Garamendi, set up government-regulated state and local health alliances that would negotiate costs and quality of service with a limited number of managed care plans and HMOs. Americans would automatically belong to an alliance and could choose one of these plans through the alliance. The alliance would also offer a regular fee-for-service alternative. The Starr-Zelman plan built upon the existing American system of health care, but it provided both universal access and the power to control costs and ensure quality.

Since the mid-1980s, support for a national health insurance plan had been growing. When Clinton announced his plan in September 1993, a *Washington Post*/ABC poll found that 67 percent supported it and only 20 percent were opposed.[16] The *New York Times* declared the plan was "alive on arrival."[17] After Hillary Rodham Clinton had appeared on Capitol Hill to present the plan, Republican Senator John Danforth declared categorically, "We will pass a law next year."[18] Under the leadership of SEIU's John Sweeney, the unions in the AFL-CIO resolved their differences over the various plans and agreed to back Clinton's. Businesses that were part of Simmons's National Leadership Coalition, including the major auto companies, backed the Clinton plan. More important, the NAM, the Business Roundtable, and the Chamber of Commerce were meeting regularly with Magaziner and other administration officials to iron out disagreements over the plan. The Chamber, led by Robert Patricelli, the CEO of a Connecticut health benefits management company and the chairman of the Chamber's Health Committee, had declared "that all employers should provide and help pay for insurance on a phased-in basis."[19] The Clinton plan looked as if it couldn't possibly lose. Yet by the end of February 1994, barely five months after Clinton introduced his plan, it was dead and buried, and no health care reform plan would pass Congress that year or even be voted upon.

What happened was that the ideal of dramatic, systematic economic reform that the bill represented—reform that would permanently alter the structure of authority in health care delivery and redistribute income downward—ran up against the reality of political and interest group power. The advocates of reform discovered that while the Reagan revolution was, indeed, over, the old alliance between conservatives and the business lobbies of K Street could still be revived—not as a governing coalition, but as a powerful veto against an ambitious program of reform.

The defeat of Clinton's health care plan was sparked by conservative political operatives and politicians who had little knowledge of or interest in health care legislation, but who feared that through the passing of health care reform, Clinton would create a lasting Democratic majority. The plan was also killed by the efforts of businesses that were directly threatened by health care reform. These included small family-owned businesses that did not provide their employees with health care, small health insurance providers that under the Clinton plan would be squeezed out by the larger, more cost-efficient firms, and corporations that owned subsidiaries that did not provide health insurance for their employees.

The key political operative in engineering Clinton's defeat was Grover Norquist, a Harvard graduate who, along with other young conservatives, had come to Washington in Reagan's first term to promote conservatism and to make his mark among the rich and powerful.[20] Norquist, after a stint with the College Republicans and the Chamber of Commerce, had formed a lobbying group called Americans for Tax Reform that demanded that candidates take a pledge not to raise taxes. When Clinton was elected, Norquist, worried that the president would be able to consolidate a new Democratic majority through passing national health insurance, began to organize against it. He set up what came to be called the "Wednesday Group"—a collection of fifty or so conservatives who met at his office every Wednesday morning over bagels and coffee to plot the destruction of the Clinton health care bill. They included lobbyists from the Christian Coalition, the National Rifle Association, home schooling organizations, term limits groups, taxpayer and property rights organizations, and also representatives from the *American Spectator*, Rush Limbaugh's talk show, and other conservative media. Norquist and the Wednesday Group did not have a single grand strategy, but they coordinated their activities against the health care bill through their weekly meetings.

The Wednesday Group was active in pressuring conservative politicians and organizations and legislators to oppose health care reform. They organized a national campaign against the Chamber of Commerce. Norquist enlisted conservative House Republicans to threaten the Chamber. At a Republican meeting in late 1993, Ohio Congressman John Boehner told Chamber president Richard Lesher and chief lobbyist William Archey that it was "the Chamber's duty to categorically oppose everything that Clinton was in favor of."[21] Norquist and his network of operatives also attempted to cripple the Clinton administration by spreading rumors of financial and personal wrongdoing.

The American Spectator, the *Washington Times*, and the *Wall Street Journal* editorial page (whose chief editorial writer, John Fund, was a close ally of Norquist) repeatedly attacked Clinton for his role in an old Arkansas land deal called Whitewater. *The American Spectator* published an article alleging that Clinton had used state troopers in Arkansas to solicit sex for himself. Limbaugh promoted the *American Spectator* articles (its circulation almost tripled that winter) and accused the Clinton administration of covering up aide Vincent Foster's murder. Limbaugh even drew a direct connection between Whitewater and health care:

> I think Whitewater is about health care. Most people think that health care is a good idea, but they haven't read the plan. They're taking the President's word for it. Now . . . if people are going to base their support for the plan on whether they can take his word, I think it's fair to examine whether or not he keeps his word.[22]

These attacks, which recalled the scurrilous Republican attacks against the New Deal in the late 1930s, diverted the Clinton White House during the crucial winter months when it should have been persuading the public of the merits of its health care plan. They also rallied the right to oppose the Clinton plan and sowed doubts in the public mind about the administration's integrity and effectiveness.

The two most important business groups that opposed the Clinton health bill were the National Federation of Independent Business (NFIB) and the Health Insurance Association of America (HIAA). Founded in San Mateo in 1943, the NFIB had long been the kid brother to the U.S. Chamber of Commerce. It was composed of pizza-store owners, service station operators, and other proprietors of small, unincorporated businesses. In the early 1990s it had about three times as many members as the Chamber of Commerce—600,000 versus 220,000—but a fraction of the dues. The Clinton health care reform provided the organization with a new opening to gain influence and represent its members, who were adamantly opposed to any employer-mandated health insurance. The NFIB threw its resources into lobbying Democratic and Republican House members who were uncomfortable with the Clinton plan but willing to back a compromise.

The NFIB joined a coalition organized by another organization, Citizens for a Sound Economy, and coordinated on Capitol Hill by Georgia senator and former insurance executive Paul Coverdell. This coalition included the National American Wholesale Grocers Association, the National Retailers Federation, and businesses like General Mills that had subsidiaries that didn't provide health insurance to their employees. The coalition also included the HIAA, the health insurance lobby that was unequivocally opposed to the Clinton plan. The HIAA spent $50 million trying to defeat the Clinton plan. It set up a dubious organization called the Coalition for Health Insurance Choices that hired organizers to pressure House members in their districts and spent about $15 million on a series of national television commercials that featured two characters named "Harry" and "Louise." The commercials depicted a couple worrying that the Clinton plan would deprive them of a choice of doctor by putting the government in charge of health care. The commercials were highly misleading. Americans were already losing their choice of doctor because of the growth of managed care within the private health industry. But they struck a chord among the public, which was wary of a new government bureaucracy, and helped to precipitate a sharp decline in the Clinton plan's popularity. The Gallup Poll found that from September 24, 1993, to February 26, 1994, Americans in favor of Clinton's plan fell from 59 to 46 percent, while those opposed rose from 33 to 48 percent.[23]

If the corporate executives that had backed universal health insurance had remained steadfast, then the efforts of Norquist, the NFIB, and the HIAA might have been in vain. The Clinton bill might not have passed, but a meaningful compromise would have been reached. But unlike earlier generations of business leaders, who had been willing to break ranks, the CEOs were more concerned about unity within their lobbying ranks than with championing a program that might be in the national interest. They allowed those businesses that were fiercely opposed to health care reform to define the position of the business community.

Clinton had counted on the Business Roundtable to play a leadership role in winning health care reform. The great majority of its members already paid for health insurance and stood to benefit from a reform that would contain their rising costs. But within the Roundtable, a minority who strongly opposed the Clinton plan were able to determine the organization's position. They worked through the organization's Health, Welfare, and Retirement Task Force, which was chaired by Robert C. Winters, the CEO of Prudential Insurance. At least eighteen of the companies on the task force either were in the health business or did not insure their workers, and they got the task force and then the entire organization to reject the Clinton plan.[24] The NAM followed course.

With the Roundtable and the NAM in opposition, the Chamber of Commerce buckled to pressure from conservative Republicans and from the NFIB, which had begun to raid their members. Chamber president Richard Lesher ordered Patricelli to inform the House Ways and Means Committee that the Chamber "cannot support any of the mandate proposals that have been advanced in legislation by President Clinton and members of Congress." The Chamber's board of directors then voted to oppose not only employer mandates but also universal coverage.* Without support from any significant business organization, and with the health industry now either neutral or lined up against it, the Clinton bill could not pass.

In the past, elites within the business community had intervened to prevent the most venal interests from dominating Congress. In 1946, the Committee on Economic Development, acting not as another business group but as an elite organization committed to the national interest, rescued the Employment Act. There were, however, no comparable organizations and no comparable leadership that could have rescued health care reform from oblivion. The CED itself had been overshadowed by the

*Lesher moved not only to change the Chamber's position on health care, but to reposition it as the loyal ally of conservative Republicans. On April 5, Lesher fired William Archey, who had been the Chamber's chief lobbyist and who had favored a "pragmatic" stance toward the Clinton administration, and replaced him with a veteran conservative, Bruce Josten. Soon afterward, Patricelli resigned as the chairman of the Chamber's Health Committee.

Business Roundtable and the American Enterprise Institute. The National Leadership Coalition had prestige but no clout and couldn't agree on the specifics of the Clinton plan. The sympathetic foundations, such as the Henry J. Kaiser Family Foundation, feared that if they got deeply involved, they would be attacked by conservatives for violating the tax laws.

The defeat of the Clinton plan emboldened his opponents on K Street and in Congress. When Clinton proposed his welfare reform plan in June 1994, tying a work requirement to $9.3 billion in new funding for jobs and job training, the plan never even made it out of committee. Congress would eventually pass a welfare reform bill that would include the work requirement but no additional money for jobs and job training. Its spirit was that of nineteenth-century individualism rather than early-1960s communitarianism.

The defeat of these measures dashed the illusions that Bill Clinton, Hillary Rodham Clinton, Ira Magaziner, Robert Reich, and the other post-sixties policy intellectuals harbored about what kind of reforms would be possible in the new post-Reagan political era of the 1990s. In the future, Clinton would revert to the cagey Southern politician. He would avoid undertaking reforms that would threaten the entrenched power of major business interests and that might expand the reach of government.

The Two Faces of Revolution

In November 1994 the Republicans captured both the House and Senate for the first time since 1952. The margin was still narrow—230 to 204 in the House and 53 to 47 in the Senate—but the House Republican and conservative leadership drew far-reaching conclusions from their surprising success. The new speaker-elect of the House, Newt Gingrich, told CNN, "It is such an historic change that it's almost impossible to believe just how big it really is."[25] Grover Norquist maintained that the election was a turning point. "Winning control of the House of Representatives is as historic a change as the emergence of the Republican Party with the election of Lincoln or the creation of the Democratic

Party majority in the 1930–1934 period with the Depression and Franklin Roosevelt."[26]

The highbrow Hudson Institute, known for founder Herman Kahn's claims of prophecy, put out an anthology, *The New Promise of American Life,* based on the premise that the Progressive Era in American politics that Croly defined had finally ended in November 1994 and had been replaced by a new conservative era that would last well into the twenty-first century. William Kristol, a former aide to Vice President Dan Quayle who would later become editor of Rupert Murdoch's *The Weekly Standard,* summed up the central idea: "November 8, 1994, could be said to cap and conclude the Progressive Era of American history. We have fulfilled the 'promise' of Herbert Croly's vision. We now have a chance to shape a new era, informed by a new promise."[27]

These pronouncements, like those of Clinton after his election in November 1992, were based on a profound misunderstanding of what was politically possible. Gingrich and his followers had ridden to victory in November primarily on the basis of Clinton's mistakes and miscues and the failure of the economy to rebound from the recession of 1991. They had advanced a program, but it was primarily directed at arousing antigovernment populism. It was fundamentally different from the conservative legislative program they would subsequently attempt to enact.

In the campaign, Republicans exploited the fact that Clinton's difficulties had rekindled voters' general hostility to the federal government. Using Ross Perot's pollster Frank Luntz, they devised a national platform, "The Contract With America." Its leading provisions—pledging to create term limits for Congress members and a balanced budget amendment—were intended to appeal to the distrust of government. The Republicans evoked the historic hatred of special interests against Clinton. "We are united here today," Representative Dick Armey, who would become majority leader, told the aspiring 367 Republican House candidates gathered on the Capitol steps, "in the belief that the people's House must be wrested from the grip of special interests."[28] Political scientist Gary Jacobson summed up the successful Republican strategy:

> Voters in 1994 were angry with government; Democrats were the party of government, not only because they were in charge,

> but also because their party believes in government. Republican candidates . . . offered themselves as vehicles for expressing anti-government rage by taking up the banner of structural panaceas—terms limits, a balanced budget amendment, cuts in Congressional staff and perks—that were broadly popular and had special appeal to the alienated voters who had supported Perot.[29]

But except during the election, Gingrich and the conservative leadership had little interest in government reform. They were never serious about term limits, the most ballyhooed of the Contract measures.* Like Reagan, they used Jacksonian appeals to promote an agenda that was much closer to Coolidge and Mellon. They saw themselves carrying forward and expanding the alliance between conservative political organizations and K Street business lobbies that had backed Reagan and that had spearheaded the defeat of the Clinton health care bill.

Reagan, of course, had succeeded in the 1980 and 1984 elections in presenting himself as the worthy successor of Jackson and the coonskin populists, but by the end of his two terms, the public had become wise to this ruse. As a result of the lobbying and banking scandals, most Americans realized that what the Reagan revolution really promised was not self-rule, but rule by K Street special interests. Gingrich and the Republicans would attempt the same deception, but this time it would take the public barely a year to see through it.

*The proposal for term limits had been circulating for several decades, but political consultant Eddie Mahe and Gingrich had revived it as a means of dislodging the Democrats from their House majority. If it had been adopted, its actual effect would have been to continue the shift of power in Washington toward K Street, which would have then enjoyed a monopoly of expertise and experience. Mahe, Gingrich, and the other term limits proponents gulled grassroots conservatives and some wealthy financiers into joining them. In the 1994 election, groups favoring term limits spent $1.5 million to try to defeat Democrats. After the Republicans won the House that November, the House leadership lost interest in term limits and failed to pass a bill.

The Contract with K Street

Gingrich himself had a fertile imagination that allowed him to frame the most mundane and craven strategies in the rhetoric of political revolution. Unlike Clinton, who belonged to the generation that admired John Kennedy, Gingrich was a child of the late sixties who as a history graduate student at Tulane in 1969 had opposed the Vietnam War and led a protest against the college administration because it had censured the campus humor magazine for publishing nude photos. Even as a conservative, his thought was marked by an apocalyptic spirit that identified change with revolution and the status quo with decline and even disaster. As he stood at the Capitol with Armey in September 1994 promoting the Contract With America, he said, "Today on these steps we offer this Contract as a first step toward renewing American civilization. If America fails, our children will live on a dark and bloody planet."[30]

Gingrich was deeply influenced by futurist Alvin Toffler, whose work he had discovered in the early 1970s. Toffler argued that American society was undergoing a transition from an industrial Second Wave to a postindustrial Third Wave. Gingrich saw himself doing for the Third Wave what William McKinley, Mark Hanna, and Theodore Roosevelt had done in accelerating the transition from the First Wave of traditional agriculture to the Second Wave. Gingrich sought to marshal K Street lobbies and his fellow Republicans behind a strategy of gutting the Second Wave programs of the New Deal, the Great Society, and the regulatory reforms of the Nixon era.[31]

Few of Gingrich's allies and followers in Congress shared his precise views. Some of them, like Armey, who had become a disciple of Milton Friedman during the sixties, favored their own version of conservative revolution. But others, like Texans Thomas DeLay and William Archer, simply represented extremely wealthy districts. When they sided with business or favored the rich, they were doing constituent service.

The key to the conservative Republican strategy was building powerful lobbying coalitions that would help enact K Street's and the Republicans' agenda. Gingrich invited business lobbies to help him eliminate any government regulations that got in their way. Gingrich told the members of the NAM in a speech in May 1995 that he intended to go to major multinationals and say, "Tell us under what circumstances you'd put the next thousand high value-added jobs in the U.S. What do we need to do to regulation, taxation, litigation, education, welfare, the structure of bureaucracy? You tell us how we make this the best place in the planet to invest." He confided to NAM members that he had already met with "eight major providers" to develop "a new product line in Medicare." And he had invited the pharmaceutical industry to develop a bill to rein in the Food and Drug Administration. "We told them, 'You bring us the bill, we'll do it.' "[32]

Norquist and DeLay, who became majority whip and later the power behind Gingrich's successor Dennis Hastert, contributed an important other element to the strategy. They believed that the Democrats had preserved their majority through incumbents' access to campaign money and the effective use of Congressional staff. Norquist and DeLay wanted to create a Republican monopoly on K Street. "There are major corporations in town with twenty lobbyists, only two of whom are Republicans. It will change," Norquist declared after the election.[33] Norquist and DeLay, along with Paul Beckner of Citizens of a Sound Economy, Bruce Josten, William Archey's successor at the Chamber of Commerce, and Congressman John Boehner organized a "Thursday Group" composed of key House and Senate Republicans, lobbyists from major businesses and trade organizations, and representatives of the conservative organizations that attended Norquist's Wednesday meetings. The Thursday Group planned legislative strategy and coordinated campaign contributions.

In the Senate, the House Republicans had strong support from Georgia's Paul Coverdell, a member of the Thursday Group, and presidential candidate Phil Gramm. Majority Leader Bob Dole, an "old guard" conservative leery of revolutionary pretensions, might have been expected to counter the House Republicans, but Dole was planning to run for president and was very worried about a challenge from Gramm on his right. (Gramm would write in a fund-raising letter attacking Dole, "Republicans cannot waffle on this Contract and expect to win the confidence of Americans in 1996.")[34] Dole used his support of the House agenda to establish his bona fides with Republican conservatives and also to strengthen his fund-raising among business groups.

Gingrich and the Republican leadership found an eager reception among Washington business groups. Out of the Thursday Group, Republicans set up coalitions to promote their legislation. DeLay organized over 350 lobbyists into Project Relief, which was designed to help draft and promote the Republicans' antiregulatory legislation. The Republicans and the lobbyists also set up the Coalition for Our Children's Future to back their budget, the Coalition for America's Future to support their tax bill, and the Coalition on Legal Reform for what was called "tort reform," which consisted of limiting the damage awards that citizens could win in civil suits against businesses. Business groups also responded with cash. In the first six months of 1993, with the Democrats in charge, the business PACs associated with Project Relief had given Republicans $2.6 million. In the first six months of 1995, the business PACs gave the Republicans $5.36 million.[35]

In the winter of 1995, the House and Senate Republicans introduced a moratorium on new regulations; new draconian requirements for the enforcement of regulations on labor health and safety, pesticides, poisons in food, clean air, and clean water; drastic reduction in funding for the EPA, the NLRB, OSHA, and other regulatory agencies; and limits on the damages that citizens could win in lawsuits against businesses. Together, these measures—embodied in separate legislation or attached as riders to appropriations bills—would have overturned many of the reforms that Congress passed from 1967 to 1974. In addition, House committees also proposed the elimination of the Commerce, Energy, and Education Departments, the Council of Economic Advisors, and the National Endowment for the Arts and for the Humanities. William Archer's Ways and Means Committee proposed massive tax cuts for capital gains and the elimination of the Earned Income Tax Credit—a liberal measure included in Clinton's first budget that helped workers climb off the edge of poverty. The labor and education committees called for gutting what remained of the War on Poverty, including Head Start. The Republicans would later recoil when Democrats accused them of favoring the rich, but their agenda clearly reflected the self-interest of their high-bracket constituents and the narrow interests of the K Street lobbies.

Many of these measures were drafted by lobbyists. Project Relief member Gordon Gooch, a lobbyist for petrochemical companies, wrote the first draft of the House bill establishing a moratorium on new regulations. Peter Molinari, a lobbyist for Union Carbide, and Paul Smith, a lobbyist for UPS, revised Gooch's draft.[36] Charles W. Ingram, associate manager of environmental policy at the Chamber of Commerce, helped draft a bill weakening the Clean Water Act.[37] Oil Industry lobbyists helped produce a draft relaxing standards for the cleanup of hazardous waste.[38] The Senate was no better. Dole's major antiregulatory bill was drafted by lobbyist C. Boyden Gray, a former Bush White House official who was representing Hoechst Celanese, a German chemical company engaged in a pitch battle with the EPA, and was also the chairman of Citizens for a Sound Economy and a prime mover in Project Relief.[39]

That summer, in devising a balanced budget for the year 2002, Gingrich also took the fateful step of trying to undermine the Medicare program. As part of the Republican attempt to balance the budget, Gingrich proposed to cut projected Medicare costs by $270 billion. Guided by health insurance lobbyists, he raised premiums and devised cuts that would have weakened and eventually crippled the program. Gingrich established a new "Medicare-Plus" plan for senior citizens to use their premiums to enroll with the insurance companies' managed care programs and HMOs. Under Medicare-Plus, senior citizens could also join what were called "medical savings accounts," a gimmick devised by one of the Republicans' principal contributors, Patrick Rooney of Golden Rule Insurance, to siphon off healthy and well-to-do seniors into private plans.[40]

Both Medicare-Plus options threatened the Medicare system. Health insurance systems work by using the premiums from the healthy to pay for the costs of treating the sick, but if the pool of the insured becomes limited to the sick, then the costs of insurance become prohibitive. Both HMOs and medical savings accounts would draw healthier senior citizens out of the regular Medicare system. The HMOs would attempt to keep their costs down by screening out senior citizens who were more likely to become sick, while the savings accounts would only attract senior citizens who were or thought they were healthy. Premium costs in the regular system would continue to rise and pressures would mount to replace it by a privatized system of vouchers. It was a controversial plan, but Gingrich and the House Republicans were determined to see it passed even if they had to shut down the government.

Initial versions of the Republicans' deregulatory agenda made their way through House and Senate committees, but in June, the bills began to encounter stiff opposition from environmental groups. Even organizations like the Wilderness Society, which had been close to Republicans, began strenuously lobbying against the bills and widely publicizing their opposition. Spurred on by environmental groups and by news reports of deadly *E. coli* bacteria in hamburgers, Republican moderates in the House and Senate began to back away from Gingrich's and Dole's regulatory reform bills. The public also began to get alarmed. After a warning of pesticide contamination in baby food, a bipartisan poll conducted by Republican pollster Ed Goeas of the Tarrance Group and Democrat Celinda Lake of Lake Research found that 78 percent of voters wanted the elimination of pesticide residues from baby food even when told that this would mean "higher costs to businesses that are passed on to consumers."[41] Luntz wrote a memo to the House leaders warning that 62 percent of American voters and 54 percent of Republican voters wanted to protect the environment rather than cut regulations. "The public may not like or admire regulations, may not think more are necessary, but puts environmental protection as a higher priority than cutting regulations," Luntz wrote.[42]

In the Senate, Dole found that he couldn't break a filibuster. In the House, Gingrich faced a revolt led by Representative Sherwood Boehlert of New York and other members of the "Tuesday Lunch Bunch," a weekly gathering of Republican moderates. On July 28, the Republican moderates joined Democrats to kill seventeen riders restricting the EPA that DeLay had attached to an appropriations bill. Over the next months, Republican moderates would join Democrats in blocking other parts of the Gingrich agenda—from the closure of the cabinet departments to the defunding of the EPA, OSHA, and the NLRB. The Gingrich revolution had suffered its first major setback—at the hands of the public and the environmental movement. Gingrich's next defeat would come during the struggle over the budget.

The American Association for Retired Persons (AARP) and consumer health care lobbies like Families U.S.A. recognized the danger that Medicare-Plus posed to Medicare. But what finally turned the public against Gingrich's plan was that the tax cuts in the Republican budget, totaling $245 billion, almost exactly equaled the amount the Republicans hoped to prune from Medicare. It seemed as though Gingrich was trying to pay for the tax cuts, most of which would benefit the Republicans' wealthier constituents, by raising Medicare premiums and reducing medical services. The public might not support a complicated new government health care initiative, but it backed Social Security and Medicare and wouldn't countenance any changes in coverage and premiums unless they appeared to make the programs more viable. As Clinton and the Democrats seized hold of this combustible issue, Gingrich and the Republican Congress's popularity plummeted. Clinton, the Democrats, and the movements that had backed them began to pull themselves out of the abyss into which they had been cast by the 1994 elections.

By the end of 1995, Gingrich and the Republican leadership had lost the trust they had gained. Armey had promised that "the people's House must be wrested from the grip of special interests," but the Republicans had merely changed which special interests held Congress in thrall. People saw the hand of K Street in the Republican program, and recoiled. A *Times-Mirror* survey found that 72 percent of the public thought that lobbyists' influence over Congress was equal to or greater than what it was before.

Labor Revolt

The Republican takeover of Congress and Gingrich's attempted revolution also provoked a leadership crisis in the AFL-CIO, which was reeling from almost two decades of steady decline under President Lane Kirkland. From 1979 to 1989, the proportion of workers unionized had fallen from 23 percent to 16.4 percent.[43] By 1995, labor union membership nationally was at 15.5 percent, lower than it had been since the early 1930s. The main factor in this decline was the militant opposition of business to the very existence of unions. During the late 1980s, workers were illegally fired in one out of every three NLRB elections.[44] In the 1980s, employers also adopted a tactic they had not used for fifty years. Inspired by Reagan's response to the air controllers' strike, management began hiring permanent replacements for strikers.

Many of the unions, faced with fierce employer opposition, gave up trying to recruit new members. In 1970 unions held about 8,000 elections to establish new locals; by the 1990s they were holding only 3,000 a year and were spending on average only 3 percent of their resources on organizing.[45] This spirit of resignation was echoed at the top of the federation. Kirkland not only abandoned trying to organize workers, but also trying to get new legislation through Congress. Union members had to go around Kirkland to get the federation to back legislation, drafted by a Democratic House member, to outlaw the use of striker replacements.

By the early 1990s labor leaders were privately comparing Kirkland to former Soviet premier Leonid Breznhev, who had also held onto power well after he had outlived his effectiveness, but none of them was willing to challenge Kirkland publicly. Then came the Republican takeover, which raised the specter of new antilabor legislation that would virtually destroy the movement. Gerald McEntee, the highly successful president of the American Federation of State, Municipal and County Employees, decided to organize a group of unions into the "95 Project," designed to win back the House. When Kirkland refused to support the effort, McEntee and John Sweeney, the president of the Service Employees International Union, lined up nine other union presidents to demand that Kirkland step down in favor of his secretary-treasurer, Tom Donahue. Kirkland fought back, and Donahue took his side, but once the issue became public, other union leaders joined Sweeney and McEntee in demanding Kirkland's retirement. In May, twenty-one union presidents—already commanding a majority of the federation's members—announced that they would back Sweeney for president against Kirkland. In June, Kirkland resigned. That October, Sweeney was elected the new president of the AFL-CIO.

Sweeney immediately demonstrated the federation's commitment to organizing and to winning back Congress for the Democrats. He drastically upped the federation's organizing budget from 3 percent to 33 percent of a total budget of $95 million and urged member unions to follow suit. He also started a "Union Summer," modeled on the civil rights movement's 1964 "Freedom Summer," to attract the college students of the 1990s to the union cause. These efforts attracted publicity and created some excitement in union ranks, but failed to stem the erosion of actual union membership nationally. Sweeney's political efforts were more immediately successful. In February 1996, Sweeney got the unions to contribute $35 million to a new political committee, Labor '96, aimed at defeating Republican House members in 1996. Twenty million dollars was to go into advertising and the rest into putting organizers into Congressional districts where a strong labor vote could make the difference in defeating an incumbent Republican. Sweeney and Steve Rosenthal, a veteran of the new left, whom he made the federation's political director, committed unions to working with the Sierra Club, Citizen Action, and other organizations that had grown out of the sixties. Sweeney and the AFL-CIO also threw their weight into blocking the Republicans' agenda.

The AFL-CIO's political reawakening in 1995 meant that the Democrats, with the support of labor, environmental, consumer, and civil rights groups, could arouse a generally sympathetic public to block conservative Republican efforts to gut regulatory agencies, privatize Medicare, and impose the Christian right's social agenda. But the end of Gingrich's revolution didn't mean that Clinton and the Democrats could simply revive the reform agenda of the 1992 campaign. Republicans still controlled Congress, and business and its K Street lobbies were more powerful than labor and the other liberal movements. The public remained supportive of the older New Deal programs, but leery of ambitious new ones. If anything, Gingrich's failure had increased public cynicism about new government initiatives. In 1996, labor's political revival didn't transform American politics but merely showed that liberal reformers could block the efforts of conservative reactionaries with the same aplomb that conservatives had blocked liberal efforts. American politics remained mired in the confusion of the Bush years, with one foot still firmly planted in the Reagan era and the other in an uncertain future.

[10]

Sleepwalking Toward the Millennium

Even after the debacle of his first two years, Bill Clinton could not give up the idea that his presidency was the reincarnation of one of America's great reform eras. As he regained his popularity in 1996, as the economy rebounded, and as Congress passed legislation that he favored, Clinton began to suggest that he was the agent of a "new Progressive Era in America."[1] On the eve of his second inaugural, he compared his administration to Theodore Roosevelt's.[2] Sadly, these were delusions of grandeur. There were striking similarities between the economic, social, and diplomatic conditions of the early 1900s and the 1990s, but there were equally striking differences between the way Americans of each era responded to those conditions.

The two periods faced similar far-reaching challenges. In the 1890s, America emerged as a global power amid a world being divided up by European imperialism. It had to replace an obsolete model of American diplomacy that went back to Washington's Farewell Address. In the 1990s the nation has had to adjust to a post–Cold War world lacking in immediate military threats, but fraught with unstable international economic arrangements and riven by ethnic and national conflicts that had been submerged during the Cold War.

In both periods Americans witnessed dramatic changes in the structure of industry, the nature of work, and the fabric of daily life. In the early 1900s the nation had to come to terms with large-scale industrialization and the rise of the giant corporation, the growth of cities and eclipse of the farm, and the rapid growth of a blue-collar working class, composed largely of Eastern and Southern European immigrants. The heightened strife between business and labor and the widening gap between rich and poor challenged the premises of American democracy. American democracy could no longer be based on the promise of roughly equal property ownership, but would have to make do with, and seek to mitigate, the inequalities of wealth and power intrinsic to corporate capitalism.

In the 1990s the nation has had to adapt to the gnawing insecurity created by the global mobility of capital and to the threat to democracy posed by powerful multinationals that could play communities, states, and even national governments off against each other. Americans have also had to come to terms with office automation, the growth of electronic commerce, the growing bifurcation of the working class into highly skilled professionals and menial service workers, the obsolescence of the older industrial cities, and a new influx of immigrants from Latin America and Asia. Not least, Americans have had to replace the older ethic of self-denial and otherworldly salvation with a new ethic of self-expression and fulfillment and of worldly happiness.

In both periods the economic conditions for reform were propitious. About the time Roosevelt took office in 1901, the economy finally recovered fully from the depression of 1893. The recovery removed the pressures for brute survival that had made the consideration of reform difficult. Over the next fifteen years, Americans would address aggressively and comprehensively the economic and social problems that had surfaced during the depression. Similarly, in the last year of Clinton's first term, the economy finally recovered from the 1991 recession. By 1998 unemployment had dipped to 4.5 percent, annual growth was at 4 percent, and productivity, spurred by the introduction of information technology, was increasing over 2 percent annually.[3] Chronic budget deficits gave way to projected trillion dollar surpluses. The fears of national decline were replaced by a spirit of triumphalism. Yet in these circumstances, political and social reform did not take place. On the contrary, the government became even more paralyzed and ineffective than before. Instead of addressing the great challenges they faced, Americans ignored them.

Some American leaders had difficulty adjusting to the prosperity of the late 1990s. They were overcome by caution. But the main reason for failure was that the political system was dysfunctional. It continued to be dominated by lobbyists and irresponsible elites backed by conservative Republicans. Their presence on Washington's K Street discouraged reform and discouraged active public participation in politics. As a result, while the economy hurtled forward, political America sleepwalked into the next century.

Failure of Reform

The Progressive Era, along with the New Deal and the 1960s, represented a high-water mark of American democratic reform. It saw the creation of the Federal Trade Commission and the Federal Reserve banking system, the establishment of a progressive income tax, federal standards for food safety, the conservation of natural resources, the adoption of the initiative and referendum and the direct election of U.S. senators—as well as myriad state reforms in social insurance and labor relations that the national government adopted during the New Deal. The 1990s, by contrast, were remarkably barren of reform legislation. Clinton's effort at health care reform was repudiated. The legislation passed has been either cosmetic or reactionary. Significant reforms were proposed, but they were peremptorily rejected.

Perhaps the classic cosmetic bill of the Clinton years was the Kassebaum-Kennedy Health Insurance Portability and Accountability Act, which was passed in 1996. In signing the bill that August, Clinton declared, "With this bill, we take a long step toward the kind of health care reform our nation needs."[4] Senators Nancy Kassebaum and Edward Kennedy claimed that their bill protected individuals who lost their insurance after they left a job and either remained unemployed or were not hired by a business that provided health insurance, but in most cases, it did not do so. Under pressure from insurance companies, Kassebaum and Kennedy had failed to cap the premiums that insurers could charge to individuals who left their jobs. An insurance company didn't have to refuse coverage; it could just charge more than an unemployed worker with a preexisting medical condition could possibly afford. A year and a half after the bill passed, a study by the General Accounting Office confirmed the problem. The GAO found that in the thirteen states that had tried to implement Kassebaum-Kennedy, some carriers initially "discouraged people from applying for the coverage or charged them as much as 140 to 600 percent of the standard rate."[5]

Many of the basic problems that the Clinton campaign first cited in 1992 remained, and some had even worsened, in spite of the economic upturn. From 1993 to 1997, the number of Americans who lacked health insurance climbed from 39.7 to 43.4 million, or from 14.2 to 16.1 percent.[6] Between 1989 and 1997, the share of wealth held by the top 1 percent grew from 37.4 to 39.1 percent of the national income, while the share held by middle-class families—those in the middle fifth—fell from 4.8 to 4.4 percent. More than 85 percent of the benefits from the increase in stock prices between 1989 and 1997 went to the richest 10 percent of households. From 1989 to 1997, CEO salaries went from 56 times to 116 times that of the average worker.[7] The economy of the 1990s was much more like that of the 1920s, when the benefits of growth were distributed unequally, than like the halcyon 1950s and 1960s when the gap between rich and poor visibly narrowed.

In the face of these inequalities, Republicans in Congress proposed measures that would widen rather than reduce them, including tax breaks for investors and the fragmentation of the Medicare system. The Clinton administration, led by Secretary of Treasury Robert Rubin, resisted the most egregious Republican efforts to reward their constituents, but the administration went little further on its own. After the 1993 budget, which included the Earned Income Tax Credit, the administration drew back from redistributive tax plans and agreed to a mildly regressive Republican plan in 1997.

The growth of budget surpluses should have made it possible to contemplate the large increases in public investment Clinton had championed during the 1992 campaign but then repudiated in the face of projected budget deficits. These surpluses could be used to widen access to health care and education, improve public transportation, and fund research and development into the next generation of science and technology. But spending on education, transportation, and high technology continued to lag during the Clinton years. If spending on education and training had not been increased but had held constant, with increases for inflation, from 1976 to 1998, it would have been $26.1 billion higher than it was.[8]

There was growing public support for measures that would reduce the threat to jobs, wages, and regulations from the unlimited movement of multinational corporations. When the administration, backed by business, proposed extending NAFTA to Chile, liberals, backed by labor and environmental organizations, proposed to attach labor and environmental safeguards to any new free trade treaties. (Chile had draconian labor laws that dated from dictator Augusto Pinochet's attempt to crush the country's unions.) Clinton was initially receptive, but, under pressure from business and from Republicans, he did not include these provisions in a "fast-track" proposal he made for negotiating the treaty. No measure passed, and the treaty was never negotiated. In his last two years, Clinton joined European leaders in backing labor and environmental accords, including a global warming treaty, but these measures met with stiff opposition from a Republican Congress and K Street.

Businesses and their lobbies were able to dictate the provisions of measures that directly affected them. In 1998, Congress passed, and the administration signed, a measure establishing a three-year moratorium on new Internet taxes and setting up a nineteen-member commission, controlled by Republican appointees, to recommend a new tax structure that could make up the $10 billion in annual sales taxes that states were expected to lose annually from purchases made over the Internet. The states themselves and consumer organizations justifiably feared that the commission would slight their concerns about lost revenue, but were unable to counter a powerful coalition that included Microsoft, America-on-Line, Charles Schwab, and IBM. The Clinton White House ignored consumer groups in determining how to police consumer privacy on the Internet. Instead of setting rules that the government had to enforce, the administration chose to leave enforcement up to industry itself—a laissez-faire approach that recalled the 1870s or the 1920s rather than the Progressive Era.[9]

The Clinton administration attempted to strengthen some environmental protections even in the face of Congressional and K Street opposition, but it found itself stymied. Under EPA regulations, the states are responsible for policing pollution violations, but when the EPA did an independent study of violations, they found five times more "significant violators" than the states discovered.[10] The EPA also found itself blocked by the courts, which remained dominated by Reagan era appointees. In July 1997, the EPA, acting in accordance with the Clean Air Act of 1990, issued stricter limits on ozone and small soot particles in the lower atmosphere. But the lawyers for affected companies, led by the ubiquitous Boyden Gray, took the EPA to court, and a three-judge panel for the U.S. Court of Appeals for the District of Columbia threw out the rules on the same grounds that the court had killed early New Deal programs.[11] The court's decision was likely to be overturned, but it would delay implementation of the regulations into the next century.*

This inordinate influence by business and its lobbyists was facilitated by the system of campaign finance. By the late 1990s it cried out for reform. Court rulings in the 1990s had destroyed the last vestige of the 1974 reform bill by allowing interest groups and wealthy individuals to campaign on behalf of candidates without any restriction on their expenditures as long as they didn't explicitly say, "Vote for candidate X." Funded by unrestricted "soft money" grants, parties could also wage their own unlimited campaigns on behalf of candidates. In effect, the campaign

*Business continued to employ a two-track strategy against the regulation of business. On the one hand, it sought to weaken the regulatory agencies themselves by cutting their budgets, limiting their scope, and reducing their authority. On the other hand, it tried to reduce the power of consumers to sue companies directly for malpractice or product liability. The strategy was redolent with hypocrisy and irony. In 1997 pharmaceutical lobbyists succeeded in getting Congress to pass a law, the FDA Modernization Act, that reduced the scope and authority of the Food and Drug Administration over new products. At the same time, the lobbyists championed a "tort reform" measure that prohibited consumers from suing companies for selling a defective or dangerous product if the product had been approved for use by a government agency.

financing system was little better than what Theodore Roosevelt had found in 1905 when he persuaded Congress to pass an eminently avoidable ban on corporate contributions. There were no longer any restrictions on what businesses and other groups could spend on candidates and parties. Instead of countering the inequality of the economic system, the political system reinforced it.

In the wake of the 1996 election, there was public support for reform. A September 1997 CNN/Gallup poll showed that by a margin of 55 to 35 percent, Americans wanted campaign reform legislation passed by the end of the year.[12] With White House support, a group of Democrats and Republicans in the Senate and House proposed a modest plan, but the Republican majority, which benefited more than Democrats from the existing system, blocked even these measures.

Politics by Other Means

The Progressive Era was characterized by a lively and politically mobilized citizenry—evidenced not merely by voting, but by participation in political movements and in organizations on a local, state, and national level. There were viable third parties and fourth parties, two national labor organizations, farm groups, business groups, and a broad-based movement for woman suffrage.[13] Party rivalry was based partly on region and religion, but in the elections of 1896 and 1912, the parties represented far-reaching democratic alternatives. The election of 1912, in which Theodore Roosevelt's Progressive Party and Eugene Debs's Socialist Party challenged the Republican and Democratic regulars, was fought over the terms of reform, and laid the basis for Wilson's climactic first term.

Politics seemed to revive in the early 1990s—evidenced in Ross Perot's third-party effort, the rise of the Christian Coalition, and the revival of the consumer and environmental movements. But by the decade's end, the signs of decay overshadowed those of rebirth and revitalization. Perot squandered his movement by turning it into a vehicle for his own thwarted ambition. The environmental movement's largest grassroots organization, Greenpeace, abandoned its local chapters in 1996 and became a Washington letterhead group, financed by direct mail. In 1996,

Ralph Nader embarked on a desperate, ill-fated presidential campaign on the Green Party ticket, securing only 1 percent of the vote. Citizen Action, which had united many of the state and local community organizing efforts during the 1980s and early 1990s, dissolved in 1997 under a cloud of scandal. The AFL-CIO's membership continued to decline and was rocked by a major scandal involving the Teamsters. Ralph Reed quit the Christian Coalition after having failed to convert it from an evangelical interest group into a popular nonsectarian movement. Its membership plummeted, and it fell into financial arrears.[14] It remained powerful primarily in name, and operated as a narrow pressure group within the embattled and divided Republican Party.

There was a general decline in popular interest and involvement in politics. This showed up in declining election turnout, but also in the UCLA studies on incoming freshmen. In 1970, 52.8 percent thought it was important to "keep up to date with political affairs." By 1997 only 30 percent did. In 1971 (the first year the question was asked) 42.9 percent ranked becoming "involved in programs to clean up the environment" an essential objective. By 1997 only 19.6 percent did. The lack of involvement in the late 1990s reflected in part a certain complacency born from economic recovery, but it was equally, if not more, driven by cynicism about government and democracy.

During the 1990s the political parties gained an important role in fund-raising because of loopholes in the campaign laws allowing unlimited contributions to parties, and court rulings that these funds could be used to support candidates. But the parties' newfound power did not improve the functioning of the political system. That was particularly the case with the national Republican Party, which by the late 1990s was following the path from movement to sect that new left Democrats had traveled in the late 1960s.

Having won control of Congress in November 1994, conservative Republicans faced the task of developing policies that would address the national interest. Instead, they fell back upon representing their most vocal constituents and interest groups. Their economic policy reflected the wealthy and K Street; their social policy the religious right; and their foreign policy the narrow isolationism of the small town provincial that had dominated the party earlier in the century, but had largely disappeared during the Cold War. When they found themselves falling in public esteem, they fought back by attempting to discredit their political opponents in the White House.

In 1994, Republicans had attempted to undermine the administration's legislative agenda by currying scandal over Whitewater, the death of Vincent Foster, and Clinton's alleged sexual liaisons in Arkansas, including the Paula Jones sexual harassment case, a questionable suit that was financed by Richard Mellon Scaife and that was eventually thrown out of court. The cloud of scandal weakened Clinton in 1994, but by 1996 the public had been immunized against the Republican attacks on Clinton's character, and he easily won reelection. Frustrated by their failure to capture the White House, the Republicans replayed the script of the Republicans of 1949, who after winning the Congress in 1946 had lost the presidency in 1948. Like the McCarthy-era Republicans, they launched investigations—most of them into the administration's fund-raising practices.

The campaign finance investigations failed to discredit the administration, but in 1998 the House Republicans and their conservative allies tried to exploit a sexual scandal in the White House. When independent counsel Kenneth Starr charged Clinton with lying about his affair with White House intern Monica Lewinsky in his deposition in the Paula Jones case and with obstructing the investigation of the affair, the House Republicans launched an impeachment drive against Clinton, even though Starr's charges did not remotely meet the Constitutional test of "high crimes and misdemeanors." There was little public support for impeachment, and in November the party lost seats in the House. Yet still the Republicans refused to turn back. Prodded by the Christian Coalition and by conservative ideologues, House Republicans became completely consumed by a cultural crusade against Clinton as a symbol of the sixties counterculture. House majority whip Tom DeLay declared that the impeachment debate was "about relativism versus absolute truth." Former judge Robert Bork promised that impeachment would "kill off the lax moral spirit of the Sixties."

Clinton's impeachment by House Republicans highlighted their subservience to the religious right and isolated them from public opinion.

Party rivalry—which was theoretically supposed to dramatize and clarify the larger choices that Americans faced—paralyzed Washington. Within the Republican Party, it exacerbated the divisions between the Congressional party and the state-based party, which was dominated by governors who were either more moderate or more prudent in their politics. As the 2000 election approached, these governors became determined to win control of the party by nominating one of their own, Texas's George W. Bush, as president. But even if they were to succeed, the bitter infighting would be likely to persist.

The Abdication of the Elites

In the Progressive Era, there were politicians, bankers, businessmen, lawyers, and intellectuals who devoted themselves in a disinterested manner to reconciling the interests of different groups and classes. Robert Brookings, Theodore Roosevelt, Elihu Root, Woodrow Wilson, Louis Brandeis, and Mark Hanna, whom Gingrich completely misunderstood, sought to reconcile business and labor rather than to represent one against the other. They tried to accommodate America's democratic ideal to the structure of corporate capitalism. There are certainly similar leaders today, but like international investor George Soros, they exist on the margins of respectable discourse. Almost all the post-1960s intellectuals who came to Washington with Clinton departed at the end of the first term—most of them, like Robert Reich, unhappy with their inability to effect change.* And the capitulation of the elites to K Street continued unabated during the same time.

Unlike their immediate predecessors, the business leaders of the 1990s did not have to worry about rising energy costs and falling profits, but the absence of a threat to their survival did not make them more inclined to civic involvement. If anything, they came to see themselves as

*The one exception proves the rule. Ira Magaziner stayed during the second term to become the administration's Internet czar. But in his negotiations with business over government regulation of the Internet, Magaziner took exactly the opposite tack he had taken with health care. He now wholeheartedly embraced the principles of laissez-faire. See John B. Judis, "Magaziner On-Line," *The New Republic,* Dec. 28, 1998.

part of a competitive global economy whose concerns often did not mesh with those of American workers or purely American-based companies. By the mid-1990s, many of the largest corporations, including Coca-Cola, General Motors, and Ford, had abolished the distinction between their American and international divisions to emphasize that they were global rather than purely American companies, and the CEOs saw themselves as world citizens.

Herb Stein, who had worked with the Committee on Economic Development for two decades, bemoaned the lack of national leadership from businessmen and bankers. "I think there was a period when there were businessmen outside the government who had some authority and who were respected, and who had a genuine national patriotic concern with the problems of the country," he said. "I can't think of a single name now of such a person."[15] Many of those business leaders who became politically involved embraced a kind of irresponsible individualism that was antithetical to the spirit of twentieth-century elites. Fred Smith of Federal Express and John Malone of Tele-Communications Inc. were among those drawn to the Cato Institute, a libertarian think tank that rejected the progressive income tax, Social Security, and the welfare state.

During the sixties, law school graduates from Harvard and Yale had flocked into public interest work, but the new generation of lawyers displayed little evidence of public-spiritedness. They even lost interest in occasional pro bono work. When Robert Gordon asked partners in big law firms why they didn't any longer offer associates a chance to do public interest law, they told him, "Too many of the most talented associates we would like to attract to the firm only pay attention to the bottom line."[16] Young lawyers who worked Capitol Hill for House members and senators and for policy committees saw their service as a means of bolstering their legal résumés. One former Congressional tax expert admitted to *Wall Street Journal* reporter Jeffrey Birnbaum that serving on Capitol Hill "became more of a means to an end while I was there. People coming up see it as a way to move up: become lobbyists and probably double their salary."[17]

Some CEOs and recipients of inherited wealth ran for office, but they seemed to do so for the sheer celebrity or power of the office. Oil heir Michael Huffington, who had never held public office, spent

$5.4 million in 1994 to win a House seat in California. Two years later, he spent a record $28 million trying to win a Senate seat. Huffington ran as a right-wing Republican, but two years later he revealed that he was gay and was considering becoming a Democrat. His political career was an exercise in frivolity, made possible by lax campaign finance regulations.[18] Steve Forbes, the heir to his father's billion-dollar publishing and real estate empire, ran twice for president using his own fortune to veil his utter lack of qualification for the nation's highest office. Forbes was raised in the "horse country" of western New Jersey where, since the beginning of the twentieth century, wealthy aspirants to an image of the old English aristocracy had lived on secluded estates and ridden to the fox. Some of these children, like Kennedy's Secretary of the Treasury C. Douglas Dillon or New Jersey Governor Christine Todd Whitman, had inherited a spirit of noblesse oblige from their parents. Like the children of the Rockefellers who had entered politics after World War II, they sought public service as a means of exercising the overall social responsibility that they believed their class standing bestowed on them. They didn't seek narrowly to protect their own, but to promote a society in which wealth, and the benefits of wealth, were more widely shared.

But Forbes was a creature of the Reagan era. He entered the family business after graduating from Princeton in 1971 and rose to be second in command to his father. After his father's death in 1989, he took over the family business. In 1995, at the same age his eccentric father had taken up motorcycling, he suddenly declared his candidacy for president. Rather than seeking to finance his campaign through contributions that the federal government would match, he threw the power of his wealth into the campaign, spending almost $50 million to advertise his name and positions and to attack his opponents. His program was a throwback to Andrew Mellon rather than Nelson Rockefeller. He espoused a regressive flat tax plan that would most benefit his own class, advocated the elimination of the inheritance taxes enacted under Franklin Roosevelt, and called for the privatization of Social Security and Medicare.

On K Street, the Charls Walker of the 1990s was C. Boyden Gray, the heir to the Reynolds tobacco fortune. The Harvard-educated Gray vividly demonstrated how far the American upper class of Theodore

Roosevelt and Dean Acheson had fallen. Gray's early career appeared promising. After graduating from the University of North Carolina Law School in 1968, he clerked for Chief Justice Earl Warren. Then, after almost a decade at Wilmer, Cutler & Pickering, he joined the Reagan administration as counsel to Vice President Bush and to the Task Force on Regulatory Relief. When Bush became president in 1988, Gray became his White House counsel. But after the 1992 election he rejoined Wilmer, Cutler & Pickering and became the principal lobbyist for companies trying to gut the EPA and the FDA. His zeal for clients earned him the nickname of "Billable Hours."

Gray specialized in using front groups for lobbying so that the public would not realize that the positions it was hearing were self-interested statements. He helped set up lobbying coalitions called the Alliance for Reasonable Regulation (to promote Dole's antiregulatory legislation, which Gray wrote) and the Air Quality Standards Coalition (to *block* EPA air quality standards). At a January 1997 meeting of the Air Quality Standards Coalition, he advocated a campaign that would "not have Beltway fingerprints." According to notes taken at the meeting, Gray said that "you can't do this with PAC or lobby money. Need grassroots money, will need lots of air time."[19]

Gray also chaired the Citizens for a Sound Economy, the archetypal K Street organization of the 1990s. It was founded in 1984 and strengthened by the arrival in 1992 of refugees from Quayle's Council on Competitiveness. It styled itself a think tank, but it was really a front for corporations and trade associations, which paid it to lobby under its name rather than theirs. Its annual budget rose from $4 million in 1991 to $17.6 million in 1996, surpassing Heritage and the AEI.[20] Its contributors included scores of the largest American companies, as well as trade associations. These businesses and business associations employed it for "grassroots organizing."[21] Gray himself used Citizens for a Sound Economy as his own front group. When he appeared to testify before the House of Representatives in July 1995 on behalf of regulatory reform, he was not identified as a lobbyist for Hoechst Celanese, but as the "chairman of Citizens for a Sound Economy," which Gray blithely described as a "250,000 member nonpartisan, non-profit consumer advocacy group that promotes market-based solutions to public policy problems."[22] Likewise, when Gray appeared on television, he was identified either as a former White House counsel or as chairman of Citizens for a Sound Economy.*

In the 1990s, there was also a steady growth in organizations like Citizens for a Sound Economy that masqueraded as policy institutes, think tanks, and research organizations but were in fact lobbying fronts for business. The Competitive Enterprise Institute, which was funded by Scaife, the Koch family (whose privately owned oil company was engaged in constant battles with the EPA), and a host of businesses and business foundations, put out op-eds, broadcast advertorials, and published polls and studies backing up business opposition to regulation. As part of a corporate campaign against the global warming treaty that the United States and other industrialized nations had agreed to in Kyoto in December 1997, it ran radio ads that grossly misrepresented the position of scientists on the treaty. "Thousands of scientists agree there's no solid

*A host of other former Bush administration officials migrated to K Street after the November 1992 election, and after only two years, Clinton administration officials also began their own exodus. Former aides of Vice President Al Gore, who helped get the administration to back the Telecommunications Act in 1996, became lobbyists for telecommunications companies and trade associations. These included Roy Neel, Jack Quinn, Greg Simon, and Sally Aman.

Former Secretary of the Treasury Lloyd Bentsen joined Verner, Lipfert, Bernhard, McPherson, and Hand, where he represented Merrill Lynch and the American Financial Services Association. Laura Tyson, fresh from chairing the Council of Economic Advisors and the National Economic Council, sold her services to Northwest Airlines, which was trying to prevent the Department of Transportation from investigating predatory pricing practices by major airlines.

Perhaps the most depressing example was former Senate majority leader and presidential candidate Bob Dole, who, after the 1996 election, went to work as a lobbyist for the Project to Promote Competition and Innovation in the Digital Age (PROCOMP for short), which was run by one of his former aides and was funded by computer companies that were striving to demonstrate that Microsoft was acting illegally as a monopoly. When he was still majority leader in 1995, Dole had denounced the Justice Department for using its "antitrust authority" against Microsoft in a "frightening manner." Referring to "Microsoft's updated windows software package and its new on-line service," Dole remarked, "If somebody makes something and somebody wants it, you sell it. You do not have to go to the Department of Justice to get their approval." But now in April 1998, Dole was accepting pay to denounce Microsoft for violating antitrust laws. Microsoft, Dole said, "can't be allowed to violate antitrust laws that protect consumers by using that monopoly to then stifle competition and to slow down innovation and leverage itself into monopolies in other markets."

evidence of a global warming problem," the organization declared in one ad.[23]

The Political Club for Growth was founded by multimillionaire Wall Street consultant Richard Gilder, who had been influenced by Jude Wanniski's supply-side economics. Its membership was composed primarily of wealthy financiers and real estate developers. They met monthly to consider which candidates and organizations to fund. They were advised by Wanniski and by John Fund from the *Wall Street Journal* editorial page. They gravitated to causes that would reduce the power of government over private capital and that would provide tax breaks to speculators. They funded Gingrich's political organization, GOPAC, the Cato Institute, and term limits organizations. They operated in secret, like a political equivalent of a gated community.

Some of the promising elite organizations that had begun at the end of the Reagan era floundered or lost their independence during the 1990s. They were products of the perception of American decline, but after the economy revived, they lost their defining purpose. With John Young's departure, the Council on Competitiveness shrunk to a letterhead. Clyde Prestowitz's Economic Strategy Institute continued to be influential during the first Clinton term, but Prestowitz increasingly came under siege from corporate funders who, no longer so concerned about national competitiveness, wanted the institute to do research to supplement their lobbying efforts. Several of the institute's best researchers resigned.

The Democratic Leadership Council saw its most important initiatives—the national citizens corps, welfare reform, and reinventing government—altered virtually beyond recognition, but instead of going into critical opposition, it declared victory. By Clinton's second term, it was emphasizing those parts of its program on trade and Social Security that mimicked Republican conservatism and that were most congenial to its own corporate funders. The older think tanks and policy groups like Brookings and the CED found themselves competing for funds and attention not only with the AEI and Heritage, but also with organizations like Citizens for a Sound Economy. In response, they began to conceive themselves as businesses that were marketing ideas. They saw themselves competing with the other institutions for customers (politicians and reporters) and investors (funders). They saw researchers as producers of products for a market, and measured their success by their sales (ranging from the number of books sold to the number of mentions in the press). Such changes inevitably undermined their historic role.

At Brookings, the most dramatic changes began in 1995 after the institution's trustees, who had become critical of its lack of influence on public affairs, brought in former Bush administration official Michael Armacost as the president. Armacost appointed another former Bush official, Richard N. Haass, as the head of foreign policy studies. Reflecting the wishes of the trustees, Armacost and Haass began to move the institution away from the older Brookings toward a market model. They frequently used the word "entrepreneurial" and talked about "marketing" to describe their efforts. "We market ideas," said Haass. "We don't turn out widgets, we turn out ideas, and we've got to be entrepreneurial."[24] Brookings, too, became subject to pressure from its contributors. One investment banker on the board of trustees tried to eliminate the funding for a study on corporate governance that he did not approve of. The funding was approved, but at a lower level than requested. In 1996, Brookings established a chair in international trade and economics endowed by Toyota on the stipulation that it would be filled by a free-trade economist—a clear breach of the wall between the funders and scholars that Robert Brookings had erected.[25]

In the 1990s the great newspapers and magazines were also shaped by the spread of high-powered corporate capitalism. Most newspapers and magazines had been run for a profit, but the best of them prided themselves on placing public service on a par with making a profit. They adhered to a strict policy of separating the news and editorial departments from the advertising and business departments of the publication. At *Time,* Henry Luce pioneered the idea of a "church-state separation" between the business and editorial functions of the magazine; when he died in 1967 he stipulated in his will that his company remain "principally a journalistic enterprise . . . operated in the public interest as well as the interest of its stockholders."[26] But this wall of separation began to break down in the 1970s and virtually crumbled in the 1990s, subjecting the news department to pressure from advertisers and from corporate owners.

At *Time,* the merger between *Time* and Warner created an entertainment conglomerate in which the editor in chief of *Time* reported to the officers and directors of a multinational corporation.* At the *New York Times,* publisher Arthur Sulzberger, Jr., established regular meetings between advertising executives and the news department, contending that news editors had to understand that "since we have a clear responsibility to make a profit, they can't succeed if they have an adverse impact on the profit margins of the paper."[27] The *Times* also continued to penalize reporters who appeared too critical of business.†

The introduction of the Internet only accelerated the merger of business and editorial functions. Asked whether advertisers would dictate content on new-media web pages, Sulzberger responded, "New media are by definition transactional. We need to work more closely with

*At Time Inc. under Luce, the editor in chief reported directly to the board of directors of Time Inc., on which the editor in chief also served, not to the CEO of Time Inc., who was responsible for the companies' financial health. Whenever the CEO made decisions that would bear on the companies' editorial operations, he had to consult with the editor in chief. In 1989, under editor in chief Jason McManus, Time Inc. took the fateful step of merging with Warner, which was already a media conglomerate. *Time* and *Fortune* became underlings in a family that included major movie, cable, and publishing holdings. In 1996, in the wake of the Telecommunications Act, Time-Warner merged with Ted Turner's CNN and TNT, adding not only television, but also toy companies, amusement parks, and sports teams to its $25 billion empire. In 1994, Time-Warner selected former *Wall Street Journal* managing editor Norman Pearlstine to succeed McManus in Luce's old job of editor in chief of Time Inc. Pearlstine was a brilliant editor who had been responsible for the *Wall Street Journal*'s news pages during the tumultuous scandals of the 1980s. In 1994, Pearlstine agreed to a new definition of the role of editor in chief. While the editor in chief sat on the board of directors and was still the co-equal of the Time CEO, he reported to the Time-Warner CEO. Three years later, after the wake of the merger with Turner's CNN, the board removed the last vestige of autonomy from the editor in chief. Pearlstine now reported directly to Time CEO Don Logan, and he no longer served on the board of directors.

†In 1991, *Times* reporter Philip Shabecoff, who covered the environment, was told, "New York is complaining. You're too pro-environment and they say you're ignoring the economic costs of environmental protection. They want you to cover the IRS."

advertisers and marketers to create content that meets their needs. We must develop new ground rules."[28]

But the breakdown was most dramatic at the *Los Angeles Times*. In the 1960s, Otis Chandler transformed it into one of the country's best newspapers, but after Chandler's retirement in 1980, the newspaper's profit margins began to decline. In 1996 the newspaper's parent company, the Times-Mirror Co., appointed Mark Willes the CEO, and in 1997 Willes made himself publisher of the *Los Angeles Times*. Willes, who had never worked for a newspaper—he was a director of the Federal Reserve for eleven years and an executive with General Mills for fifteen years—began merging the business and editorial departments. He appointed general managers from the business side to serve as "partners" for the editors. He demanded profit-and-loss statements from each section, and he established bonuses for editors based on how profitable each section was. These kinds of changes have made it more difficult for the elite newspapers and magazines to mediate, arbitrate, and assess objectively the conflicts between business and labor and between business and consumers.

In the past, publishers and top editors had considered themselves to be mainstays of the nation's political elite. They had belonged to the Council on Foreign Relations. Many of them conferred regularly with the president and top administration officials. But in the 1990s newspaper publishers like Willes and the *Washington Post*'s Donald Graham saw themselves simply as businessmen selling a product in an increasingly competitive market. When in January 1998 a reporter interviewed Graham, the grandson of Eugene Meyer, about the paper's achievements under his leadership, he talked entirely about its circulation figures. Wrote the *New York Times*'s Iver Petersen, "What is missing in this inventory of success are accounts of the articles themselves."[29] The *Washington Post*'s executive editor Leonard Downie professed to have no political opinions whatever. Time Inc. editor in chief Norman Pearlstine admitted he was much closer to Hollywood moguls than to Washington officials and that he did not participate in any policy groups. He felt closest, he admitted, to the Cato Institute.

As the great newspapers, magazines, and television news networks became obsessed with their bottom line, they abandoned their responsibility as guardians of the national interest. Beginning with the exposure of Democratic presidential candidate Gary Hart's marital infidelity in 1987, they allowed the barrier separating the elite media from the tabloid press to crumble. From the Clinton campaign in 1992 through the Lewinsky affair in 1998, they printed or broadcast unsubstantiated rumors; they intruded into areas of private life that had formerly been marked off; they blithely published illegal leaks. During the McCarthy investigations, some of the same publications and CBS News under Edward R. Murrow and Fred Friendly had led the effort to expose the Wisconsin senator's baseless charges, but as the drive to impeach the president grew during 1998, the great publications and networks became accessories to the campaign being waged against the Clinton administration. They shared blame with the Republican conservatives for the travesty of Constitutional government that finally took place.

Intellectual Drift and Reaction

In the Progressive Era, there was intense intellectual ferment. Herbert Croly, Walter Lippmann, William Weyl and *The New Republic,* John Dewey, Thorstein Veblen, John Commons, Richard Ely, and Charlotte Perkins Gilman grasped the challenge that corporate capitalism posed to America's older democratic ideal. In the 1990s, there was no shortage of brilliant social scientists and journalists, but the political journals lost their focus on larger questions, and the loudest strains of political thought were either apologetic or reactionary.

In the Progressive Era, *The New Republic* had played a vital role in defining and seeking to resolve the conflict between democracy and corporate capitalism. With greater or less success, it had maintained this focus through the New Deal, the Eisenhower era, the sixties, and the Reagan years, but with the Cold War's end, and the election in 1992 of a Democratic president pledged to reform, the magazine, ironically, lost its focus. As the editorship rapidly changed hands, the magazine became distinguished primarily by its advocacy of an aggressive foreign policy and by eclectic political causes that were not directly related to or contradicted the magazine's original project. It helped, for instance, the effort to derail national health insurance in 1994 and was either opposed or indifferent to campaign finance reform during Clinton's second term. Conservative journals failed to define the choices Americans faced. While Buckley's *National Review* had presented a philosophical counter to progressive reform, the conservative journals of the 1990s were either an extension of television punditry or tabloid journalism. *The American Spectator,* which claimed the largest circulation, had originally been designed as the successor of *National Review,* but during the Clinton years, it became known for publishing sordid and irresponsible exposes of the president's sex life.

In books and magazines, op-ed pages of newspapers, and talk shows, political discussion was extraordinarily shallow, dominated by celebrity glitz, speculations about scandal, and predictions of political success or failure. It was typified by *Washington Post* reporter Bob Woodward's insider books about the Bush and Clinton administrations. There was much discussion of economics, but most of it resembled the kind of naïve boosterism that characterized the discussion in the 1920s. AEI fellow James Glassman co-authored a book claiming that the Dow-Jones average of stock market prices would rise to 36,000. New magazines like *Wired* and *Fast Company* promoted the idea of a "long boom" that would last well into the twenty-first century. When *Rolling Stone* columnist Bill Greider published a study of the world economy, *One World, Ready or Not,* warning of overcapacity and financial instability in world markets, he was roundly criticized in *The New York Times Book Review* and *Foreign Affairs.*

Even the higher level debate about democracy and government was shallow and reactionary. Two decades after Kristol and the AEI had taken to the stump, the country's political debate was still dominated by a naïve conception of the relationship between state and market. It found its clearest expression in the revival of interest in Alexis de Tocqueville. Both Bill Clinton and Newt Gingrich declared that *Democracy in America* was one of their favorite books. Tocqueville even acquired his own web page, and C-SPAN staged a year-long bus tour to retrace Tocqueville's journey. Tocqueville, a great political thinker, has been deservedly credited with the insight that American democracy has not simply depended on the election of the rulers by the ruled, but on a welter of intermediate political and civil associations. The political associations of the 1990s were very different from those in Tocqueville's days, but if the Frenchman's point were taken generally, it was certainly relevant to understanding what ailed democracy. In Robert Putnam's acclaimed essay, "Bowling Alone," he used Tocqueville's thesis to argue that America's "democratic disarray may be linked to a broad and continuing erosion of civic engagement that began a quarter century ago."[30]

But liberals and conservatives who cited Tocqueville did so on behalf of a theory of contemporary democracy that was wildly inappropriate. They argued that because of the rise of computer automation, America was becoming similar to the country that Tocqueville visited in the 1830s. Wrote Gingrich in *To Renew America,* "The Information Revolution is breaking up these giants and leading us back to something that is—strangely enough—much more like de Tocqueville's 1830s America."[31] Michael Barone of *U.S. News & World Report* put it this way: "Today's postindustrial America in important respects more closely resembles the preindustrial America Tocqueville described in *Democracy in America* than the industrial America in which most of us grew up."[32]

At the same time, these political thinkers urged that Americans do whatever they could to speed this "return to Tocquevillian America."[33] Blaming the problems of American democracy on the increase in the power of the national government—on what former Tennessee governor Lamar Alexander called "hypercentralism"—they called for reducing the power of government by devolving its functions back on states, cities, businesses, charities, neighborhood groups, and families.[34]

Moderates and liberals espoused very similar views. In 1996 the Democratic Leadership Council published a manifesto, *The New Progressive Declaration,* in which it offered a "political philosophy for the information age." It extolled "the information revolution's tendency to diffuse power from large, hierarchical institutions to decentralized, self-adapting systems." It advised Americans that "as big institutions lose their power to deliver security and stability, Americans need to fall back on the support of strong families and networks of mutual aid." It argued that "today's dispersal of economic power suggests a corresponding diffusion of political power, away from central institutions to people and local institutions."[35]

These views, which ran directly counter to the insights of the Progressive Era, were almost entirely mistaken. There was very little resemblance between Tocqueville's America and the America of the 1990s. In 1831, when Tocqueville visited the United States, ten out of eleven Americans still lived on small farms. There were only a few large businesses, and Andrew Jackson had closed down one of the most powerful, the Bank of the United States. Tocqueville's theory of American democracy—adapted from Jackson and Thomas Jefferson—held that political equality rested on the remarkable economic equality that prevailed among white Northern Americans in the 1830s. Democracy was the means by which a roughly equal populace could inoculate itself against governmental tyranny.

One hundred sixty years later, the top 500 manufacturing and mining firms accounted for 82 percent of all sales in the United States.[36] Many of these firms were multinationals with assets around the globe and the ability to play one government off against another. In the 1990s, capital became more concentrated, while the distribution of wealth became even more unequal. A massive wave of mergers occurred in telecommunications, banking, health care, aircraft, retail sales, and autos. In 1998 four of the five largest mergers in American history occurred.

Barone, Gingrich, and the authors of *The New Progressive Declaration* confused the dispersion of *production,* which has been occurring because of the mobility of capital, with the dispersion of *control.* If anything, control over the national economy has become more concentrated in a few giant corporations and banks, which in the last three decades have become even more removed from local, popular control. Political power has devolved from the national government, but not toward the states and neighborhoods. It has become increasingly lodged in multinational corporations and international finance. In Washington, it has shifted away from the federal bureaucracy toward the issue networks that are dominated by K Street.

Weakening the federal government still further—whether through privatizing its functions or by abolishing regulatory agencies—would not shift power to workers, consumers, and local entrepreneurs, but to large corporations and banks and their lobbyists in Washington. The government remains the only national institution through which the inhabitants of Camden or Peoria can contest the power of IBM, Ford, or Caterpillar.

The conservative champions of civil society were equally mistaken in blaming the decline of civil society and of Tocqueville's intermediate associations on the growth of the national government. Those periods in which private, voluntary, local activity has flourished—for instance the 1930s and 1960s—were exactly those times when the national government grew and was strengthened.[37] In twentieth-century America, the growth of government power and of civil society occurred in tandem rather than in opposition to each other. The decline in civil society was as much symptom as cause of our democratic distemper. Its cure won't be found in dismantling but in strengthening the structure of democratic pluralism that emerged over the first half of the century.

The Courage to Be Rich

During the Progressive Era, there was a Christian revival inspired by the social gospel and more broadly by a spirit of altruism toward the poor. New schools and universities were founded to promote social Christianity. Black colleges and high schools were established by Northern mission societies. Women's clubs and moral reform movements were founded. The common goal of the era's diverse religious movements, historian William G. McLoughlin wrote, was "to use religion and science together to 'uplift the masses' rather than to levee them to the mercy of laissez-faire individualism."[38] This kind of spirit was highly conducive to a political reform movement. There were, of course, pockets of social reform in the 1990s, and there was a large conservative evangelical movement, but its basic outlook was hostile to social reform.

The dominant spirit of the late 1990s was a return with a vengeance to the Reagan years' obsession with becoming wealthy and successful. Everything and everyone had a "bottom line." One of the best-selling authors was a West Coast financial consultant, Suze Orman, the author of *The Courage to Be Rich* and *The Nine Steps to Financial Freedom*. Orman's books were a pilgrim's program, but to an ATM machine rather than the gates of heaven. Her male counterpart was Stephen R. Covey, the author of *The Seven Habits of Highly Effective People* and other books on how to succeed in life and business.

The major response to this new narcissism was a curmudgeonly conservatism based on a nostalgia about America before the sixties. Robert Bork, William Bennett, *Washington Post* columnist Charles Krauthammer, *U.S. News & World Report* columnist John Leo, Irving Kristol and his son William, Richard John Neuhaus, Marvin Olasky, and Myron Magnet argued that whatever ailed American culture was the fault of the movement of the sixties. In *Slouching Towards Gomorrah,* Bork charged that the sixties introduced a spirit of "radical individualism," which encouraged a "rootless hedonism," and a spirit of "radical egalitarianism," which could lead to "collectivist tyranny."[39] Irving Kristol made a similar indictment. Identifying the radicalism of the sixties with the "liberal ethos," he charged that "sector after sector of American life has been corrupted by the liberal ethos. It is an ethos that aims simultaneously at political and social collectivism on the one hand, and moral anarchy on the other."[40] Magnet, who would influence Texas Governor George W. Bush, blamed the existence of an underclass on the "cultural revolution" promoted by the sixties.[41]

In response to this cultural revolution, conservative critics put forth their own version of narcissism. After leaving the Reagan administration, former Secretary of Education William Bennett marketed himself as a professional moralist. While Covey made his living advising people how to become effective at work, Bennett became an expert in good behavior, publishing among other books *The Book of Virtues, The Children's Book of Virtues, The Book of Virtues for Young People, The Children's Book of Heroes, The Moral Compass* and *Anecdotes from the Book of Virtues.* Both men encouraged the preoccupation with private at the expense of public life. Both men reinforced Americans' self-absorption.

The 1990s also displayed the kind of unseemly fascination with luxury that Thorstein Veblen pilloried in *The Theory of the Leisure Class.* When the economy finally began to pick up in 1996, the sales of luxury goods increased 21 percent, while overall sales increased only 5 percent. New magazines like *Luxe* and *Success* joined stalwarts from the 1980s like Forbes' *FYI.* The *Wall Street Journal* inaugurated a Friday section that dealt with luxury goods. A typical feature was on the "Five Hundred Dollar a Night Hotel Room."[42] *House and Garden* did a special issue titled "It's All About Luxury." In 1996, *The Wine Spectator*'s auction index, which measures what prices buyers will pay for premium wines, grew 40 percent.[43] Sales in luxury watches rose 13 percent in 1997. Most of these were in the $25,000 to $75,000 range, but some cost as much as $300,000.[44] In Texas there was a run on recreational vehicles that cost over $500,000.[45]

The conspicuous consumers of the 1990s identified status and happiness with the power to buy and display very expensive goods. Like the $300,000 Patek Phillipe watch, they were coveted for their symbolic value rather than for their superior beauty or utility. This spirit was antithetical to political reform, which is based upon an understanding that individual happiness is inextricably linked to social well-being. Reform depends upon the recognition that the protection of the air and water from pollution, the preservation of forests and streams, and the elimination of poverty and economic insecurity is as important to happiness as the acquisition of a prestigious watch or the construction of a Gatsby-like castle in the Hamptons.

[11]

Conclusion

In America, periods of massive industrial consolidation and dramatic technological innovation have always been followed by periods of political and social reform. One eventually creates the need for the other, as the economic changes produce social conditions that come into conflict with democratic ideals. The United States has now had thirty years—comparable to the post–Civil War decades—in which the structure of industry and America's relation to the world have been thoroughly transformed. During the Bush administration and during Clinton's first years in office, some new and some older social problems have emerged. In the past, the nation did not seem to have the resources to deal with them. With budget deficits soaring, how could it afford to complete the funding of Headstart, reduce teacher-student ratios, make college education affordable, subsidize urban rapid transit systems, broaden access to health care and improve antipollution technology? Now it does have the resources, but still nothing happens.

The reason is the political system, which was supposed to be purged of corruption during the reforms of the late 1960s and early 1970s, but is increasingly driven by big money. There was an inkling in the early 1990s of a new reform era, but it quickly vanished—a casualty of the revival of the alliance between K Street and Republican conservatives. Clinton's projection of a new New Deal, Gingrich's boasts of revolution, and Clinton's later claim of a new Progressive Era all proved equally ill-founded. It is not clear when, or under what circumstances, Americans might embark on the kind of reforms that would once again bring the country's ideals to bear on its political system and economy. One, however, can describe the conditions that could make a genuine new era of reform possible.

COUNTERVAILING POWER American democracy has functioned best when workers, consumers, and citizens have acquired countervailing power against the might of business and business leaders, who enjoy an inherent advantage because of their hold over the economy, the wealth at their disposal, and the relative ease with which they can organize themselves. During the Progressive Era, the New Deal, and the 1950s, labor unions provided the principal countervailing power to business. They wielded power within the workplace and industry, but also exerted political power by rallying citizens to pass laws that significantly improved Americans' living conditions. The minimum wage, unemployment insurance, and Medicare all owe their existence to the political power marshaled by labor unions.

During the 1960s, the scope of politics expanded to include consumer protection, environmental regulation, and the guarantee of sexual and racial equality. Labor unions were joined by civil rights organizations, feminists, consumer activists, and environmentalists, as well as a host of single-issue groups. These movements and organizations had an indelible effect on the Johnson years and the first Nixon administration, laying the basis for the civil rights laws of 1964 and 1965 and the environmental and consumer legislation passed from 1967 to 1974. But labor and the movements of the 1960s never fully recovered from the business counteroffensive that began in the early 1970s and that coincided with and also contributed to the rise of K Street. Over the last two decades, many of these movements have learned to play the new game of K Street politics by running focus groups, hiring public relations and media experts, testifying before Congress, and setting up political action committees. They have even learned to write web pages, and to get information out over the Internet. But they cannot hope to create countervailing power without a mobilized base outside of Washington. Just as business's power depends ultimately upon its ability to move elsewhere or close down if it doesn't get its way, the power of labor and citizen movements depends upon their ability to disrupt the normal pattern of life—whether through strikes, demonstrations, marches, or boycotts. To fulfill the promise of democracy—to create genuine countervailing power—America needs a rebirth of popular movements.

In the case of unions, that may be difficult without passing the kind of labor law reform that business lobbies defeated in 1978—a defeat that signalled a new era in American politics. In the 1990s, there was growing support among workers for unionization, but businesses continued to take advantage of loopholes in labor law to frustrate union organizing. According to a study commissioned by the National Labor Relations Board, a third of the private companies being organized illegally fired union backers and half of them threatened to close down their plants.[1] Increasing the penalties to discourage illegal company tactics would not merely help unions grow. It would also strengthen the foundation of democratic pluralism.

POLITICAL REFORM Political parties and even elections sometimes precipitate and ratify the need for significant structural changes (as in the elections of 1912, 1932 and 1936, 1964, and 1980). But more often they have taken second place to the struggle among interest groups and the influence exercised by elites and elite organizations. In the last decades, the electoral process has increasingly come under the control of business lobbyists and political action committees that have used their superior financial resources to influence candidates and manipulate public opinion. Instead of serving as a counterweight to the inequality of the economic system, the political system has reinforced it. It has also created a vicious circle. Voters, believing that elections are being controlled by "special interests," have stopped participating, reinforcing the domination of the same interests.

To restore the original function of the electoral system, it is important to limit severely the role that wealth and concentrated economic power play. This means either overturning the Supreme Court's decision in *Buckley* v. *Valeo* prohibiting limits on campaign spending or enacting a voluntary public finance provision for Congressional as well as presidential races. The public has balked at taxpayer financing, but it could become more receptive if reformers made clear how much the lack of public financing costs in favors that large contributors extract from politicians and parties. The cost of public finance pales before the cost to the taxpayer of unwarranted subsidies to ethanol producers or to overseas banks and corporations. (In 1995, DLC economist Robert Shapiro estimated that eliminating unnecessary subsidies could save taxpayers $265 billion in five years.)[2]

ELITES AND ELITE ORGANIZATIONS In 1956, C. Wright Mills touted the existence of a power elite or political establishment as a contradiction to the American ideal of democracy. It certainly was a contradiction to the ideal of one-man, one-vote electoral democracy then taught in high school civics classes, but not to the actual functioning of American democracy in the twentieth century. Those periods when democracy has most clearly flourished—the Progressive Era, the New Deal, and the 1950s and 1960s—were also the times when a political establishment was most active and influential. Elites and elite organizations have served as the repository for a set of values that have been essential to American democracy: the determination to stand above class, party, region, race, and religion; the respect for social science; and the commitment to the unique American ideal of social equality. At their best, elites and elite organizations have promoted an idea of the national interest that could bind together citizens and unite conflicting interest groups. They have allowed citizens—who don't have the time or inclination to read every clause of an arms control treaty or every provision of a bill—to put their trust in a dispassionate group of experts. Trust in their wisdom and expertise has been essential to trust in government itself. As the would-be members of the nation's establishment have opted to become advocates for special interests, the public has become justifiably cynical about government and about public service.

It's hard to imagine measures that might inspire civic responsibility. What distinguishes a disinterested elite is that it acts without monetary incentive. But it's not hard to imagine measures that might discourage irresponsibility. These would include much stricter laws regulating Washington lobbyists and lawyers—closing the revolving door between lobbyists and government, requiring full disclosure of activity at the time it is undertaken. A lobbyist like Boyden Gray who appears on a television talk show or authors an op-ed article would have to disclose fully any lobbying activity that bore on the subject he was discussing.

THE NATIONAL GOVERNMENT During the Progressive Era and the New Deal, those movements that sought to mitigate the inequality created by corporate capitalism saw the government as an instrument of reform rather than of tyranny. They thought of government regulatory agencies like the Federal Trade Commission and the National Labor Relations Board not as a constraint on individual freedom, but as a bulwark against the superior power of private corporations. Through the Wagner Act and the NLRB, government even took over the task of promoting democratic pluralism. On the other side, business and business organizations have attempted to curb government—and to convince the public that it is an evil—in order to enhance their own power and weaken that of their adversaries. The Administrative Procedure Act of 1946 and the Taft-Hartley Act of 1947 fundamentally altered the role of government and public administration, transforming government administrators from representatives of the national interest into referees in the ongoing struggle among interest groups, a struggle in which business lobbies had an intrinsic advantage. Today, American political debate is dominated by antigovernment nostrums—and by simple-minded proposals such as term limits for legislators. Government needs continual reform in its operations—the DLC's initiative to reinvent government was entirely appropriate—but its critics have attempted to restrict its purview and power rather than make it more efficient. To make democracy work, Americans have to affirm the importance of government as an instrument of popular, democratic power and restore the original mission of agencies like the NLRB.

Americans also need to affirm the importance of government work. The natural tendency of capitalism has been to generously reward those who assiduously defend the interests of business—the lobbyists, public relations experts, and policy wonks—while attempting to stigmatize and penalize those who are appointed, elected, or hired to carry out the people's business in Washington. In periods of upheaval and crisis, Americans have rallied around the national government, and America's top businessmen, lawyers, and academics have come to Washington to serve on behalf of the national interest; but at other times, Americans have accepted without challenge or even endorsed the canard that America's ills are the result of its government being too powerful and its officials being irresponsible and unaccountable. One very modest way to encourage the best and brightest to serve rather than sell out would be to make the salaries of government officials remotely comparable to those of K Street lobbyists. Paying a public servant and politician only a fraction of what a peer in business or law makes is an invitation to corruption.

THE NEW MILLENNIALISM America remains a Protestant nation, and its dreams belong to the millenarian legacy of the Puritans. Since the seventeenth century, the attempt to create a "new Israel" and a "city on the hill" in America has inspired the finest moments of our politics—from the Revolution to abolitionism to the social reforms of the Progressive Era and the New Deal. It informed Americans' sense of social responsibility as a nation. In the twentieth century, what was once a specifically Christian ideal became a secular objective with Christian millennial undertones. And what was once a dream of making America a model for the world became a dream of remaking the world after the model of America. When Henry Luce proclaimed the American century in 1941, he was unconsciously invoking the early Puritan dreams, but doing so in largely secular and global terms. America's sense of mission during the Cold War derived its underlying fervor and urgency from these same millennial themes. With the Cold War's end, however, Americans have become uncertain about their mission at home and in the world.

The irony is that Americans stand poised to realize the dream of Wilsonian internationalism: to create a world capitalism no longer threatened by either imperialist rivalries or by Communism. The United States has good reason to complete this mission—not out of pride, but out of a realization that democracy and prosperity within the United States depend, finally, upon their spread overseas. Yet the last decade has seen the reemergence of an older isolationism. Echoing the Republicans of the 1920s, some of today's politicians have insisted that currency collapses in East Asia and ethnic cleansing in the Balkans are none of America's business.

At home, Americans also stand poised to carry forward the mission of the Progressive Era, the New Deal, and the great society: to make good on the original promise of liberty and equality within the constraints of corporate capitalism. But Americans' sense of mission has been threatened by narcissism and selfish individualism and by the narrow moralism of the religious right. Contemporary Americans seek either wealth or moral perfection. This new schizophrenia of spirit has been well represented by Representative Tom DeLay and the "young Turks" of the Republican House, who walk along the corridors of the Capitol with a check from a corporate political action committee in one hand and a Bible in the other and who find it unthinkable that the country should expend its considerable resources on ending poverty at home or combating tyranny abroad. Americans need a rebirth of postmillennialism—not necessarily in its original Christian form, but in the form of a renewed commitment to democracy at home and overseas.

THE QUALITY OF LIFE Some Americans still have not accepted that the security of old age, the opportunity for employment, the protection of the environment, the safety of the workplace, and the quality and safety of products depend on powerful government programs and vigilant public agencies. Right-wing radicals have called on these programs to be "privatized"—under the absurd contention that private charities, which are already over-burdened and underfunded, can better care for the poor, unemployed, and disabled.[3] K Street policy groups have suggested that Social Security and Medicare have unduly shifted the nation's resources toward the undeserving aged rather than the young—as if Americans had to choose between the two. And in the name of deregulation, they attack consumer, workplace, and environmental protections for inhibiting economic growth—an unlikely contention in an era in which business makes money by enhancing people's quality of life.

In this case, as elsewhere, the lobbies and think tanks are twisting knowledge to their own ends. The real situation is entirely different. Like the Americans of the 1920s, the Americans of the late 1990s have faced a problem of abundance rather than scarcity—of finding consumers willing to purchase the avalanche of new products that global advances in manufacturing productivity have made possible and of finding worthy social programs that can put this vast surplus to use. Social programs don't act to undermine capitalism, but to maintain its prosperity in the face of a recurring threat of overcapacity. If properly designed, they can also reduce the overall costs of providing services. If anything, Americans of the twenty-first century have to think about expanding the reach of our social programs—for instance, from Medicare to universal health insurance and from piecemeal college loans to a national citizens' corps—and widen the scope of regulation to meet threats like global warming.

THE PURSUIT OF HAPPINESS There is a reluctance to accept that in the twentieth century, American culture irrevocably turned a corner away from the Protestant work ethic that dominated American life since the seventeenth century. The change dates as far back as the 1920s when advertising man Bruce Barton suggested that the way to combat godless Soviet Communism was to "give every Russian a copy of the latest Sears-Roebuck Catalogue and the address of the nearest Sears-Roebuck outlet."[4] In the sixties, a new American most clearly emerged. For this new American, the goal of life was not salvation in the afterlife but happiness in this life. The satisfaction of bodily pleasures, through sex, sports, social activity, entertainment, and eating, was no longer viewed as sinful but as an integral part of happiness. Work itself was not dutiful toil directed at the glory of God but an important source of self-fulfillment and a means to achieve comfort and security for oneself and one's family. Leisure was not a temptation to sin but a reward for work.

Conservatives regard this new ethic as a symptom of moral and cultural decline. But it is far preferable to worry about how to achieve happiness on earth than to tolerate unhappiness and even misery in the pursuit of an imagined afterlife. It is also a decided advance that the average American can now take advantage of activities and opportunities that were once reserved for the upper classes—like travel, education, psychotherapy, athletics, and preventive medicine. Most Americans, and not simply a fortunate few, can now enjoy the aesthetic dimension of fine clothes, comfortable housing, and good food. And Americans can participate freely in sexual activities that were formerly performed secretly under a burden of crippling guilt.

The conservative culture war against the 1960s—like the struggle in the early twentieth century against the evils of drink and urban industrial culture—will eventually meet defeat at the hands of inexorable social and economic change. But in the meantime, it has prevented Americans from adapting to the reality of our circumstances. America needs to put the sixties behind it—not by repudiating them but by incorporating what was positive in their legacy. The key question for the twenty-first century will not be whether to pursue happiness in this life, but how to do so—whether through the individual quest for riches, immortalized in Suze Orman's *The Courage to Be Rich,* or through the enhancement of our communities, cities, nation, and the planet itself. The mark of civilization is not the wealth of a single individual or family, but that of a nation and is measured in its ability to protect its citizens from the unbridled power of nature and from the ravages of poverty, untended illness, and old age.

POST–BRETTON WOODS AMERICA No one knows how long today's seemingly unbounded prosperity—based in part on stock prices wildly inflated by foreign money and by native dreams—will last. America's objective should be to make sure that all its citizens enjoy its benefits. We should also do what is possible to ensure that when it does finally end, the nation will not suffer a disastrous crash. This depends on how America maneuvers within the post–Bretton Woods world economy that emerged in 1971, to which our fate is inextricably tied.

The largest challenge facing America today is to adapt our democratic ideals to this new world economy of multinational corporations, floating exchange rates, and fierce international competition. This means erecting the new "financial architecture" that Clinton promised during the Asian crisis of 1997–98, but then forgot about it after the crisis abated. Besides discouraging the kind of currency speculation that precipitated the Asian crisis, it would also enable the spread rather than the constriction of labor rights and environmental and consumer regulation. America's approach to the post–Bretton Woods economy would also cushion workers against insecurity through national health insurance and through programs, on and off the job, that allowed lifetime learning. There is nothing particularly novel about these approaches. Most of them were part of Clinton's unsuccessful reform efforts in his first two years in office, but, except for the occasional rhetorical flourish, they were abandoned after the 1994 elections.

Business leaders and economists have argued that any attempt to regulate the new economy of runaway shops, downsizing, and temporary employment will jeopardize its benefits and plunge the country back into the stagflation of the 1970s. It is the same argument that the leaders of the newly founded National Association of Manufacturers made a century ago against government intervention and union recognition. But of course the reforms of the Progressive Era and the New Deal and the rise of the labor movement didn't destroy capitalism, they preserved, humanized, and democratized it. These periods in our history demonstrated that it was possible to reconcile democratic pluralism with the new corporate industrial economy. It will be the task of Americans of the twenty-first century to demonstrate that the nation need not forsake its democratic ideals, including its commitment to social equality, in order to enjoy the fruits of the new world economy.

Notes

INTRODUCTION

1 Center for Responsive Politics, *Influence Inc.,* Washington, D.C., 1999.

2 Dick Morris, *Behind the Oval Office: Winning the Presidency in the Nineties,* New York, 1997, p. 13.

3 See C. Eugene Steurele, Edward M. Gramlich, Hugh Heclo, and Demetra Smith Nightingale, *The Government We Deserve,* Washington, D.C., 1998, p. 114.

1. THE PARADOX OF DEMOCRACY

1 Clinton Rossiter, *Parties and Politics in America,* New York, 1960, p. 11.

2 Arthur F. Bentley, *The Process of Government,* Chicago, 1908, p. 258.

3 Quoted in *Time*, Aug. 7, 1978.

4 See James Weinstein, *The Corporate Ideal in the Liberal State: 1900–1918,* Boston, 1968; and Samuel Hays, "The Politics of Reform in Municipal Government in the Progressive Era," *Pacific Northwest Quarterly,* Oct. 1964.

5 See Daniel T. Rodgers, *Contested Truths: Keywords in American Politics since Independence,* New York, 1987, ch. 6.

6 Quoted in Michael Schudson, *Discovering the News: A Social History of American Newspapers,* New York, 1978.

7 See Sidney Blumenthal, *The Permanent Campaign,* Boston, 1980.

8 See William Leuchtenburg, *Franklin Roosevelt and the New Deal,* New York, 1963, p. 190.

9 Interview with author.

10 See Lawrence R. Jacobs and Robert Y. Shapiro, "Myths and Misunderstandings about Public Opinion Toward Social Security," paper delivered at the National Academy of Social Insurance, January 29–30, 1998.

11 See Philip Stern, *The Best Congress Money Can Buy,* New York, 1988, ch. 8.

12 See John B. Judis, "The Contract with K Street," *The New Republic,* Dec. 4, 1995.

13 Quoted in David B. Truman, *The Governmental Process,* New York, 1951, pp. 58–59.

14 Allan J. Cigler and Burdett A. Loomis, *Interest Group Politics,* Washington, D.C., 1991, p. 11.

15 See Joseph Goulden, *The Superlawyers,* New York, 1971, ch. 6; and Hugh Heclo, "Issue Networks and the Executive Establishment," *The New American Political System,* ed. Anthony King, Washington, D.C., 1980.

16 See Robert A. Kagan, "Adversarial Legalism and American Government," *The New Politics of Public Policy,* ed. Mark K. Landy and Martin A. Levin, Baltimore, 1995.

17 E. E. Schattschneider, *The Semi-Sovereign People,* Hinsdale, Ill., 1960, p. 38.

18 See Walter Guzzardi, Jr., "Business Is Learning How to Win in Washington," *Fortune,* March 27, 1978.

19 E. Pendleton Herring, *Group Representation Before Congress,* Baltimore, 1929, ch. 4.

20 John Kenneth Galbraith, *American Capitalism,* Boston, 1952, p. 111.

21 Herring, *Group Representation.*

22 Robert Dahl, *A Preface to Democratic Theory,* Chicago, 1956, p. 137.

23 See Paul M. Sweezy, *The Theory of Capitalist Development,* New York, 1942.

24 C. Wright Mills, *The Power Elite,* New York, 1956, p. 11.

25 Ibid., p. 18.

26 For an analysis of Mills's *The Power Elite* along these lines, see Daniel Bell, "*The Power Elite* Reconsidered," *American Journal of Sociology,* Nov. 1958.

27 E. Digby Baltzell, *The Protestant Establishment,* New York, 1964, and *Philadelphia Gentlemen,* Glencoe, Ill., 1958.

28 See G. William Domhoff, *Who Rules America?,* Englewood Cliffs, N.J., 1967.

29 "*The Power Elite* and its Critics," *C. Wright Mills and the Power Elite,* ed. G. William Domhoff and Hoyt B. Ballard, Boston, 1968, p. 276. After he wrote *Who Rules America?,* Domhoff became familiar with the work of historians James Weinstein and David Eakins, who argued that in the twentieth century American elites exerted their influence through their control of policy groups, foundations, and think tanks, and that much of what had been seen as antibusiness legislation had either emanated from or been endorsed by these "corporate liberal" organizations. In his subsequent works, Domhoff tried to explore in detail how these institutions influenced particular laws, such as the Social Security Act of 1935 and the Employment Act of 1945.

30 See Gordon Wood, *The Radicalism of the American Revolution,* New York, 1991, p. 207.

31 *The Federalist Papers,* No. 35., New York, 1961, p. 216.

32 Quoted in Jordan A. Schwarz, *The New Dealers: Power Politics in the Age of Roosevelt,* New York, 1993, p. 136.

33 Louis Brandeis, "The Opportunity in the law," *American Law Review,* 1905.

34 Weinstein, *Corporate Ideal,* p. 10.

35 Walter Lippmann, *Drift and Mastery,* Englewood Cliffs, N.J., 1961, p. 150.

36 Quoted in Olivier Zunz, *Why the American Century?,* Chicago, 1998, p. 27. See also A. James Reichley, *Religion in American Public Life,* Washington, D.C., 1985, ch. 5; and William G. McLoughlin, *Revivals, Awakenings and Reforms,* Chicago, 1978, ch. 5.

37 See Andrew Carnegie, *The Autobiography,* Boston, 1920 (reissued 1986), p. 72.

38 On the history of the National Civic Federation, see Weinstein, *Corporate Ideal;* Robert Wiebe, *Businessmen and Reform,* Chicago, 1962, ch. 7; and the National Civic Federation collection in the New York Public Library.

39 Mary O. Furner, "The Republican Tradition and the New Liberalism," *The State and Social Investigation in Britain and the United States,* ed. Michael J. Lacey and Mary O. Furner, Washington, D.C., 1993, p. 215.

40 Marcus Hanna, "Socialism and the Labor Unions," *National Magazine,* Feb. 1904.

41 Herbert Croly, *Marcus Alonzo Hanna: His Life and Work,* New York, 1912, ch. 25. Croly's early and authorized and somewhat uncritical biography is still the best source on Hanna's life, because soon after it was published, Hanna's papers were either destroyed or lost.

1 paradox

42 Weinstein, *Corporate Ideal,* p. 10.

43 "The Work of the National Civic Federation," New York Public Library Collection, 12.

44 David Hammack and Stanton Wheeler, *Social Science in the Making,* New York, 1994, p. 3

45 Ibid.

46 National Bureau of Research, *Retrospect and Prospect: 1920–1935,* New York, 1936, p. 7.

47 Ibid.

48 Donald T. Critchlow, *The Brookings Institution: 1915–1952,* DeKalb, Ill., 1985, ch. 3.

49 Ibid., ch. 4.

50 Quoted in Schudson, *Discovering the News,* ch. 3.

51 Ibid.

52 Quoted in David Seidman, *The New Republic,* New York, 1993, p. 14.

53 See Charles Forcey, *The Crossroads of Liberalism,* New York, 1961, p. 193.

54 Quoted in Nelson Aldrich, *Old Money,* New York, 1988, p. 213.

55 Financial journalist Frank A. Vanderlip, speaking in 1902, before the Commercial Club of Chicago, as quoted in Martin J. Sklar, "Thoughts on Origins and Implications of the 'American Century': A Twice-Told Tale," 1998, unpublished manuscript.

56 Quoted in Robert D. Schulzinger, *The Wise Men of Foreign Affairs: The History of the Council on Foreign Relations,* New York, 1974, ch. 1.

57 Quoted in Leonard Silk and Mark Silk, *The American Establishment,* New York, 1980, p. 189.

58 Laurence H. Shoup and William Minter, *Imperial Brain Trust,* New York, 1977, p. 89.

59 John Franklin Campbell, "The Death Rattle of the Eastern Establishment," *New York Times Magazine,* Sept. 20, 1971.

60 *Federalist Papers,* No. 10, p. 82.

61 Woodrow Wilson, "The Study of Administration," *Political Science Quarterly,* June 1887.

62 Ibid.

63 John Dewey, *The Public and Its Problems,* Chicago, 1927, p. 71.

64 Quoted in Felix Frankfurter, *The Public and Its Government,* New Haven, 1930, p. 148. See also Frederick C. Mosher, *Democracy and Public Service,* 2d ed., New York, 1982.

65 Earl Latham, *The Group Basis of Politics,* Ithaca, N.Y., 1952, pp. 35–36.

66 Robert Reich, "Policy Making in a Democracy," *The Power of Public Ideas,* Cambridge, Mass., 1988, p. 129.

67 Heclo, "Issue Networks."

68 James Landis, *The Administrative Process,* New Haven, 1938, p. 36.

69 Ruy Teixeira, *Why Is American Voter Turnout So Low?,* Washington, D.C., 1992, p. 9.

70 Quoted in Matthew Josephson, *The Politicos,* New York, 1938, p. 364. See also Michael E. McGeer, *The Decline of Popular Politics,* Oxford, 1986, chs. 1 and 2.

2. THE DEVELOPMENT OF DEMOCRATIC PLURALISM

1 Quoted in John B. Judis, *Grand Illusion: Critics and Champions of the American Century,* New York, 1992, p. 15.

2 See Thomas Cochran and William Miller, *The Age of Enterprise,* New York, 1961.

3 See James Weinstein, *The Corporate Ideal in the Liberal State,* Boston, 1968, p. 63.

4 Alexis de Tocqueville, *Democracy in America,* New York, 1945, vol. 2, p. 171.

5 Quoted in Cochran and Miller, *Age of Enterprise,* p. 171.

6 On the history of the corporation and the law, I have benefited from Scott Bowman, *The Modern Corporation and American Political Thought,* University Park, Md., 1996; on "corporate individualism," see p. 8.

7 Quoted in Harold U. Faulkner, *Politics, Reform and Expansion: 1890–1900,* New York, 1959, p. 141.

8 See Thomas B. Brooks, *Toil and Trouble,* New York, 1964, chs. 6 and 7.

9 See Steven J. Rosenstone, Roy L. Behr, and Edward Lazarus, *Third Parties in America,* Princeton, 1984, ch. 3.

10 See James Weinstein, *The Decline of Socialism in America: 1912–1925,* New York, 1967, ch. 2.

11 See Elisabeth S. Clemens, *The People's Lobby,* Chicago, 1997, ch. 4.

12 Reprinted in a National Civic Federation pamphlet, "The Social Problem," New York, 1914, New York Public Library collection.

13 See Robert Wiebe, *Businessmen and Reform,* Chicago, 1989, p. 31.

14 See Woodrow Wilson, *The State: Elements of Historical and Practical Politics,* Boston, 1889.

15 On the differences between Roosevelt and Wilson, see Martin J. Sklar, *The Corporate Reconstruction of American Capitalism,* Cambridge, Mass.,

1988, part 2; and John Milton Cooper, Jr., *The Warrior and the Priest,* Cambridge, Mass., 1983, ch. 14.

16 Quoted in George F. Mowry, *The Era of Theodore Roosevelt,* New York, 1958, p. 101.

17 Quoted in Cooper, *Warrior and the Priest,* p. 254.

18 Woodrow Wilson, "Politics," *Atlantic Monthly,* Nov. 1907.

19 Brooks, *Toil and Trouble,* p. 134.

20 Weinstein, *Decline of Socialism,* p. 115.

21 William Leuchtenburg, *The Perils of Prosperity,* Chicago, 1958, p. 67.

22 Weinstein, *Decline of Socialism,* p. 206.

23 See Irving Bernstein, *The Lean Years,* New York, 1966, ch. 3; and Cochran and Miller, *Age of Enterprise,* p. 333.

24 Quoted in Cochran and Miller, *Age of Enterprise,* p. 331.

25 On the early history of public relations, see Eric Goldman, *Two-Way Street,* New York, 1948.

26 Quoted in Cochran and Miller, *Age of Enterprise,* p. 332.

27 Quoted in Edward Epstein, *The Corporation in American Politics,* Englewood Cliffs, N.J., 1969, p. 75.

28 E. Pendleton Herring, *Group Representation Before Congress,* Baltimore, 1929, ch. 4.

29 Quoted in Bernstein, *Lean Years,* p. 88.

30 Quoted in Cochran and Miller, *Age of Enterprise,* p. 343.

31 Ibid., p. 342.

32 See Allan Nevins, "Andrew William Mellon," *Dictionary of American Biography,* New York, 1958.

33 See Leuchtenburg, *Perils of Prosperity,* p. 98; and George Soule, *Prosperity Decade,* New York, 1947, pp. 131–32.

34 Quoted in Arthur Schlesinger, Jr., *The Crisis of the Old Order,* Boston, 1957, p. 62.

35 Quoted in Leuchtenburg, *Perils of Prosperity,* p. 189.

36 Herring, *Group Representation,* ch. 4.

37 Quoted in Leuchtenburg, *Perils of Prosperity,* p. 203.

38 Quoted in Michael E. Parrish, *Anxious Decades,* New York, 1992, p. 52.

39 See Herbert Hoover, "Rugged Individualism" speech, Oct. 22, 1928, *Documentary History of the United States,* ed. Robert D. Heffner, New York, 1952. p. 265.

40 The *National Civic Federation Review* contained this blurb: "The National Civic Federation Review deals with current issues of paramount importance; sinister forces seeking to undermine American democratic in-

stitutions; international affairs; problems of reconstruction period requiring co-operation of constitutional and humanitarian forces for their solution."

41 See Frederick Lewis Allen, *Only Yesterday,* New York, 1931, p. 147.

42 See Weinstein, *Decline of Socialism,* chs. 4 and 5; and Theodore Draper, *The Roots of American Communism,* chs. 9 and 10, New York, 1957.

43 Bernstein, *Lean Years,* p. 84.

44 Soule, *Prosperity Decade,* p. 318.

45 Soule, *Prosperity Decade,* p. 317.

46 Quoted in Bernstein, *Lean Years,* p. 63. The author of the Brookings study, *America's Capacity to Consume,* wrote, "it appears that . . . income was being distributed with increasing inequality, particularly in the later years of the period."

47 Ruy Teixeira, *The Disappearing American Voter,* Washington, D.C., 1992, p. 9.

48 Felix Frankfurter, *The Public and Its Government,* New Haven, 1930, pp. 2–3.

49 Walter Lippmann, "The Causes of Political Indifference Today," *Atlantic Monthly,* Feb. 1927.

50 Bernstein, *Lean Years,* p. 147

51 Ibid.

52 Herbert Croly, "The New Republic Idea," *The New Republic,* Dec. 6, 1922.

53 Walter Lippmann, *Preface to Morals,* New York, 1929, p. 62.

54 Bureau of Labor Statistics figure.

55 Leuchtenburg, *Perils of Prosperity,* pp. 247–48.

56 Quoted in Ron Chernow, *The House of Morgan,* New York, 1990, p. 322.

57 Quoted in William Leuchtenburg, *Franklin Roosevelt and the New Deal,* New York, 1963, p. 22.

58 Ibid., p. 22.

59 Stuart Chase, *A New Deal,* New York, 1932, p. 2.

60 Charles Beard, "The Myth of Rugged Individualism," *New Deal Thought,* ed. Harold Zinn, Indianapolis, 1966, p. 10.

61 Ernest Gruening, "Capitalist Confiscation," *The Nation,* Feb. 1, 1933.

62 Franklin D. Roosevelt, "Message to Congress," April 29, 1938.

63 See Kenneth Finegold and Theda Skocpol, *State and Party in America's New Deal,* Madison, Wis., 1995, p. 136.

64 Leuchtenburg, *Franklin Roosevelt,* pp. 98–100.

65 Irving Bernstein, *The Turbulent Years,* Boston, 1971, p. 217.

66 On Frankfurter's life, see Jordan A. Schwarz, *The New Dealers:*

Power Politics in the Age of Roosevelt, New York, 1993; and Leonard Baker, *Brandeis and Frankfurter,* New York, 1984.

67 Frankfurter, *Public and Its Government,* p. 163.

68 Ibid., p. 135.

69 Alan Brinkley, *The End of Reform,* New York, 1995. p. 51.

70 Quoted by Leuchtenburg, *Franklin Roosevelt,* p. 21.

71 Quoted by Karen Lewis, "NAM Turns Programmatic, *National Journal,* June 3, 1972.

72 For my analysis of the Wagner Act and the second hundred days, I have drawn heavily on David Plotke's *Building a Democratic Political Order,* Cambridge, Mass., 1996, and Finegold and Skocpol's *State and Party in America's New Deal.* On the Wagner Act, see also Domhoff's retraction of his own earlier views in *The Power Elite and the State,* New York, 1990, chs. 3 and 4.

3. THE GREAT AMERICAN CELEBRATION

1 A. M. Schlesinger, "The Tides of History," *Yale Review,* Dec. 1939.

2 Harold Ickes, *The Secret Diary of Harold Ickes,* New York, 1953, p. 705.

3 After winning election in 1932, Roosevelt told friends, "We'll have eight years in Washington. By that time there may not be a Democratic party, but there will be a progressive one." Quoted in James MacGregor Burns, *The Deadlock of Democracy,* Englewood Cliffs, N.J., 1963, p. 167.

4 On the post-1936 leadership of the Roosevelt administration and on causes of the New Deal's decline, see Brinkley, *The End of Reform,* New York, 1995.

5 Broadus Mitchell, *Depression Decade,* New York, 1947, p. 92.

6 See Samuel Lubell, *The Future of American Politics,* New York, 1951, ch. 7.

7 See Irving Bernstein, *The Turbulent Years,* Boston, 1971, p. 663.

8 Ibid., pp. 666ff.

9 See Christopher L. Tomlins, *The State and the Unions: Labor Relations, Law and the Organized Labor Movement in America, 1880–1960,* Cambridge, Mass., 1985, p. 207.

10 Robert M. Collins, *The Business Response to Keynes: 1929–1964,* New York, 1981, pp. 91, 41.

11 On the history of the Employment Act, see Brinkley, *End of Reform;* Collins, *Business Response;* and Domhoff, "Conflict over the Employment Bill," *The Power Elite and the State,* New York, 1990.

12 See Nelson Lichtenstein, "From Corporatism to Collective Bargaining," *The Rise and Fall of the New Deal Order,* ed. Steve Fraser and Gary Gerstle, Princeton, 1989.

13 See Burton R. Fisher and Stephen B. Withey, *Big Business as the People See It,* Ann Arbor, 1951, pp. 20–22.

14 See Robert Griffith, "Forging America's Postwar Order: Domestic Politics and Political Economy in the Age of Truman," *The Truman Presidency,* ed. Michael Lacey, New York, 1989.

15 Ibid., p. 101.

16 See files for Michael Ross, CIO staff director of the International Affairs Department at the George Meany Library, Silver Spring, Md.

17 See V. O. Key, *Politics, Parties, and Pressure Groups,* New York, 1958, p. 86.

18 Philip H. Burch, Jr., "The NAM as Interest Group," *Politics and Society,* fall 1973.

19 On Hoffman, see Alan R. Raucher, *Paul G. Hoffman: Architect of Foreign Aid,* Lexington, Ky., 1985. On Benton, see Sidney Hyman, *The Lives of William Benton,* Chicago, 1969.

20 Karl Schriftgiesser, *Business Comes of Age,* New York, 1960, p. 29.

21 Collins, *Business Response,* p. 85.

22 Paul Hoffman, "The Corporation as a Social Instrument," in Bronson Batchelor, *The New Outlook in Business,* New York, 1940, pp. 108–09.

23 Quoted in Karl Schriftgiesser, *Business and Public Policy,* Englewood Cliffs, N.J., 1967, p. 22.

24 See Schriftgiesser, *Business and Public Policy,* p. 161.

25 See Tomlins, *State and the Unions,* p. 282.

26 Ibid., p. 287.

27 See Stephen Breyer, *Regulation and Its Reform,* Cambridge, Mass., 1982, pp. 378–79.

28 See Joseph C. Goulden, *The Superlawyers,* New York, 1971, pp. 186–87; and Foster H. Sherwood, "The Federal Administrative Procedure Act," *American Political Science Review,* Feb. 1947.

29 See Lynn Eden, "Capitalist Conflict and the State: The Making of United States Military Policy in 1948," in *State Making and Social Movements,* ed. Charles Bright and Susan Harding, Ann Arbor, 1984.

30 Quoted in Laurence A. Shoup and William Minter, *Imperial Brain Trust,* New York, 1977, p. 35.

31 Quoted in Schriftgiesser, *Business and Public Policy,* p. 115.

32 Arthur Larson, *A Republican Looks at His Party,* New York, 1956, p. 9.

4 60s

33 David Riesman, *The Lonely Crowd,* New York, 1953, p. 199.

34 Key, *Politics, Parties, and Pressure Groups,* pp. 144, 158.

35 David B. Truman, "The American System in Crisis," *Political Science Quarterly,* Dec. 1959.

36 E. E. Schattschneider, *The Semi-Sovereign People,* Hinsdale, Ill., 1960, p. 35.

37 Larson, *Republican Looks at His Party,* p. vii.

38 Charles C. Alexander, *Holding the Line: The Eisenhower Era, 1952–1961,* Bloomington, Ind., 1975, p. 103.

39 See Frank Levy, *New Dollars and Dreams,* New York, 1998, pp. 25–26.

40 Frederick Lewis Allen, *The Big Change,* New York, 1952, pp. 251–52.

41 Murray Kempton, *Part of Our Time,* New York, 1955, p. 297.

42 See Louis Hartz, *The Liberal Tradition in America,* New York, 1955.

43 Quoted in James A. Smith, *The Idea Brokers,* New York, 1991, p. 128.

44 On RAND, see James A. Smith and Paul Dickson, *Thinktanks,* New York, 1972, ch. 5.

45 Quoted by Dickson, *Thinktanks,* p. 86.

46 Baltzell, *The Protestant Establishment,* p. 302.

47 AFL-CIO papers, pp. 31–32, George Meany Library, Silver Spring, Md.

48 Quoted by David Eakins, "Policy-Planning for the Establishment," *The New History of Leviathan,* ed. Ronald Radosh and Murray Rothbard, New York, 1972, p. 199.

4. THE LEGACY OF THE SIXTIES

1 Robert H. Bork, *Slouching Towards Gomorrah,* New York, 1996, p. 32.

2 See Todd Gitlin, *The Sixties,* New York, 1987, p. 39.

3 On foundations and civil rights, see Waldemar Nielsen, *The Big Foundations,* New York, 1972, ch. 18.

4 Richard Barber, "The Great Partnership," *The New Republic,* Aug. 13, 1966; and David Vogel, *Fluctuating Fortunes,* New York, 1989, pp. 32–34.

5 Vogel, *Fluctuating Fortunes,* p. 25.

6 Robert Lekachman, "The Automation Report," *Commentary,* May 1966.

7 E. E. Schattschneider, *The Semi-Sovereign People,* Hinsdale, Ill., 1960.

8 Reprinted in James Miller, *Democracy Is in the Streets,* New York, 1987, p. 333.

9 Taylor Branch, *Parting the Waters,* New York, 1988, p. 73.

10 Robert Sam Anson, *McGovern,* New York, 1972, p. 51.

11 The quotations are from "The Triple Revolution," which was reprinted in *Liberation*, April 1964.

12 Kim Moody, *An Injury to All,* London, 1988, p. 210.

13 Francis A. Walker, *First Lessons in Political Economy,* New York, 1889, p. 64.

14 I am drawing much of my account of this new economy from Martin J. Sklar, "Some Political and Cultural Consequences of the Disaccumulation of Capital," *The United States as a Developing Country,* Cambridge, Mass., 1992, which was first published in the May–June 1969 issue of *Radical America;* and James Livingston, *Pragmatism and the Political Economy of Cultural Revolution: 1850–1940,* Chapel Hill, N.C., 1994, part 1. See also Daniel Bell, *The Coming of Post-Industrial Society,* New York, 1976, and *The Cultural Contradictions of Capitalism,* New York, 1976. Bell's interpretation, however, is significantly different. I see changes in morality reflecting changes in capitalism; he sees morality and capitalism in conflict. On the work ethic, see also Daniel T. Rodgers, *The Work Ethic in Industrial America:* 1850–1920, Chicago, 1978.

15 See John B. Judis, "The Great Savings Scare," *The New Republic,* Jan. 27, 1997, and "Value-free," *The New Republic,* April 26, 1999. See also Livingston, *Pragmatism and the Political Economy,* pp. 107–08.

16 See George Soule, *Prosperity Decade,* New York, 1947, p. 325.

17 See Stuart Ewen, *Captains of Consciousness,* New York, 1976, p. 26.

18 Quoted in Olivier Zunz, *Why the American Century?,* Chicago, 1998, p. 83.

19 On how this new capitalism created changes in family life, see Eli Zaretsky, *Capitalism, the Family and Personal Life,* New York, 1976.

20 Paul Goodman, *Growing Up Absurd,* New York, 1960, p. 28.

21 *Historical Statistics of the United States,* Washington, D.C., 1996.

22 See Robert B. Carson, "Youthful Labor Surplus," *Socialist Revolution,* May–June 1972; and *Statistical Abstract of the United States, 1996,* Washington, D.C., 1996, p. 180. Carson argues that the increase in student enrollment after World War II didn't just reflect the needs of a more educated labor force. It was also designed to keep large numbers of workers out of a labor force that couldn't employ them. The G.I. Bill, for instance, certainly functioned in that manner.

23 See *Report of the National Advisory Commission on Civil Disorders,* New York, 1968; and Thomas Byrne Edsall with Mary D. Edsall, *Chain Reaction,* New York, 1991, ch. 3.

24 See William G. McLoughlin, *Revivals, Awakenings and Reform,*

Chicago, 1978, ch. 6. I have explored the same themes in "The Visible Saints Go Marching In," *The Progressive,* Jan. 1982, *Grand Illusion,* New York, 1992, and "The Great Awakening," *The New Republic,* Feb. 1, 1993, as has Hugh Heclo in "The Sixties' False Dawn: Awakenings, Movements and Postmodern Policy-making," *Journal of Policy History,* vol. 8, no. 1, 1996. Like many observations about the sixties, however, the point was first made by Paul Goodman in *New Reformation: Notes of a Neolithic Conservative,* New York, 1969.

25 Harold Jacobs, "The Dialectics of Liberation," *Leviathan,* July–Aug. 1969.

26 See "You Don't Need a Weatherman," SDS pamphlet, 1969.

27 George Rising, *Clean for Gene: Eugene McCarthy's 1968 Presidential Campaign,* Westport, Conn., 1997, p. 63.

28 Goodman, *New Reformation,* p. 52.

29 On the "riot ideology," see Fred Siegel, *The Future Once Happened Here,* New York, 1998, ch. 1.

30 See Terry H. Anderson, *The Movement and the Sixties,* New York, 1995, pp. 366–67.

31 See Walter Isaacson and Evan Thomas, *The Wise Men,* New York, 1986, chs. 22–23.

32 Nielsen, *Big Foundations,* ch. 5.

33 See Frank K. Kelly, *Court of Reason: Robert Hutchins and the Fund for the Republic,* New York, 1981.

34 See Joseph C. Goulden, *The Money Givers,* New York, 1971, ch. 8; and Siegel, *Future Once Happened Here,* ch. 3.

35 See Sara M. Evans, *Born for Liberty,* New York, 1989, pp. 277–92. See also *Feminist Chronicles* (www.feminist.org/research/chronicles).

36 See Robert Cameron Mitchell, "From Conservation to Environmental Movement: The Development of the Modern Environmental Lobbies," in *Government and Environmental Politics,* ed. Michael J. Lacey, Washington, D.C., 1991.

37 Interview with author.

38 Ibid.

39 See Teresa Celsi, *Ralph Nader: The Consumer Revolution,* New York, 1991.

40 Charles McCarry, *Citizen Nader,* New York, 1972.

41 See Mark Dowie, *Losing Ground,* Cambridge, Mass., 1995, pp. 34–35.

42 Waldemar Nielsen, *The Golden Donors,* New York, 1985, p. 69

43 U.S. Department of Commerce, *Long Term Economic Growth,* Washington, D.C., 1973.

44 Vogel, *Fluctuating Fortunes.*

45 See William G. Mayer, *The Changing American Mind,* Ann Arbor, 1992, p. 478.

46 See Seymour Martin Lipset and William Schneider, *The Confidence Gap,* Baltimore, 1983, p. 30.

47 Robert S. Diamond, "What Business Thinks," *Fortune,* Feb. 1970.

48 Alexander Astin, Sarah A. Parrott, William S. Korn, and Linda J. Sax, *The American Freshman: Thirty Year Trends,* Los Angeles, 1997.

49 Daniel Yankelovich, *Generations Apart,* New York, 1969.

50 Daniel Yankelovich, *The New Morality: A Profile of American Youth in the '70s,* New York, 1974, p. 57.

51 Charles Reich, *The Greening of America,* New York, 1970, p. 340.

52 See Murray Bookchin, "Listen Marxist," a pamphlet circulated in 1969.

53 Ibid., p. 340.

54 Ibid., p. 383.

55 Goodman, *New Reformation,* p. 47.

56 Theodore Roszak, *The Making of a Counter Culture,* New York, 1969, p. 215.

57 Bell, *Cultural Contradictions of Capitalism,* p. 25. On this point see also Heclo, "The Sixties' False Dawn."

58 Tom Wolfe, "The Me Decade and the Third Great Awakening," *Mauve Gloves & Madmen, Clutter & Vine,* New York, 1976.

5. BUSINESS AND THE RISE OF K STREET

1 *Economic Report of the President,* Washington, D.C., 1991.

2 See Bennett Harrison and Barry Bluestone, *The Great U-Turn,* New York, 1988, p. 7; Philip Armstrong, Andrew Glyn, and John Harrison, *Capitalism Since World War II,* London, 1984, ch. 11; and Susan Strange and Roger Tooze, *The Industrial Politics of Surplus Capacity,* London, 1981.

3 Joyce Kolko, *America and the Crisis of World Capitalism,* Boston, 1974, p. 85.

4 See John B. Judis, *Grand Illusion: Critics and Champions of the American Century,* New York, 1992, ch. 7; and Robert C. Angel, *Explaining Economic Policy Failure,* New York, 1991.

5 See Robert Brenner, "The Economics of Global Turbulence," *New Left Review,* May–June 1998, p. 229.

6 Dani Rodrik, "Sense and Nonsense in the Globalization Debate," *Foreign Policy,* summer 1997. See also Dani Rodrik, *Has Globalization Gone Too Far?,* Washington, D.C., 1997.

5 K Street

7 See Peter B. Levy, *The New Left and Labor in the 1960s,* Urbana, Ill., 1994, ch. 8.

8 *Nation's Business,* July 1969.

9 *Business Week,* Dec. 6, 1969.

10 Interview with Murray Weidenbaum.

11 Elizabeth R. Jager, "The Changing World of Multinationals," AFL-CIO papers, Silver Spring, Md.

12 Kolko, *America and the Crisis of World Capitalism,* p. 43.

13 Richard L. Barovick, "The Washington Struggle over Multinationals," *Business and Society Review,* 1976.

14 AFL-CIO files, Silver Spring, Md.

15 David Rockefeller, "What Is the Future of the Multinational Corporation?," May 1, 1972, Burton Historical Collection, Detroit Public Library.

16 *Journal of Commerce,* Aug. 31, 1972.

17 Powell memorandum provided by U.S. Chamber of Commerce.

18 Reprinted in Irving Kristol, *Two Cheers for Capitalism,* New York, 1978, ch. 2.

19 Ibid., p. 14.

20 Ibid.

21 Ibid., p. 134.

22 William Simon, *A Time for Truth,* New York, 1978, p. 246.

23 Robert H. Malott, *Harvard Business Review,* July–Aug. 1978.

24 *National Journal,* Jan. 5, 1974.

25 Thomas B. Edsall, *The New Politics of Inequality,* New York, 1984, ch. 3.

26 See Thomas Howell, William A. Noellert, Jesse G. Kreier, and Alan W. Wolff, *Steel and the State,* Boulder, 1988, ch. 7.

27 See Kim McQuaid, "The Roundtable: Getting Results in Washington," *Harvard Business Review,* May–June 1981. On the history of the Roundtable, see also Sar A. Levitan and Martha R. Cooper, *Business Lobbies: The Public Good & the Bottom Line,* Baltimore, 1984, ch. 3.

28 *Harvard Business Review,* July–August 1981.

29 Baroody was little quoted in the fifties and spoke cautiously after 1965 when asked about the AEI's purposes. My own account is drawn from interviews with Herbert Stein, Seymour Martin Lipset, and Murray Weidenbaum, who knew Baroody, and from contemporary profiles and articles in the press. These include Daniel Balz, "Washington Pressures/AEI, Hoover Institution," *National Journal,* Dec. 22, 1973; and Myra MacPherson, "The Baroody Connection," *Washington Post,* Aug. 17, 1975. In his book on

think tanks, *The Idea Brokers* (New York, 1991), James A. Smith also interviewed AEI fellows who knew Baroody.

30 Balz, "Washington Pressures."

31 *The Economist,* March 2, 1979.

32 The story of Weyrich and Feulner's breakfast is told in Lee Edwards, *The Power of Ideas,* Ottawa, 1997. For my account of Heritage I have relied on interviews with Ed Feulner, Herb Berkowitz, Adam Meyerson, and Burton Pines.

33 Edwards, *Power of Ideas,* p. 9.

34 See Karen Rothmyer, "Citizen Scaife," *Columbia Journalism Review,* July–Aug. 1981.

35 See Gregg Easterbrook, "Ideas Move Nations," *Atlantic Monthly,* Jan. 1986.

36 Interview with author.

37 Easterbrook, "Ideas Move Nations."

38 *The Structure of Power in America,* ed. Michael Schwartz, New York, 1988, p. 207.

39 Quoted in Joseph D. Pescheck, *Policy Planning Organizations,* Philadelphia, 1987, p. 187.

40 Reginald Jones, *Harvard Business Review,* Sept.–Oct. 1975.

41 Interview with Murray Weidenbaum.

42 William G. Mayer, *The Changing American Mind,* Ann Arbor, 1992, p. 483.

43 Ibid., p. 485.

44 Ibid., p. 465.

45 Levitan and Cooper, *Business Lobbies.*

46 "Swarming Lobbyists," *Time,* Aug. 7, 1978; Robert H. Salisbury, "The Paradox of Interest Groups," *The American Political System,* ed. Anthony King, Washington, D.C., 1980; Hedrick Smith, *The Power Game,* New York, 1988.

47 Hugh Heclo, "Issue Networks and the Executive Establishment," *The American Political System,* ed. Anthony King, Washington, D.C., 1980.

48 Robert H. Salisbury, "Washington Lobbyists," *Interest Group Politics,* ed. Allan J. Cigler and Burdett A. Loomis, Washington, D.C., 1986.

49 *Newsweek,* June 20, 1988.

50 "Swarming Lobbyists," *Time,* Aug. 7, 1978.

51 Gerald Ford, *A Time to Heal,* New York, 1979, p. 259.

52 Carl Bernstein, "King of the Hill," *Vanity Fair,* March 1998.

53 See Marc Galanter and Thomas Palay, *Tournament of Lawyers,* Chicago, 1991, pp. 66–67.

6 Conservatism

54 For Walker's biography see Ralph Nader and William Taylor, *The Big Boys,* New York, 1986; and Elizabeth Drew, "Charlie," *The New Yorker,* Jan. 9, 1978. I also interviewed Walker myself.

6. THE TRIUMPH OF CONSERVATISM

1 Kevin P. Phillips, *The Emerging Republican Majority,* New Rochelle, N.Y., 1969, p. 25.

2 See Henry S. Farber, "The Extent of Unionization in the United States," *Challenges and Choices Facing American Labor,* ed. Thomas A. Kochan, Cambridge, Mass., 1986, p. 16.

3 Ibid.

4 See Richard Freeman, "Why Are Unions Faring Poorly in NLRB Representation Elections?," *Challenges and Choices,* ed. Kochan, p. 53.

5 See "Business Lobbying," *Consumer Reports,* Sept. 1978; and Mark Green, "Why the Consumer Bill Went Down," *The Nation,* Feb. 25, 1977.

6 David Vogel, *Fluctuating Fortunes,* New York, 1989, pp. 161–62.

7 *CQ Almanac,* Washington, D.C., 1978, p. 474.

8 Carter Presidential Files, "Labor Law Reform," Atlanta, Ga.

9 Sar A. Levitan and Martha R. Cooper, *Business Lobbies: The Public Good & the Bottom Line,* Baltimore, 1984, p. 135.

10 Interview with author.

11 See Thomas Ferguson and Joel Rogers, "Labor Law Reform and Its Enemies," *The Nation,* Jan. 6, 1979; Thomas Edsall, *The New Politics of Inequality,* New York, 1984, ch. 7; D. Quinn Mills, "Flawed Victory in Labor Law Reform," *Harvard Business Review,* May–June 1979; and Carter Presidential Files, "Labor Law Reform."

12 *Fortune,* March 27, 1978.

13 Whittaker Chambers, *Witness,* New York, 1952.

14 Interview with author.

15 Quoted in Frances Fitzgerald, "Ministers and Marches," *The New Yorker,* May 18, 1981. On this history, see George M. Marsden, *Understanding Fundamentalism and Evangelicism,* Grand Rapids, Mich., 1991; and A. James Reichley, *Religion in American Public Life,* Washington, D.C., 1985.

16 Reichley, *Religion in American Public Life,* p. 321.

17 See Alan Crawford, *Thunder on the Right,* New York, 1980, p. 102.

18 Jude Wanniski, "The Mundell-Laffer Hypothesis," *Public Interest,* spring 1975.

19 See Vogel, *Fluctuating Fortunes,* p. 209. Calculation is mine.

20 Associated Press, Sept. 9, 1980.

21 Interview with Herbert Stein.

22 Thomas Edsall, "The Reagan Legacy," *The Reagan Legacy,* ed. Sidney Blumenthal and Thomas Byrne Edsall, New York, 1988, p. 38.

23 See Charles O. Jones, "The New, New Senate," *A Tide of Discontent,* Washington, D.C., 1981, p. 102.

24 David Stockman, *The Triumph of Politics,* New York, 1986, p. 248.

25 Edsall, "Reagan Legacy," p. 45.

26 Lawrence Mishel et al., *The State of Working America, 1996–1997,* Washington, D.C., 1997, p. 110.

27 Mark Dowie, *Losing Ground,* Cambridge, Mass., 1995, p. 92.

28 Vogel, *Fluctuating Fortunes,* p. 270.

29 Ronald Reagan, *An American Life,* New York, 1990, pp. 226–27.

30 *Washington Post,* Nov. 13, 1981.

31 William G. Mayer, *The Changing American Mind,* Ann Arbor, 1992, p. 443.

32 Cyra McFadden, *The Serial,* New York, 1977, p. 92.

33 Alexander W. Astin, Sarah A. Parrott, William S. Korn, Linda J. Sax, *The American Freshman: Thirty Year Trends,* Los Angeles, 1997, pp. 56–57.

7. THE APOSTASY OF THE ELITES

1 Quoted in Sally Covington, *Moving a Public Policy Agenda,* Washington, D.C., 1997.

2 Irving Kristol, *Two Cheers for Capitalism,* New York, 1978, p. 134.

3 Pat Buchanan, *Conservative Votes, Liberal Victories,* New York, 1975, pp. 45, 77.

4 On Brookings's life, see Donald T. Critchlow, *The Brookings Institution: 1916–1952,* De Kalb, Ill., 1985, ch. 3.

5 See Karen Rothmyer, "Citizen Scaife," *Columbia Journalism Review,* July–Aug. 1981; and Robert Kaiser and Ira Chinoy, "The Right's Funding Father," *Washington Post,* May 2, 1999.

6 See George M. Marsden, *Understanding Fundamentalism and Evangelicism,* Grand Rapids, Mich., 1991, pp. 73–74.

7 See Saloma, *Ominous Politics,* New York, 1984, pp. 53–54.

8 Ford Foundation, *A Time to Choose,* Cambridge, Mass., 1974, pp. 326, 329.

9 Richard H. K. Vietor, *Energy Policy in America since 1945,* Cambridge, Mass., 1984, p. 314.

10 Ford Foundation, *A Time to Choose,* appendix, p. 381.

11 Ford Foundation, *A Time to Choose,* appendix.

12 Institute for Contemporary Studies, *No Time to Confuse,* San Francisco, 1975.

13 Ibid., p. 330.

14 Ford Foundation files.

15 Ibid.

16 Quoted in *The American Establishment,* New York, 1980, pp. 147–48.

17 Ford Foundation, *Energy: The Next Twenty Years,* Cambridge, Mass., 1979.

18 *Washington Post,* Sept. 14, 1979.

19 See Mark Green, *The Other Government,* New York, 1975, p. 274.

20 Quoted in David Vogel, *Fluctuating Fortunes,* New York, 1989, p. 214.

21 Chris Argyris, *Behind the Front Page,* San Francisco, 1974, p. 173. Sulzberger and Oakes confirmed their identity in Argyris's book to author Joseph Goulden.

22 Ibid., p. 176.

23 Joseph Goulden, *Fit to Print,* Secaucus, N.J., 1988, p. 210.

24 Katharine Graham, *A Personal History,* New York, 1997, p. 579.

25 *Washington Post,* Feb. 7, 1978.

26 Interview with author.

27 *Washington Post,* March 1, 1978.

28 Carol Feisenthal, *Power, Privilege and the Post,* New York, 1993, p. 362.

29 Richard Viguerie, "Ways and Means," *The New Right Papers,* ed. Robert W. Whitaker, New York, 1982, p. 31.

30 Interview with author.

31 Interview with author.

32 American Center for the Study of Business, brochure, n.d. (1970s).

33 See Murray L. Weidenbaum and Robert DeFina, *The Cost of Federal Regulation of Economic Activity,* Washington, D.C., 1978; and Murray Weidenbaum, "Time to Control Runaway Inflation," *Reader's Digest,* June 1979.

34 See Stephen Kelman, "Regulation That Works," *The New Republic,* Nov. 25, 1978.

35 Julius W. Allen, "Estimating the Costs of Federal Regulation," Congressional Research Service, Sept. 26, 1978.

36 *People,* Feb. 14, 1983.

37 Mary Ann Glendon, *A Nation Under Lawyers,* New York, 1994, p. 29. See also Marc Galanter and Thomas Palay, *Tournament of Lawyers,* Chicago, 1991.

38 Robert W. Gordon, "The Independence of Lawyers," *Boston University Law Review,* Jan. 1988.

39 *Washington Representatives,* Washington, D.C., 1989.

40 Interview with author.

41 Interview with author.

42 Interview with author.

43 Charles R. Babock, "Haig Discloses Earnings," *Washington Post,* May 25, 1987.

8. THE CONSERVATIVE CRACK-UP

1 Rowland Evans and Robert Novak, *The Reagan Revolution,* New York, 1981, p. 3.

2 MIT consultant John Krafcik estimated that an average plant in Japan turned out a car with 20.3 hours of labor, while it took 24.3 hours in the United States. According to J. D. Power & Associates, in 1987, American cars had an average of 177 defects in the first ninety days compared to 129 for Japanese cars. *Fortune,* Oct. 23, 1989.

3 Ibid.

4 Michael L. Dertouzos et al., *Made in America,* Cambridge, Mass., 1989, p. 217.

5 *Economic Report of the President,* Washington, D.C., Feb. 1992.

6 See John B. Judis, "The Red Menace," *The New Republic,* Oct. 26, 1992.

7 See *Economic Report of the President,* Washington, D.C., Feb. 1997.

8 The story of the establishment of the commission and of Young's role in it is told in Max Holland, *The CEO Goes to Washington,* Knoxville, 1994, ch. 1.

9 *Washington Post,* Oct. 20, 1992.

10 *Industry Week,* Nov. 14, 1983.

11 Holland, *CEO Goes to Washington,* p. 18.

12 Clyde Prestowitz, *Trading Places: How We Allowed Japan to Take the Lead,* New York, 1988, p. 18.

13 Interview with author.

14 Interview with author.

15 This account of the origins of the Economic Strategy Institute and its first years is based on author's interviews with Clyde Prestowitz, Alan Tonelson, and John Nash.

16 See Clyde Prestowitz, Ronald Morse, and Alan Tonelson, eds., *Powernomics,* Lanham, Md., 1991.

17 See Mark A. Peterson, "The Politics of Health Care Reform," *The Great Divide,* ed. Margaret Weir, Washington, D.C., 1989.

18 See John B. Judis, "Moon: Rising Political Influence," *U.S. News & World Report,* March 27, 1989.

19 See John B. Judis, "Charge of the Light Brigade," *The New Republic,* Sept. 29, 1986.

20 Ibid.

21 See Anthony Harrigan and William R. Hawkins, *American Economic Pre-Eminence,* Washington, D.C., 1989; and Anthony Harrigan, ed., *Putting America First: A Conservative Free Trade Alternative,* Washington, D.C., 1987.

22 For Buchanan's story, see John B. Judis, "White House Vigilante," *The New Republic,* Jan. 26, 1987, and "Taking Pat Buchanan Seriously," *GQ,* Dec. 1995.

23 Patrick Buchanan, *The Great Betrayal,* Boston, 1998, p. 18.

24 See John B. Judis, "The Conservative Crackup," *American Prospect,* fall 1990.

25 Interview with author.

26 Patrick Buchanan, "Come Home America," *Washington Post,* Sept. 8, 1991.

27 I was present at this convention and at Robertson's 1988 meeting with his followers.

28 Paul Kennedy, *The Rise and Fall of the Great Powers,* New York, 1987; and Kevin Phillips, *The Politics of Rich and Poor,* New York, 1990. Lest I be accused of letting myself off the hook, I also wrote considerably on the subject of America's decline, including a 1992 book, *Grand Illusion,* which focused on America's attitude toward its own rise and then decline as a world power. My book, however, had considerably less impact than Kennedy's or Phillips's.

29 Stanley Greenberg and Celinda Lake, *Defining American Priorities,* Washington, D.C., May 18, 1989.

30 See James B. Stewart, *Den of Thieves,* New York, 1991.

31 See *Los Angeles Times,* April 13, 1986.

32 See Everett Carll Ladd and Karel Bowman, *What's Wrong?,* Washington, D.C., 1998, pp. 109–10.

33 Gordon Black and Benjamin Black, *The Politics of American Discontent,* New York, 1994, p. 110.

34 Ibid., p. 111.

35 Gary Burtless and Lawrence Mishel, "Recent Wage Trends," Social Science Research Council Policy Conference, Nov. 1993.

36 Edward Wolff, "The Rich Increasingly Get Richer," Economic Policy Institute, Washington, D.C., 1993.

37 Phillips, *Politics of Rich and Poor,* p. xviii.

38 Alexander W. Astin, Sarah A. Parrott, William S. Korn, and

Linda J. Sax, *The American Freshman: Thirty Year Trends,* Los Angeles, Feb. 1997, pp. 56–57.

39 Jay Letto, "One Hundred Years of Compromise," *Buzzworm,* March 1992.

40 *Time,* April 23, 1990.

41 Christopher J. Bosso, "Adaptation and Change in the Environmental Movement," *Interest Group Politics,* ed. Allan J. Ciglar and Burdett A. Loomis, Washington, D.C., 1991.

42 Ibid.

43 See John B. Judis, "Can Labor Come Back?," *The New Republic,* May 23, 1994.

44 See Ladd and Bowman, *What's Wrong?,* p. 105.

9. THE FRUSTRATION OF REFORM

1 "Key Quotes from Clinton Interview," Gannet News Service, Aug. 12, 1992.

2 "Clinton's Revolution," *Newsweek,* March 1, 1993.

3 *This Week with David Brinkley,* April 2, 1995.

4 On the history of the DLC, I have relied on interviews with Al From and Will Marshall; documents and statements; an article by political scientist Jon F. Hale, "The Making of the New Democrats," *Political Science Quarterly,* no. 2, 1995; and an unpublished doctoral dissertation by Kenneth Baer, "Reinventing Democrats."

5 Democratic Leadership Council, *Citizenship and National Service,* Washington, D.C., 1989.

6 See David Osborne and Ted Gaebler, *Reinventing Government,* Reading, Pa., 1992.

7 David Maraniss, *First in His Class,* New York, 1995, p. 242.

8 See Robert B. Reich, ed., *The Power of Public Ideas,* Cambridge, Mass., 1988, for an extended discussion by Reich and other new left policy experts on the role of government.

9 Robert B. Reich, *The Work of Nations,* New York, 1991, p. 3.

10 Ibid., p. 8.

11 Ibid., pp. 312–13.

12 Robert B. Reich, "Up the Workers," *The New Republic,* May 13, 1991.

13 See "Education or Strong-Arming? Companies Lobby Workers, Suppliers for NAFTA," Associated Press, Sept. 28, 1993.

14 See Gary Hufbauer and Jeffrey Schott, *NAFTA: An Assessment,*

Washington, D.C., 1993; and Keith Bradsher, "Trade Pact Job Gains Discounted," *New York Times,* Feb. 22, 1993.

15 Quoted in Mark A. Peterson, "The Politics of Health Care Reform," *The Great Divide,* ed. Margaret Weir, Washington, D.C., 1989.

16 Peterson, "Politics of Health Care Reform."

17 *New York Times,* Oct. 3, 1993.

18 Quoted in Theda Skocpol, *Boomerang,* New York, 1996, p. 5.

19 See John B. Judis, "Abandoned Surgery: Business and the Failure of Health Care Reform," *The American Prospect,* spring 1995.

20 See John B. Judis, "Newt's Gang," *GQ,* May 1995.

21 See Judis, "Abandoned Surgery."

22 Quoted in Haynes Johnson and David S. Broder, *The System,* Boston, 1996, pp. 276–77.

23 See Lawrence R. Jacobs and Robert Y. Shapiro, "Don't Blame the Public for Failed Health Care Reform," *Journal of Health Politics, Policy and Law,* summer 1995.

24 On the story of the Business Roundtable, see Judis, "Abandoned Surgery."

25 *Inside Politics,* Nov. 10, 1994.

26 Grover Norquist, *Rock the House,* Fort Lauderdale, 1995, p. 2.

27 William Kristol, "The Politics of Liberty, the Sociology of Virtue," *The New Promise of American Life,* ed. Lamar Alexander and Chester Finn, Indianapolis, 1995.

28 See John B. Judis, "The Contract with K Street," *The New Republic,* Dec. 4, 1995.

29 Gary C. Jacobson, "The 1994 House Elections in Perspective," *Political Science Quarterly,* vol. 3, no. 2, 1996.

30 Quoted in Dick Williams, *Newt,* Marietta, Ga., 1995, p. 149.

31 See John B. Judis, "Inside Newt's Brain," *The New Republic,* Oct. 9, 1995.

32 Newt Gingrich, speech to the NAM in Washington, May 18, 1995.

33 Interview with author.

34 Quoted in Elizabeth Drew, *Showdown,* New York, 1996, p. 278.

35 See Judis, "Contract with K Street." Figures cited are from the Center for Responsive Politics.

36 See Judis, "Contract with K Street."

37 *Special Access for Special Interests,* Washington, D.C., 1995.

38 See Gary Lee, "House Votes to Strengthen Clean Water Act," *Washington Post,* June 26, 1993.

39 See John B. Judis, "The Bill," *The New Republic,* June 3, 1996.

40 See John B. Judis, "The Gold Standard," *The New Republic,* Nov. 6, 1995.

41 Congressional Press Releases, July 26, 1995.

42 *Cleveland Plain Dealer,* Oct. 22, 1995.

43 See *Statistical Abstract of the United States,* Washington, D.C., 1996, p. 436.

44 *CQ Researcher,* June 28, 1996.

45 *Business Week,* Feb. 17, 1997.

10. SLEEPWALKING TOWARD THE MILLENNIUM

1 *New York Times,* May 19, 1996.

2 *Washington Post,* Jan. 20, 1997.

3 Bureau of Labor Statistics Data (BLS web site).

4 *Health Line,* Aug. 22, 1996.

5 General Accounting Office, "Health Insurance Standards: Implications of New Federal Law for Consumers, Insurers, Regulators," March 19, 1998.

6 Census Bureau figures.

7 Figures are from Lawrence Mishel, Jared Bernstein, and John Schmitt, *The State of Working America, 1998–99,* Ithaca, N.Y., 1999.

8 See Dean Baker, *The Public Investment Deficit,* Washington, D.C., 1998.

9 See John B. Judis, "Magaziner On-Line," *The New Republic,* Dec. 28, 1998.

10 John Fialka, "EPA Probers Find Big Flaws," *Wall Street Journal,* Dec. 28, 1999.

11 See John B. Judis, "Deregulation Run Riot," *The American Prospect,* Sept.–Oct. 1999.

12 CNN polls, Sept. 29, 1997.

13 See Eldon J. Eisenach, *The Lost Promise of Progressivism,* Lawrence, Kans., 1994.

14 Laurie Goodstein, "Coalition's Woes May Hinder Goals of Christian Right," *New York Times,* Aug. 2, 1999.

15 Interview with author.

16 Robert W. Gordon, "The Independence of Lawyers," *Boston University Law Review,* Jan. 1988.

17 Jeffrey Birnbaum, *The Lobbyists,* New York, 1992, p. 128.

18 See Howard Kurtz, "Huffington Declares his Homosexuality," *Washington Post,* December 6, 1998.

10 now

19 Minutes obtained from participant.

20 See Hanna Rosin, "Shades of Gray," *The New Republic,* April 14, 1997.

21 Information provided by the Clearinghouse on Environmental Advocacy and Research.

22 Testimony before the House Small Business Committee, July 18, 1995.

23 See John B. Judis, "Irresponsible Elites," *The American Prospect,* Jan.–Feb. 1999.

24 Quoted in Burt Solomon, "Ferment at Brookings," *National Journal,* Oct. 18, 1997.

25 See *Brookings,* autumn 1996. Details of negotiations over the chair were provided in a confidential interview with one of the participants.

26 Quoted in Lester Bernstein, "Time Inc. Means Business," *New York Times Magazine,* Feb. 26, 1989.

27 Quoted by David Shaw, *Los Angeles Times,* March 31, 1998.

28 See MSNBC web site, May 5, 1999.

29 *New York Times,* Jan. 12, 1998.

30 Robert D. Putnam, "Bowling Alone," *Journal of Democracy,* Jan. 1995.

31 Newt Gingrich, *To Renew America,* New York, 1995, p. 57.

32 Michael Barone, "The Road Back to Tocqueville," *Washington Post,* Jan. 7, 1996.

33 *Washington Post,* Jan. 7, 1996.

34 Lamar Alexander, "Restoring the American Dream," The Civil Society Project, vol. 98, no. 1.

35 See Democratic Leadership Council, *The New Progressive Declaration,* Washington, D.C., July 1996.

36 See Scott Bowman, *The Modern Corporation and American Political Thought,* University Park, Md., 1996, p. 17.

37 See Theda Skocpol, "Building Community," *Brookings Review,* fall 1997.

38 William G. McLoughlin, *Revivals, Awakenings and Reform,* Chicago, 1978, p. 163.

39 Robert H. Bork, *Slouching Towards Gomorrah,* New York, 1996, Introduction.

40 Irving Kristol, "My Cold War," *The Public Interest,* spring 1993.

41 See Myron Magnet, *The Dream and the Nightmare,* New York, 1993.

42 *Wall Street Journal,* April 30, 1999.

43 For more examples, see Robert Frank, *Luxury Fever,* New York, 1999.

44 *San Diego Union-Tribune,* March 10, 1998.

45 *Dallas Morning News,* Feb. 20, 1998.

11. CONCLUSION

1 See Aaron Bernstein, "All's Not Fair in the Labor Wars," *Business Week,* July 19, 1999.

2 See John B. Judis, "Clinton's Second Act," *GQ,* Aug. 1996.

3 See Marvin Olasky, "Franklin D. Roosevelt: How His New Deal Undermined Charity," *Philanthropy, Culture and Society,* April 1999.

4 See Warren Susman, *Culture as History,* New York, 1984.

Acknowledgments

I had considerable help getting this book from initial draft to final form. Dan Frank is proof that some editors at publishing houses still edit. His advice was invaluable. James Gilbert, Michael Lacey, Martin Beiser, Robert Angel, Paul Starobin, Ruy Teixeira, and Eli Zuretsky read the manuscript and were enormously helpful. I tried to give credit where due in footnotes, but I'd like to single out the works of Martin J. Sklar on the Progressive Era and twentieth-century American capitalism; James Weinstein on the Progressive Era; Alan Brinkley, Theda Skocpol, and David Plotke on the New Deal and its aftermath; David Vogel and Thomas Edsall on business and politics; and Hugh Heclo on the way Washington works. I also want to thank belatedly G. William Domhoff. Our views have sharply diverged over the decades, but many years ago, Domhoff awakened my interest in how the American political system works.

I needed time off from my regular jobs to write this book, and I was very fortunate to receive a year's fellowship from the Wilson Center in Washington—an institution that has encouraged other attempts to reintepret our past, but that is presently under seige by short-sighted legislators who want to turn it into another Congressional Research Service. While at the Center I profited from conversations with Michael Lacey, Samuel Beer, Wilfred McClay, Seymour Martin Lipset, and Donald Wolfensberger.

Eric Behrns gathered research materials from the library. Hanna Rosin and Jonathan Cohn lent me their valuable files. Kenneth Baer sent me his excellent doctoral dissertation on the Democratic Leadership Council. Lee Sayrs at the George Meany Memorial Archives of the AFL-CIO, Alan Divack at the Ford Foundation Library, and Robert Bohanan and others at the Carter Library helped me find documents. Gary Fink of Georgia State University helped me understand George Meany and Jimmy Carter. At Pantheon, Jennifer Weh, Walter Havighurst, and Susan Norton readied the manuscript for publication.

I first broached many of this book's themes and ideas in articles I wrote for *The New Republic*, where I benefited from a succession of excellent editors. When I was struggling to get the book finished, Martin Peretz, the owner of *The New Republic,* and Charles Lane, the editor, allowed me the extra time I needed. Kathy Robbins negotiated my contract for the book. My wife, Susan Pearson, and my daughters, Hilary and Eleanor, tolerated me during the writing process. At a crucial time, my friends Larry Lynn and Lisa Saks lent me a room in their house. I got the idea for the book and wrote the first chapter while I was in Florida staying with my ailing father-in-law. I regret that John Pearson, one of my most critical but most supportive readers, did not live to see it concluded.

Index

About the Author

John B. Judis is a senior editor at *The New Republic* as well as a writer-at-large for *GQ* and a columnist for *The American Prospect*. He is the author of *William F. Buckley, Jr.: Patron Saint of the Conservatives* and *Grand Illusion: Critics and Champions of the American Century*. His work has appeared in numerous publications, including the *New York Times Magazine, Washington Post, Foreign Affairs, Washington Monthly, The Wilson Quarterly,* and *Dissent*. He lives in Maryland with his wife and two teenage daughters.